Faleh A. Jabar was Director of the Iraq Institute for Strategic Studies in Beirut and Research Fellow at the School of Politics and Sociology, Birkbeck College, University of London. His publications in English include: *The Shi'ite Movement in Iraq* (2003), *Tribes and Power in the Middle East* (2002), and *Ayatollahs, Sufis and Ideologues* (2002). He wrote a number of books in Arabic as well as contributions to peer-reviewed edited collections and journals.

Renad Mansour is Research Fellow at The Royal Institute of International Affairs, Chatham House and the American University of Iraq, Sulaimani. He has previously been Lecturer of International Studies in the Faculty of Politics at Cambridge University and the Faculty of International Relations at the London School of Economics (LSE). He was a Senior Fellow at The Iraq Institute for Strategic Studies, Beirut.

'A very timely, well-put together work bringing together the leading scholars in Kurdish Studies.

The essays carefully embed contemporary challenges of governing diversity within Kurdish history, identity and historiography. A must-read for scholars interested in the region as well as in the political aftermath of the unitary state model.'

– Fatma Müge Göçek, Professor of Sociology and Women's Studies, University of Michigan

THE KURDS IN A CHANGING MIDDLE EAST

History, Politics and Representation

EDITORS
FALEH A. JABAR AND RENAD MANSOUR

Volume I: 'Governing Diversity: The Kurds in a New Middle East'

I.B.TAURIS
LONDON • NEW YORK • OXFORD • NEW DELHI • SYDNEY

I.B. TAURIS
Bloomsbury Publishing Plc
50 Bedford Square, London, WC1B 3DP, UK
1385 Broadway, New York, NY 10018, USA
29 Earlsfort Terrace, Dublin 2, Ireland

BLOOMSBURY, I.B. TAURIS and the I.B. Tauris logo are
trademarks of Bloomsbury Publishing Plc

First published in Great Britain 2019
This paperback edition published 2023

Copyright Editorial Selection © 2019 Faleh A. Jabar and Renad Mansour
Copyright Individual Chapters © 2019 Hamit Bozarslan, Martin van Bruinessen,
Michael Gunter, Faleh A. Jabar, Janet Klein, Michiel Leezenberg, Renad Mansour,
David Romano, and Sami Zubaida

Faleh A. Jabar and Renad Mansour have asserted their right under the Copyright,
Designs and Patents Act, 1988, to be identified as editors of this work.

All rights reserved. No part of this publication may be reproduced or
transmitted in any form or by any means, electronic or mechanical,
including photocopying, recording, or any information storage or retrieval
system, without prior permission in writing from the publishers.

Bloomsbury Publishing Plc does not have any control over, or responsibility for,
any third-party websites referred to or in this book. All internet addresses given
in this book were correct at the time of going to press. The author and publisher
regret any inconvenience caused if addresses have changed or sites have
ceased to exist, but can accept no responsibility for any such changes.

A catalogue record for this book is available from the British Library.

A catalog record of this book is available from the Library of Congress.

ISBN: HB: 978-1-7845-3991-7
PB: 978-0-7556-5105-4
ePDF: 978-1-7867-3549-2
eBook: 978-1-7867-2549-3

Typeset in Garamond Three by OKS Prepress Services, Chennai, India

To find out more about our authors and books visit
www.bloomsbury.com and sign up for our newsletters.

This book is dedicated to the life and work of Iraqi sociologist Faleh Abdul Jabar, who passed away during its writing. He will be remembered as a leading Arab and Iraqi thinker, activist, and teacher.

أنجز هذا المشروع بأجزائه الخمسة بدعم مركز أبحاث التنمية العالمية، أوتاوا ـ كندا

The work involved in this and subsequent volumes was carried out with the aid of a grant from the International Development Research Center, IDRC, Ottawa, Canada. Iraq Studies (IIST)

دراسات عراقية ـ معهد الدراسات الاستراتيجية

CONTENTS

Note on Transliteration — ix
Note on Bibliographic References — x
Glossary of Acronyms and Abbreviations — xi

Introduction   The Kurdish Moment and the Fate of the
Unitary State in the Middle East
  Faleh A. Jabar and Renad Mansour — 1

Part I   New Society: The Kurds in a Changing Middle East

1. New and Old Dynamics in the Construction of
   Kurdish Nationhood – Some Reflections
   Faleh A. Jabar — 17

2. Problems and Outlooks of Kurdish Representation
   Renad Mansour — 41

3. Segmentation of Political Parties in Underdeveloped
   Contexts – The Case of the Kurds
   Gareth Stansfield — 68

4. The Rise of the White Kurds – An Essay in Regional
   Political Economy
   Michiel Leezenberg — 86

5. Forms and Prospects of Kurdish Armed Struggle
   David Romano — 118

Part II   Old Society: Perennial Continuity

6. Tribes and Ethnic Identity
   Martin van Bruinessen — 141

7. Tribes and Politics
   Hamit Bozarslan — 171

8. Gender, Family, Patriarchy and Women
   Sami Zubaida — 185

Part III   Reflections on the Historiography of the Kurds

9. A Critical Overview of Early British Kurdish Studies
   Michael Gunter — 205

10. Kurdish History – Not a Neutral Pursuit
    Janet Klein — 222

Contributor Biographies — 244
Index — 246

NOTE ON TRANSLITERATION

This book draws on texts and interviews in English, Arabic, Turkish and in Kurmanji Kurdish. The geographical areas that it covers are also home to a variety of languages, some of which have been politicized due to proscriptions on their public use. Therefore, using one model of transliteration applicable to all place names and organizations has not been possible. As far as possible, places commonly referred to by their Arabic names have been transliterated according to a simplified use of the system employed by the *International Journal of Middle Eastern Studies* (excluding the use of diacritical symbols). However, common spellings are employed to promote ease of understanding.

The *IJMES* model of transliteration is employed. Names of organizations are referred by their most commonly used name or acronym (see glossary of acronyms and abbreviations) so as to be the most recognizable and understandable to the reader. Where necessary or appropriate, both Arabic and Kurdish names are given. People's names are generally written as they themselves would have them transliterated.

NOTE ON BIBLIOGRAPHIC REFERENCES

Due to the current and changing nature of the subject matter, research for this book involved constant monitoring of events on the ground in many countries in the form of field research, respondents and through live news and opinions available on open-source and social-media outlets. Sources have been provided to verify facts which may not be widely known and to gauge the widest possible impression of opinions of people in these regions. These sources have been corroborated as far as possible through field observations, interviews and other open-source materials. News sources are cited within the endnotes, whilst other sources – including academic literature, publications by think tanks and organizations, political documents and interviews – are listed in the bibliographies.

GLOSSARY OF ACRONYMS AND ABBREVIATIONS

AKP	Justice and Development Party
AQI	Al Qaeda Iraq
DOS	US Department of State
FO	British Foreign Office
HDP	Peoples' Democratic Party
ICP	Iraqi Communist Party
IKF	Iraqi Kurdistan Front
IMK	Islamic Movement of Kurdistan
IOR	India Office Records
IS	Islamic State
ISIS	Islamic State of Iraq and Syria / Islamic State of Iraq and al-Sham (Syria and Lebanon)
KCP	Kurdistan Conservative Party
KDP	Kurdistan Democratic Party
KDPI	Kurdistan Democratic Party of Iran
KDP-I	Democratic Party of Iranian Kurdistan
KDP-S	Democratic Party of Syrian Kurdistan
KNA	Kurdistan National Assembly
Komala	Organization of Revolutionary Toilers of Iranian Kurdistan
KRG	Kurdistan Regional Government
KRI	Kurdistan Region of Iraq
KSSE	Kurdish Students' Society in Europe
OSC	Omar Sheikhmous' Collection

PJAK	Free Life Party of Kurdistan
PKK	Kurdistan Workers' Party
PUK	Patriotic Union of Kurdistan
PYD	Democratic Union Party
Rojava	Democratic Federation of Northern Syria
TIP	Workers' Party of Turkey
TOKI	Turkish Housing Development Agency
YPG	People's Protection Unit; military wing of the PYD in Syria

INTRODUCTION

THE KURDISH MOMENT AND THE FATE OF THE UNITARY STATE IN THE MIDDLE EAST

Faleh A. Jabar and Renad Mansour

This is the first of five volumes in a grand project: Governing Diversity, the Kurds in the Middle East in the aftermath of the 'Arab Spring'. The project in general has two aspects. The first tackles the basic general issues of Kurdish diversity in terms of the history, identity, party politics and sociology of Kurdish communities in four host countries; these aspects are examined in our present volume.

The second aspect embraces problems of representation, that is, concepts of group representation, tied to conceptions of identity and forms of action to achieve representation. It comprises concrete case studies, country by country, contextualized in the framework of current conditions and developments. These cases involve Iraq, Turkey, Syria and Iran in four successive and separate volumes.

Basic Themes in Volume I

In our present, first, volume the research teams selected a few major issues drawn from all or most of the case studies. Patriarchy and tribalism, for example, are relevant to all cases. So is the spread and typical fragmentation of modern party politics. The role of modern Kurdish business classes is examined although it is mostly evident in Turkey and

Iraq, much less so in Syria or Iran. Problems of representation, while having an abstract conceptual nature, appear in different forms at different locations in different times, and range from local autonomy to federalism; to confederacies; to full independence; or, beyond all these, to a new, multi-ethnic 'autonomous democracy' as in Rojava (the Democratic Federation of Northern Syria). History and identity, or early Kurdish studies in the Anglo-American tradition, are also among the topics examined that shed light on the early problems of identity.

In a sense, this first volume is an introductory note to what we consider to be the basic current issues of the Kurds and their quest for self-representation in four host countries in the Middle East (ME).

The list of such basic issues may well be expanded or abbreviated, and the range defined here is not and cannot be exhaustive. It starts with the examination of nation-nationalism and nation-building in a failed state, Iraq, and the Kurdish endeavour towards independence; but this and other issues, crucial as they are, require a thorough examination of the profound changes that in certain cases have transformed Kurdish societies since the turn of the millennium. This is best seen in the predominance of modern forms of organization and culture, which, nevertheless, do not exclude the impact of traditional forces — in fact, they overlap and interact. Urbanization, for example, reduced the weight of the rural-peasant grounds for mountain-based guerrilla warfare and strengthened the potential of urban protest, peaceful or violent. In the words of a veteran *peshmerga* (Kurdish guerrilla), 'through urban mass protests in Iraq [March 1991], we achieved in few weeks what we could not in a half-century of armed fighting in the mountains'.[1]

The study of self-representation requires the examination of modern party politics as a set of ideological tools in expressing demands, organizing actions and serving as a medium of representation. Parties strive to obtain representation in federal/national institutions (parliaments, local governments) and deploy their candidates accordingly, but communities and localities in turn strive to be represented in the leadership or branches of these parties. No single party can claim to represent all segments of the Kurdish community. In this sense, modern political parties carry representation in a dual manner: from community to party structures, and from party to central institutions. One of the prominent features of all party politics is its peculiar fragmentation.

The expansion and role of modern middle-class strata – and, more importantly, business classes – is another factual theme to be considered. This may well apply to Turkey, where business classes have grown into political maturity, and Iraq, where another pattern of state–business alliances has been in the making. The question is in what way these sociological changes influence ethnic identity and the quest for representation.

The same question applies to the role of tribes, Sufi orders and traditional social segments in such pursuits of representation. Stronger observable inclinations towards 'ethno-Kurdish-ness' have been observed lately in the political leanings of tribal chieftains who had hitherto opted for cooperation with central authority. This will be seen in the cases of Turkey and Iraq.

The historical roots of self-ethnic-identity, and the first offshoots of British Kurdologist studies, may well serve as a general background.[2]

The Kurdish discourse of group identity in the quest for self-representation has had to face the centralist–nationalist rebuttal, that is, that of the 'dominant national group', which denies ethno-cultural diversity. In its long history, this discourse sustained continuous change – from establishing a monarchy in Sulaimaniya (1920s) to founding an independent republic (Mahabad, in the 1940s) or seeking local autonomy in Iraq as of the 1960s, moving to federalism or con-federalism. The discourse, while ethno-linguistic and purely Kurdish, has shifted in recent years.

The Unitary State in Question

The Sisyphean efforts on part of the Kurds to achieve their legitimate representation clearly testify to the fact that the unitary state model constructed in 1917 is not only faltering in 2017 but has, in fact, failed when it comes to governing diversity.

Civil wars, and the declining reach of the central government testify to this failure: civil war in Syria resulted in the disintegration of the unitary state as of 2012; much earlier, the 1991 Gulf War ended with the ethnic division of Iraq and the subsequent mutation of the unitary state into federalism. The ultimate fate of the unitary state in Syria is still shrouded in uncertainty. Sensing the tide of change around them, the unitary states of Iran and Turkey are fiercely resisting the turning away from their long-cherished, monolithic centralism; the demands for reform to allow for pluralism in these two countries may seem weak or dormant at the moment, but they continue pulsating beneath the surface. We may note that the Sykes–Picot and post-World War I arrangements are partly unravelling; the new arrangements, however, are still in limbo.

In Iraq and Syria, the drivers working at present to propel the unitary state in the Mashriq into the abyss of an uncertain future are also sending the Kurds on an uncertain trajectory. Perhaps the ethno-linguistic approach to Kurdish identity politics might invoke the notorious problem of cultural markers that make or break a national community: language. The old Wilsonian principles of self-determination were couched in the language of geographical borders of countries rather than the abstract norms of specific linguistic or cultural markers of 'nation-ness'. In anticipation of the final fate of the unitary state, the Kurds face the same problems that their Arab or Turkish oppressors did: what to do with the non-dominant, non-Kurdish groups that share their geography? One way is to manufacture a new territorial identity bereft of ethnicity: the 'Kurdistani' as an inhabitant of a Kurdistan region. Cultural-linguistic ethnicity has been the marker of Kurdish nationalism, and it continues to be the marker of territorial disputes vis-à-vis the Iraqi federal government; however, it has been discontinued in governing diversity inside the KRG (Kurdistan Regional Government) or Rojava. In short, ethnic identity is being sacrificed to accommodate non-Kurds in the KRG or in Rojava (Syria). Such a prospect may face the Kurds in Turkey and Iran once their right to some form of autonomy is recognized. This is one of the many paradoxes of governing diversity in action. What comes next is a question that we strive to answer in the next four volumes.

Kurds and the Arab Spring

When this project was conceived at the beginning of the second decade of the new millennium, the Kurds were hardly present on most maps of the Middle East. In Syria and Iran, the Kurdish question seemed dormant. In Turkey, the HDP (People's Democratic Party) was actually under the wing of the ruling Islamist AKP (Justice and Development Party) and mediating semi-clandestine negotiations between the

Turkish Government and the PKK (Kurdish Workers' Party). The only genuine exception was Iraq, where Kurds had the privilege of enjoying a unique form of federalism that verged in certain areas, such as the military, airports, and representation in embassies, on confederacy.

When the project was completed in August 2017, the Kurds seemed to have re-emerged at the heart of Middle East politics. In Iraq, a referendum for independence (25 September 2017) was conducted in defiance of native, regional and international powers and actors; in Syria, the Kurds have a vital role in the global war against IS (Islamic State), as in the administration of Rojava, in the framework of 'autonomous democracy' experimented with by the country's leading Kurdish party, the PYD (Democratic Union Party). Their contribution to the liberation of Raqqa, the capital of the IS 'Caliphate', on 17 October 2017, was a phenomenal achievement. In Iran, mass Kurdish demonstrations erupt periodically into cultural protests or in support of their Iraqi fellow-Kurds' referendum; in Turkey, the electoral success scored by the HDP in June 2015 was remarkable. This upward trajectory, however, soon turned downward. In Turkey, the HDP was disfranchised, its leaders kept behind bars in the wake of a cruel anti-Kurdish campaign. In Iraq, the referendum backfired, dividing the Kurds, with Erbil pitted against Sulaimaniya (i.e., Barzani vis Talabani blocs or centres of power); the disputed areas controlled by the KRG were soon lost and a confrontational atmosphere prevailed. Airports in Erbil and Sulaimaniya were shuttered, border outlets under the KRG control were retaken by the federal authority.

The suggested ties between Kurds and Arabs via the 'Arab Spring' may seem a historical anachronism, or even an aberration. In reality, the relationship is profound and complex.

The Arab Spring was a new, additional catalyst to Kurdish yearnings for self-representation. While it was an 'Arab' phenomenon in general, it had clear direct or indirect links with Kurdish aspirations in Syria and Iraq – and, successively, in Turkey and Iran. Kurds in Syria were directly involved in their country's protest movement for democracy; so were their PKK Turkish mentors.

Looking at the Middle East through an ethnically divided lens that separates one group from the other is a naive way of thinking about the area. This is a cultural region that shares much in common, exactly like those of Eastern Europe and Latin America in the 1980s. More often than not, we see an actual or potential 'spillover' effect in the Middle East. This is born of the region's history in the twentieth century and the early decades of the twenty-first.

Atatürk, for example, who emerged in 1920s' Turkey as a military leader-hero, was soon emulated by generals in Iran and Iraq (in the 1920s and 1930s) and, later on, even by Gamal Abdel Nasser of Egypt (1952); the last-named, in turn, was taken as an example in the Arab world during the later series of military takeovers of power in Iraq, Syria, Yemen, Libya and Algeria. Or look at the aim of the *coup d'état* organized by the giant oil companies to remove the radical prime minister Mohammad Mosaddegh in Iran: to prevent any spillover effect from his oil nationalism. Or, again, look at the Middle East itself immediately after the Iranian 'Islamic' revolution of 1979 that helped political Islam to spread more forcefully.

The Arab Spring brought the Kurds to the forefront of events in Syria and enhanced their position in Iraq. And both emboldened Kurdish groups in Turkey to run in the 2014–15 elections independently, the reactions notwithstanding.

Arab Spring protestors shattered fear of the Establishment and called for genuine reform to end the single-party system. Even the civil wars that subsequently erupted, or the rise of Islamic State as a terrorist menace, brought forth the Kurds in Syria and the KRG in Iraq as reliable allies to fight against terrorism and dictatorship. The KRG's peshmerga forces stood fast and fought back around the cities of Mosul, Kirkuk and Erbil. In Syria, the armed self-protection units of the PYD, an extension of Abdullah Öcalan's Kurdistan Worker's Party (PKK), took up arms and defended their major towns, including Kobani in the Aleppo Governorate among others, and created a self-organized federal domain inside the predominantly Kurdish areas of Syria, known in Kurdish as Rojava. Washington and its allies support both of these forces politically, militarily and financially.

The Turkey-based PKK has guerrilla groups in the northern parts of Iraq; they moved these fighters to defend Sinjar, the Yezidi district that had been overrun by IS, expanding the PKK's influence into Syria and Iraq.

The 'IS factor' drove the militarization of Kurds in Syria and enhanced their militarization in Iraq, whereas the heavy-handed crackdown on Kurdish peaceful institutional politics in Turkey has invited violent reactions from the PKK beginning in mid-2015 and continuing to this day.

Representing the Kurdish Communities

The old right of nations to statehood, the Wilsonian formula that proved difficult to fit onto the region in 1918, still faced grave difficulties in 2017. When the one-nation/one-state formula is embedded in ethno-linguistic criteria, its model immediately creates contradictions. With the existence of some 8,000 linguistic groups worldwide and less than 200 polities at present, the ethno-language form of nation-statehood becomes the exception rather than the rule. Multicultural, that is, multilingual, states have been and continue to be the real, actual model in the Middle East. The success of ethno-linguistic nationalism has been limited worldwide. That such a pattern had scored success in Europe may have been the result of the spread of industrial capitalism, with its unifying markets and cultural forces. Still, we have counter examples – Catalonia was the latest case. Beyond Europe, uniformity of language did not and could not bring about a pan-Latin American union along the lines of Arab or Slavic unions.

The Middle East was, and to some extent still is, bereft of such modern unifying forces or drivers of integration. In the Middle East, ethno-nationalism could never override parochial localism, anchored as it was in various forms of social networks, tribes, clans, extended families, guilds and Sufi orders, overlapping with religion and sect. The discourses flowing from these networks competed against that of nationalism in many intriguing ways.

Long before the Kurds, most Arabs discovered that language and history are insufficient to cement or construct, let alone hold, a new, legitimate, all-representative national entity or central polity.

If the mono-ethnic political pattern proved difficult to sustain peacefully, democracy is also not enough to sustain the viability of local autonomy, federalism or con-federalism, which are contingent on a non-existent recognition of pluralism. But where should one look for it in the Mashriq, the Levant?

When it comes to rejecting pluralism, Turkey, the oft-cited most 'advanced democratic' example in the region, currently provides a case of the breakdown of democratic checks and balances and the rise of authoritarianism. A simple move by the country's only enfranchised Kurdish party, the HDP, to obtain independent representation in the June 2015 elections invited fierce 'centralist–nationalistic' reactions on the part of the ruling Islamic party, the AKP. Furthermore, civil peace in Turkey broke down immediately. In Syria, a single-party, authoritarian-patrimonial system is still fighting to maintain the status quo, while both the secular and Islamic Syrian opposition are alien to the very idea of pluralism. The prospects indeed look grim, yet opportunities may well exist.

What is the fate of the current Kurdish quest for representation?

For Kurds as for others, representation is complex and involves multilayered forms that evolve over time and space and mutate with socio-economic and cultural configurations. Problems of representation are integrated with issues of identity, ethnic or otherwise, and, by extension, territoriality whenever and wherever autonomy, federalism or independence is on the agenda.

Various Kurdish social groups and entities have been wavering between full sovereign nationhood or federalism, decentralization or local autonomy and general participation or limited privileges. The radical case is that of Iraq, where independence is on the agenda.

There are also various sundry conceptions regarding the ways and means of achieving this objective. On the radical side are direct military rebellion (as in the 1920s), the establishment of a Kurdish polity in defiance of central power (as with the Mahabad Republic in 1946) and the reliance on a mountain-based, peasant-backed, guerrilla warfare insurgency – the last-named almost a continuous element of Kurdish folklore since early 1960s in Iraq, the 1980s in Turkey and, for a short period, in Iran right after the Islamic Revolution (1979–80).

On the opposite side, Kurds either joined the *Fursan* (knights) of Salahudin – pro-government paramilitary Kurdish battalions in Iraq (1963–91) – or the pro-government village-protection units in Turkey (1985–present). This, again, partakes of age-old folklore stemming from the *Fursan Hamidiya* of the late nineteenth century onwards. These counter examples to radical tactics indicate a political choice of cooperating with central authorities in exchange for accommodation and local privileges. Many such strategies are still alive, but hardly in a peaceful symbiosis with each other.

Since 1990, however, new trends in the Kurdish quest for representation have been at work: a turn towards urban protest against central governments or mostly urban constitutional–institutional politics, i.e., the creation of legal political parties to achieve representation in parliaments.

Political analysis or historiography usually links these new trends to the defeat of Iraq's Ba'ath regime in the 1991 Gulf War, which allowed for a de facto Kurdish state to emerge, or to the arrest of the historical leader of the PKK, Abdullah Öcalan, followed by Ankara's decentralization reforms. These political events were important; the shift, however, had more to do with profound socio-economic, cultural and demographic change, which weakened the very pillars of the old wisdom of peasant-backed, mountain-harboured guerrilla fighters. And this is an aspect of Kurdish representation that has not in the least been analyzed thus far.

A New Kurdish Society

A new society has been evolving, and with it the Kurdish community has also been mutating. Much of this change would meticulously explain why institutional politics, peaceful by definition, has gathered pace despite setbacks. But how do Kurds perceive or understand the representation of their community (either externally vis-à-vis the central government or internally vis-à-vis ruling Kurdish actors)? Internally, in addition, implies the representation of non-dominant ethnic and religious groups within predominantly Kurdish regions. These are not abstract questions but rather practical considerations in Iraq, Syria and Turkey, and they will appear on the agenda in Iran once the Kurds there come out of dormancy.

The Kurdish moment, just like the so-called Arab Spring, testifies to the need to reform the parochial nature of the century-old unitary state. However, the 'Kurdish Spring' may end up looking like a twin of its Arab counterpart, which in most cases thus far has resulted in dysfunctional states. In Syria, the Kurdish Spring could prove short-lived once the Islamic State threat is removed; in Turkey, the 'Kurdish Winter' is contingent on the outcome of the federal project in Syria and Turkish President Recep Tayyip Erdoğan's consolidation of power; and in Iraq, the Kurdish polity, the KRG, may continue to linger in the current crisis of representation, under which the presidency and the parliament are locked in stalemate.

Lastly:

Volume II: Syria is to follow, with Volume III: Turkey after that. Volumes IV and V, Iran and Iraq, conclude this project, which will have covered a civil war in Syria, political violence in Turkey, a crisis in Iraq and protests in Iran.

Structure of the Book

This will be as follows:

Part I. New Society: The Kurds in a Changing Middle East

Chapter 1: Faleh A. Jabar, New and Old Dynamics in the Construction of Kurdish Nationhood – Some Reflections

Kurds have long suffered from the construction of the nation state in Iraq; now, they face similar problems in constructing their own nationhood. This is a historical paradox, in which two models have been and will continue to be at play. There is firstly the German tradition of 'inherent', that is, non-voluntary or coercive affiliation, and secondly the French tradition of free-willed togetherness. These two traditions, an authoritarian versus a liberal conception of nationhood, are in conflict. Nations do not grow naturally but are the products of meticulous engineering, through which politics, culture and economy are intertwined. Failure to comprehend such complexities as those involved in nation-building has the potential to break rather than make nations.

Chapter 2: Renad Mansour, Problems and Outlooks of Kurdish Representation

The Kurds have long yearned to have representation. Now they enjoy it in Iraq and are seeking to enhance it in Turkey. Mansour tackles the question of representation by focusing on the claims to legitimacy that Kurdish leaders in Iraq make in order to speak on behalf of their constituents when governing at home, when negotiating with the central government or when practising diplomacy abroad. The analysis looks at four time periods: post-World War I and the creation of the

Iraqi state; 1946–75 and Mullah Mustafa Barzani's united nationalist movement in Iraq and other countries; 1975–91 and the emergence of the PUK as a challenger to the KDP; and, finally, 1991–present and the institutionalization of the Kurdish political movement in Iraq through the establishment of governmental bodies like the Kurdistan Regional Government (KRG). Mansour concludes that Kurdish leaders believe that it is important to employ a 'toolbox' of intersecting claims based on local popularity, effective control, dynasty and international support in order to prove their legitimacy as Kurdish leaders at home and abroad.

Chapter 3: Gareth Stansfield, Segmentation of Political Parties in Underdeveloped Contexts – The Case of the Kurds

Stansfield argues that today's segmentation and factionalism in Kurdish politics is neither unusual nor static, nor inherently 'bad'. Presenting a typology of segmentation that includes spatial, ideological, socio-economic and generational factors, he outlines Kurdish attempts to overcome schisms in the pursuit of greater representation and autonomy vis-à-vis their central governments. Moreover, his distinctive approach forms an analysis of the sociological context underlining the development of political parties and political life in Kurdistan to the present day. Ultimately, he asks whether the Kurdish history of segmentation is likely to repeat itself or whether the Kurds will rise above internal differences to become, for the first time, more than the sum of their parts.

Chapter 4: Michiel Leezenberg, The Rise of the White Kurds – An Essay in Regional Political Economy

Leezenberg offers updated field research on the new Kurdish business classes in Iraq and Turkey. He uses the term 'White Kurds' to refer to this new class. His argument is twofold. First, in Iraq, more than 2,000 Kurdish nouveau-riche millionaires have emerged and are moving beyond their old radical discourse and pursuing strictly business relations with the ruling political elite. Second, in Turkey, the business class is divided into two parts; those in the predominately Kurdish areas freely use their Kurdish identity in their dealings with local development projects, and those in Istanbul and other predominately ethnic-Turkish cities perceive their Kurdish identity as a liability in commerce. These new findings have major political implications for how the Kurds are represented in both constituencies.

Chapter 5: David Romano, Forms and Prospects of Kurdish Armed Struggle

Romano examines the recent Kurdish strategic shift from rural guerrilla warfare to peaceful urban politics in Turkey, and the institutional politics that has been established in Iraq since 1991. At the heart of both cases is the socio-economic and cultural change that has almost emptied the countryside and augmented the dense urban presence of an active community. Is this shift a final turn to peaceful politics or simply a conjectural moment, one that actually implies rather than excludes the adoption of urban warfare? The examination is not only empirical but also theoretical, as it invokes theories on conflict and collective violence.

Part II. Old Society: Perennial Continuity

Chapter 6: Martin van Bruinessen, Tribes and Ethnic Identity

Van Bruinssen provides a *tour d'horizon* of tribes and the evolution of ethnic identities across the Kurdish areas in the region. The competition between ethnic-identity discourse, on the one hand, and the kinship ideology of tribes, on the other hand, is problematized by another discourse: Sufism. An interplay of Sufi orders turning into tribes, political parties or socio-military organizations continues to impact on sociopolitical life in all Kurdish areas. Yet, the creation of a central administration in Iraq has resulted in the strengthening of bureaucratic, rather than tribal or Sufi, links.

Chapter 7: Hamit Bozarslan, Tribes and Politics

Bozarslan argues that Kurdish tribes are ushering in a new phase of their existence, characterized by the pursuance of ethno-national politics. This is a break from their old, changing loyalties, serving the powers that be or steering away from any manifestations of Kurdishness. This change from conformism to activism, observed since the beginning of the new millennium, is the subject matter of this socio-anthropological examination of tribes and tribal politics. The historical background is linked with current conditions, dissecting the drivers behind this long, twisting trajectory of tribal political alliances. In many ways, it supplements Bruinessen's account.

Chapter 8: Sami Zubaida, Gender, Family, Patriarchy and Women

Zubaida examines the traditional facets of Kurdish societies. He argues that the Kurdish regions share in the diversity of other Middle Eastern societies with respect to issues of gender, women, patriarchy and reform. They are diverse by dint of region, class, politics and religiosity. In the KRG, for example, the political class tries to present an image to the world of a liberal and secular government, in contrast to the religious authoritarianism of the rest of Iraq and the region. At the same time, the political classes, as well as the related military and police, are involved in complex power relations, patronage and tribal kinships and communal and religious networks — all of which grant immunity from the law for powerful persons and groups. Rapid economic development and the rise of business elites overlapping with the political class and leading families, widespread corruption in politics and business, gross inequalities in wealth and power and limited opportunities of employment for the region's youth have all contributed to the emergence of new tensions, frustrations and subjectivities. These include fear of loss of control by the patriarchal order and the family tensions and crises that produce heightened violence, killings and the more numerically important suicides and burnings. The cases of the Turkish PPK and the Syrian PYD, however, put this advocacy into practice within their own ranks.

Part III. Reflections on the Historiography of the Kurds

Chapter 9: *Michael Gunter*, A Critical Overview of Early British Kurdish Studies

Gunter traces the how, when and who of the initiation of Kurdish studies in the Anglo-Saxon tradition during the first decades of the twentieth century. The earlier generation of Kurdish studies, in a post-World War I context, comprised government employees and intelligence agents, and as such they contributed to the literature in many ways that have not been equalled let along surpassed by subsequent generations of researchers. Indeed, a review of the work of these British political officers would pay rich dividends to new scholars seeking to study and write about the Kurds. Nonetheless, the past 50 years have seen a veritable explosion of studies, some based on innovative political and sociological theories and frameworks that have enabled an opening-up of new scholarly horizons on the Kurdish issue.

Chapter 10: Janet Klein, Kurdish History – Not a Neutral Pursuit

Klein employs Eric Hobsbawm's adage of 'historians are to nationalism what poppy-growers in Pakistan are to heroin addicts: we supply the essential raw material for the market', in order to examine the role of Kurdish historians and academics in the nationalist struggle. Today, the pursuit of Kurdish history is thriving. However, from the late Ottoman period, when Kurdish researchers joined other groups in the pursuit of documenting their 'national' history, to the present day, those who research Kurdish history have been faced with roadblocks erected by states, individuals and institutions who believe that the study of the Kurds somehow constitutes a threat. Accordingly, these obstacles have included restricted access to research fields and archives, the persecution of scholars, and the banning of books and articles. The newest generation of scholars of Kurdish history is nonetheless showing promise in navigating both ongoing obstacles and new opportunities for innovative research.

Notes

1. Interview with Mla Bakhtiar, Sulaimaniya, September 2015. Mla Bakhtia, a veteran PUK leader and Peshmerga, is currently a member of the PUK's Political Bureau.
2. The focus on the British (overlooking the rich Russian or French input) is understandable in the light of the decisive role that Great Britain played as the dominant colonial power in the politics of the Middle East before, during and immediately after World War I.

PART I

NEW SOCIETY: THE KURDS IN A CHANGING MIDDLE EAST

CHAPTER 1

NEW AND OLD DYNAMICS IN THE CONSTRUCTION OF KURDISH NATIONHOOD – SOME REFLECTIONS

Faleh A. Jabar

Never has the Kurdish moment been so contradictory in the Middle East: a mixture of advances and setbacks for the largest, yet mostly disfranchised, ethnic group in the region. The Kurds of the Kurdistan Regional Government (KRG) in Iraq, the most advanced case of self-representation, face the perils of a war of attrition against the Popular Mobilization Force (PMF), poised to expand through Zimmar and its surroundings in the northwestern tiers of Mosul. Iraqi Kurdistan president Masoud Barzani has just gone through a controversial referendum on 25 September 2017, which massively voted for independence from Iraq (92 per cent, out of a 72-per cent turnout). A fierce reaction from the central government followed, and government forces regained most of the territories that the Kurdish forces, the Peshmerga, had gained during the fight against Islamic State (IS) in 2014–17. Amidst international disagreement over the referendum, and the closure of all Kurdish airports, the two regional giants, Turkey and Iran, shut down their border corridors. While the KRG as a legal, constitutional and political entity is still safe, it has lost much of the leverage that it originally had. By contrast, the Kurds in Syria have a self-proclaimed federal order, well-equipped armed units, international Western support and a measure of Russian understanding. The prospects for their inclusion in the future reform plans to restructure the country's political order may well be promising. Turkish Kurds, on the other hand, face the bleak reality of disenfranchisement. Immediately following their electoral successes in Turkey's 2015 general elections, Kurdish leaders and MPs (including the secretary of the People's Democratic Party, the HDP) were placed behind bars on the grounds of their ethnicity and ethnic pursuits, in an open war against Kurds in Turkey and beyond. Shortly before these setbacks, a measure of euphoria seemed to have prevailed among the Kurds in Iran. Their fighters paraded their return to the mountains in a bid to receive recognition and, by extension, representation in the face of threats by Iranian Revolutionary Guards to overrun Iraqi Kurdistan.

The rise and realization of Kurdish nation-ness is far from reaching the goal that each nation strives for, mainly what Ernest Gellner called the congruence of an (ethno-)cultural group and a political unit – that is, the unity of nation and state or the organization of the nation in a separate political entity. The events in Iraqi Kurdistan throughout September and October 2017 – notably, the schism separating Sulaimaniya from Erbil and the collapse of the Pesghmerga units in Kirkuk and other regions – constituted a case of failed centralization efforts or failed national (here, Kurdish) unity.

Pan-Kurdish endeavours seem reminiscent of Pan-Arabism, with its crippling segmentation, whereas the bid to build a Kurdish mini-nation state in Iraq seem to have striking similarities with the fate of pan-Iraqism: partial success followed by endless failure. The question is: what are the prospects of such yearnings for the Kurds in Iraq? In what way can the KRG serve to unite Kurdish society in 'southern' (Iraqi) Kurdistan? How far will it go to achieve this?

This is a pivotal question/problem, and its significance may well go beyond the Iraqi case into the larger Middle East.[1]

This chapter will investigate whether or not the structural flaws in many of the Middle Eastern polities – above all, in Iraq – which cause instability and schisms are active or dormant in the Kurdish case. It discusses four aspects: the first is an abstract, theoretical examination of prerequisites of nationhood; the second is the construction of nations from above as opposed to that from below; the third is the unravelling of Iraq's nation-ness and the subsequent failure to rebuild Iraqi nationalism; the fourth is the prospect for such endeavours in Iraqi Kurdistan, and whether or not it is inherently similar to the Arab-Iraqi pattern.

Through the aforementioned four aspects, then, this chapter will examine major modalities or conditions that can serve as indicators of the potential success or possible failure of nation-building. These can be represented in several dichotomies: top-down versus bottom-up nation-building; coercive assimilation versus voluntary integration; command versus market economy; homogeneous versus heterogeneous cultures; and internal versus external sovereignty. The practice of Arab and Iraqi nation-building has revealed only a partial understanding of, or else a full-blown disregard for, such complexities, which have the potential to make or break nations.

What are Nations, and How Do They Come About?

Nations do not grow naturally. Rather, they are conscious socio-economic, cultural and political constructions. They are the products of meticulous engineering that may or may not promote such grand constructions.

If the concept of 'state' is almost self-evident, involving as it does a political apparatus with control over territory (via Max Weber's successful monopoly of the means of coercion), the populace inhabiting this political unit is, or should be, the 'nation'. But what is a nation? Is it a community characterized by some common marker: language, or religion, or even race? In certain cases (Japan) all three markers are present, yet in other cases (the USA, India) none of these markers exist. The definitions of nation and state require a third element, which is the primordial 'glue': nationalism. This is a discourse/movement to bring about the unity of the two, the congruence of nation and state.

Are nations random constructions? In many senses, the answer is in the affirmative. The question as to why they emerged in the eighteenth, nineteenth and twentieth centuries invites two opposing conceptions: for Ernest Gellner, nations formed due to industrialism; for Anthony Smith, however, a longer sociocultural history, predating industrialism, explains why nations emerged.[2] The latter suggest a perennial pattern of nationalism, which seems a contradiction in terms.

Novel or perennial, a nation needs to be constructed as a socio-political and economic unit. This unit includes three distinct yet overlapping systems of integration:

1. There is a need for a material communication systems stemming from the rise of mass commercial production known as capitalism or industrialism (production, exchange, circulation, currency, railways, markets etc.). This transcends the age-old 'solitary confinement' of villages, towns and countries, and creates organic bonds of mutual, integrative dependency.
2. Another is a cultural cohesive system (lingua franca, religion) together with educational agencies, printing presses, art and literature, and other cultural artefacts. Benedict Anderson focuses on 'print capitalism' and the 'novel' (literature) as vital devices to anthropologically 'imagine', not to create, the community.
3. Lastly, a unifying administrative-political system with adequate means of violence and a strong judiciary – both embedded in widely accepted legitimacy on the basis of open, participatory institutions – is required to hold the national entity together.

Without some combination of these three, no nation state could ever arise. Modalities of nation-building are as varied as languages, histories, locations and religions. Those countries that shifted from fragmented pre-industrial conditions to modern nation-statehood primarily utilizing System 1, physical infrastructure, have been called 'natural', while those which started from System 3, that is, a centralizing political power, are often classified as 'artificial'. The dichotomy natural/artificial seems to relate to two important aspects of nationhood. National unity in the first instance, that of the so-called natural nations, stems from below and is strong enough to generate self-sustainability. Hence, consent is the basic element whereas coercion is supplementary in terms of maintaining nation states, although coercion, that is, violence, is necessary from the standpoint of other conflicts of interest not related to nationhood. In the second case, that of 'artificial nations', coercion is primary; consent is almost, as a rule, a secondary corollary. This was the case for the new Iraqi colonial state in its first phase, 1921–36.

In this context, artificiality is a peculiar concept given that nations are always constructed sociopolitical designs. It is, however, a fruitful reminder that top-down nation-building yields weak entities, which teeter on the verge of collapse. It also serves as a reminder of the limited effectiveness of coercive methods (assimilation) and the need to shift from the primacy of coercion to the primacy of consent. This is a critical stage that needs to be achieved and, more importantly, sustained. For instance, Iraq has been dubbed an 'artificial' nation state, put together at random by the British colonial administration from three distinct and disconnected Ottoman provinces: Mosul, Baghdad and Basra. This argument, however, is very loose. It condemns all nations built from above to failure in each and every circumstance. Such broad-brush, intrinsic generalizations fail to account for cases of success, or show causes of failure. The cases of nation-building from above have inherent weakness, but they also have some elements of continuity.

It could be argued, then, that nation-building from above is extremely weak, at least at the beginning, but the seeds of self-destruction in it can be neutralized. A shift from coercion to consent is possible. Finally, the terms and conditions of the pluralistic inclusion of all segments in the 'manufactured' nationhood need to be protected, refined, perfected, negotiated and renegotiated in tandem with sociopolitical and cultural changes. The failure to tend to such broad conditionality is bound to cause the disintegration of the nation state.

This is the case for the Iraq nation state: segmentation, success, disruption, failure and disintegration. It remains to be examined whether this would be the same trajectory on which Kurdish-Iraq-based nationalism may be setting out.

The Creation of Iraq: The Dilemma of State-Formation and Nation-Building

The Iraq case in the period of 1914–32, from the year of invasion to the year that Iraq joined the League of Nations, is one of a centralization effort that gradually developed into nation-state-building from above – that is, the 'artificial' type.[3] It was also largely coercion-based, narrowly anchored in consent, embedded in cultural diversity, and with a non-organic, agricultural–artisanal–mercantile economy.[4]

The new state-nation (rather than nation state) was constructed, initiated and largely implemented by the British colonial administration, under Sir Percy Cox (from 1920 to 1923) and Sir Henry Dobbs (from 1923 to 1929), two successive high commissioners. Native groups and forces, both pro or anti, were also involved in the process from the very beginning: ex-Ottoman 'Iraqi' officers; ex-Ottoman civil servants; the urban, noble and mercantile classes; tribal chieftains; clerics; Sufi leaders; and other groups. The first prime minister was a noble Sufi leader (Abdul Rahman al-Naqib of the Qadiriya Sufi order). Iraq was segmented, and its segments fragmented in every conceivable fashion. The very concept of nation or nationhood seemed a logical contradiction in definition.

The Iraqi territorial space was not only divided into three provinces (Mosul, Baghdad and Basra) but each province was segmented and fragmented in socio-economic and cultural terms. These conditions reveal the fact that centrifugal dissent was the order of the day, and that military action was more appropriate than peaceful engagement: the Najaf insurrection (1916–18) and the 1920 revolt cost the British treasury some £50 million, a staggering figure by today's prices; some 2,000 were killed and wounded on the British side, and 8,450 on the Iraqi side.[5]

Centrifugal demands had surfaced before – for instance, after the creation of the native administration that had replaced direct, colonial rule.[6] The observer, looking at this period, is struck by these glaring centrifugal forces; Basra in the south showed leanings towards a 'Basrite kingdom'[7] and the Kurds twice rebelled under Shaykh Mahmood Barzinji, with nationalist calls for independence in the garb of a Kurdish kingdom. The Turks were still occupying tracts of land and small towns in the ex-province of Mosul, notably in Rawanduz and its surroundings.[8]

Parallel to these centrifugal forces, Iraqi nationalist centripetal forces were also at work. These had a discourse with a twofold effect: firstly, enhancing the drive to centralization, if for no reason other than that of inventing the Iraqi nationalist discourse; secondly, as this discourse was responsive, anti-British and almost xenophobic, it was bound to oppose direct colonial rule and, later on, the hegemonic British 'mandate'. This line marked the opposition in the street as in parliament, but it also represented the 'ethos' and 'mentality' of the Iraqi Arab urban elite, which was inclined to work with the British colonial administration throughout the mandate period.

Iraqi nationalist, anti-British agitation continued unabated in Baghdad, opposing the British treaty so hard-pressed by Sir Percy Cox but never materializing during his term in office.[9]

After the endorsement of the treaty with the British (alongside a national constitution in 1924), Shi'i clerics in Najaf changed course; they withdrew their support for King Faysal, reversing their previous *fatwas* for an Arab Muslim prince to rule over the country. Shi'i people at large were now prohibited from working in the departments of the new state. Clerical opposition, it must be made clear, was directed not against the native government but rather against the conclusion of the Iraqi–British Treaty, which was in their eyes a colonial bondage. Many leading Iraqi politicians, including King Faysal, had similar views but were aware of the inherent weakness of the nascent state and its inability to do without, or do away with, the treaty.[10]

Nonetheless, the cleavage with Najaf, the seat of Shi'i clerical authority in the country, was glaring at this very early stage of central state formation.

Regionally, the new entity, the Iraqi Kingdom, was not yet recognized by its neighbours. Turkey fought hard to regain the Mosul province, in a case that was raised, negotiated and debated in successive international forums – Lausanne, San Remo and the League of Nations, among others.[11] Iran was grudgingly silent, and the Saudi principality to the south was unfriendly.

In short, this was a pre-national case. It concerned an agrarian society strained by cultural conflict, divided vertically by religious and communal hierarchies and torn by the city–tribe divide, with heterogeneous cultures, weak cities, a feeble artisanal–mercantile economy and strong tribes in an antagonistic, segmentary world. A few decades on, the country became riddled with newly emerging modern cleavages of class and ethnicity and a variety of nationalisms: Arab-Iraqi in Baghdad, but also Kurdish nationalism, upheld by competing Sufi/tribal leaders, and Turkmen nationalism and loyalty to Turkey. This was not a promising case for state-formation or nation-building.

Both before and after his coronation as the first monarch of Iraq, King Faysal I was painfully aware of this reality. Discussing the fate of 'Iraq', the King warned Sir Percy Cox, the British high commissioner, that giving the Kurds independence according to the Treaty of Sèvres would cut the size of the country's Sunni populace in half, and leave him with a predominantly Shi'i population.[12] After a few years as a monarch, King Faysal lamented, 'Iraq is among the countries which lack the most vital element of social life: cultural, nationalist and religious unity.'[13] To connect these elements, Basra, Baghdad, Sulaimaniya and Najaf were required to hold the fragments together.

Theoretically, a state elite was needed to hold together the two most important state institutions, the army and the administration, and a social elite was also required to hold the nation's social fabric in some sort of 'patriotic' cohabitation. The former process had to do with state-formation; the latter with nation-building. These two aspects are one and the same in homogeneous communities; in heterogeneous ones they are two relatively separate, though overlapping, aspects.

The British began with state-formation ahead of nation-building, lending making Iraq a showcase of a 'state in search of a nation'. State-formation is a question of creating agencies of governance: a monarch; cabinet; constitution; flag; currency; territory borders; and, most of important of all, civil administration, judiciary and security institutions (police, military etc.).[14]

This system was dual: partly 'Iraqi', partly British. The mandate state was a conjoined twin of native–foreign structure. The new native staff was mostly drawn from Ottoman functionaries who, by dint of a long history of the 'sacred' empire, were mostly Muslims by religion, Sunni by sect, mostly Arabs but including also Kurds and Turkmen. By definition, this narrow mix may have been a sufficient cement to hold the state together, but it was an insufficient glue to hold a newly made nation. Lacking a strong Kurdish element and strong Shi'i-Arab factors, it was inherently flawed. If the British could lay down the foundations of state-formation so easily and quickly in the years 1916–25, the building block of nationhood took at least two decades to enhance. This is best seen in the role of coercion vis-à-vis consent in the relations between state and local communities.

The British deployed 'colonial', then colonial-native, violence against dissenters in order to ensure both colonial rule and the centralization drive that they had initiated. Air power and/or ground forces were deployed against in the Kurds in 1923–4 and 1927; air power was also deployed against rebellious Arab Shi'i tribes in the south, who were opposing conscription, and against Assyrian demands for local autonomy (1932), which ended in the notorious Semele Massacre of 1937.[15]

The more we advance, the less often violence is required. The shift from highly coercive assimilation to voluntary integration in Iraq passed through two interconnected phases.

In the first phase, a social factor, the landlord class, was crucial. This class was empowered in economic (land ownership), political (in the upper chamber of the parliament) and legal (applying tribal customary law under their jurisdiction) terms. Interestingly, the composition of this landlord class, created and promoted under an intentional British design, almost matched the ethno-religious structure of the Iraqi population: around 50 per cent were Shi'i Arab; some 20 per cent Kurds (Sunni); some 20 per cent Sunni Arabs; and the rest were divided among Turkmen, Assyrians and other Christian categories.[16] It was a multi-ethnic, multi-religious, multi-sectarian landlord class; under these conditions, it was a 'universal' class that served to build the nation and constituted the social basis of the monarchy (1920–58).

In the second phase, institutional factors, a market economy and a parliamentary–constitutional polity were decisive. A feature common to both phases was the existence of open participatory mechanisms, which were opened up in political, cultural and, more importantly, economic terms. In the transition from the first to the second phase, the social weight and status of the landlord class was waning, and the traditional political class of nobles and notables also declined. However, the business and bureaucratic classes were slowly growing, and, with them, the size, number and influence of the Iraqi lower-middle classes and the urban poor (the latter mostly drawn from declining artisans and, more commonly, from the migrant peasantry). The whole system showed a remarkable degree of openness and flexibility throughout the early, difficult years of nation-building. Once in place, however, it showed little consideration for the social change brought about by state-formation – the new social structure stemming from the growth of the country's market economy, the expansion of its modern educational system and the staggering increase in the rate and tempo of urbanization. The new upper and middle classes were strong enough to adjust to the system, but the monarchy – with its nobles, notables, shaykhs and *aghas* ('lords') – was unwilling to accommodate the changes.

The demise of the Iraqi monarchy, hailed by so many historians as a triumph of the middle classes, led to contradictory outcomes.[17] In political terms, it closed the political system and shut down channels of political participation, but it opened the gates for conspiratorial and armed politics. In economic terms, it led to a state-controlled economy, closing down the market as a conduit for economic participation. True, the new ruling elite was indeed drawn from the country's middle strata, but it was confined to a narrowly based military *nomenklatura* that by dint of its own sociopolitical fragility appealed to kinship–tribal and, at times, local–communal networks. This in turn damaged, and ultimately shattered, the old mechanisms for participation. Ethnic and communal grievances directed against the monopolistic state served to reshape the political system and to re-form the mechanisms of national integration. The revolt of the Kurds (1964–75) led to the endorsement of Kurdish autonomy in the country's constitution. The 1974 Shi'i demonstrations led to partial change in its inclusion mechanisms, but these were reversed during the Iran–Iraq War (the first Gulf War) with its expulsion of Shi'as and security camps for the Kurds. The 1980s represented a declining trajectory in terms of Iraqi national unity. The best evidence for this change are the 1991 rebellions in the north and the south of the country, led respectively by Kurds–Leftists and Shi'i Islamist groups, not to mention insurrections within the army.[18] And the clearest manifestation of this profound change was the shift from ideological politics, which had characterized Iraq from the early 1940s to the late 1970s, to the identity politics that has overwhelmed it since 2003.

To sum up the modalities of this long, arduous process: Iraq has thus far gone through five major phases of state centralization and nation-building:

1. Nation-building in Iraq initially proceeded from above (1921–37), relying heavily on state power and international sovereignty (via the colonial British mandate); there was some effort to garner societal consent – mostly, but not exclusively, from Arabs. In this attempt, the French approach to build on 'common interests' and 'forgetting grievances of the past' (feuds among tribes or communities) was pursued. These are or were the only positive factors in centralization-state nation-building.[19] On the negative side stand

the agrarian–artisanal local economy, cultural diversity, tribal segmentation and ethno-religious cleavages – and the centrifugal forces flowing from them.
2. A shift from centralization per se to constructing the nation from below (up to 1958) proceeded gradually: the creation of a multi-ethno-cultural landlord class mixed well with an urban state elite to hold the system from below as from above. The development and spread of an integrative market economy was instrumental, whereas the relatively open nature of the political system allowed for the inclusion and representation of different ethnic and cultural groups.
3. The so-called revolutionary–military phase (1958–68), which developed a strain of authoritarianism, may have 'improved the representation of the middle classes', as Batatu contends, but it definitely disrupted – and subsequently almost destroyed – the country's integrative mechanisms. The accompanying military or single-party rule shut down representative institutions; monopolized political power, often in the hands of a narrow group (a junta or tribal grouping); gradually built a monopolized command economy that wedded economic and political power; and manipulated the distribution of national wealth. The monolithic nature of this political order invited opposition, and this opposition in turn encountered growing tendencies by successive military regimes to deploy coercive assimilation rather than voluntary integration. I have dubbed this change a shift from the French, common-interest state nationalism to a corecive, German, ethnic-violent state nationalism model (after Fichte, as cited in footnote 19).
4. The Ba'ath single-party regime (1968–2003) continued such policies after a short period of accommodating diversity. Indeed the Ba'ath moved for a full-fledged command economy, and imposed a party–state and state–clan hegemony that tolerated no pluralism or diversity in whatever sense, under its totalitarian regime. During this era, however, symbolic icons were created to ceremonially represent the country's Kurds, Shi'as and non-Arabs under the guise of Babylonian motifs; or under the the figure of the medieval Kurdish warrior, Salahudin; or the names of Shi'i imams, Hussain and Abbas.[20]

In short, this total hegemony brought about the demise of the Iraqi nation state as of 1991, and its expiry in 2003 was simply a

ceremonial final scene. As a cultural edifice, this discourse disintegrated immediately after the defeat in the second Gulf War, 1991. A new trend towards Islam and tribe was effected, which combined two different discourses: the kinship ideology and state-sponsored Islamism. The last bastions of state nationalism collapsed.
5. The last, and current, phase is a new search for a rebuilding of the Iraqi state-nation (rather than nation state) under various conditions – among them, the rise and militarization of identity politics – some of which preserve the seeds of conflict. As of 2003–5, the political order was redesigned into a federal polity. For the first time in history, Kurds enjoyed their own semi-autonomous statelet, enshrined in the constitution and established in reality, with a parliament, government, armed forces and presidency. Its federal status stands little short of confederacy; indeed, it has some features of that tradition. Federalism, however, is a sensitive order that thrives on equity. The authoritarian tendencies at the centre, Baghdad, have strained the realtionship between the federal government and the KRG, denying the latter its share of the national budget. The authoritarian tendencies in the KRG itself have also produced some negative effects.

Kurdish Dilemmas, Expectations and Bewilderment

Since the fall of Mosul on 9 June 2014, the Kurds in Erbil have shown more enthusiasm for full separation. Relations with Baghdad became strained as a result of the suspension of allocations to the KRG (17 per cent of the national budget was offered, but only some 12 per cent was actually delivered), and the suspension (until September 2016) of official talks coupled with a covert, mutual slander campaign. On various occasions in 2015 and 2016, the KRG president, Masoud Barzani, reiterated plans to hold a referendum – it was presumed, on Kurdish independence. The war against ISIS (the Islamic State of Iraq and Syria) and later IS (Islamic State), drew the Kurds into the web of international schemes for the 'war on terror'. US and European Union (EU) support for the Kurds in military, financial and diplomatic terms increased dramatically.

The call for independence coming from Erbil, and specifically from the Kurdistan Democratic Party (KDP), brings forth all the past experiences of the grand Sufi cleric Mahmood Barzinji. Barzani invoked the long suffering of the Kurds from the construction of Iraq as a state-nation, the heroic yearning to have their own autonomous polity and the tragedy when their labour was lost.

Of course, the Kurds had been constrained by the rise or enhancement of territorial or national states around them in the larger Middle East since 1916. The 'successes of one are the calamities of another', one Arab proverb says, in what could have served as a Kurdish axiom. And the stronger these states as systems of control and governance, the weaker the Kurds became in their endeavours. The paradox, however, was that the neighbouring nationalisms — of Arabs, Turks or Iranians — emerged almost simultaneously in pre-national societies, and in that sociological sense they had much in common with the Kurds. They all lacked the homogenizing potency of modern industrialism and they all suffered from segmented cultural diversity (be it linguistic or religious). The differences lay in the existence or, as in the case of the Kurds, absence of a state apparatus to hold together the various sociocultural segments from above in one nation state. In 1920, the Arabs of Iraq were on par with the Kurds in this crucial political condition: the lack of a unifying political system. Had it not been for the British colonial administration filling the gap, Iraq as it came to be known would not have existed. The British colonial army–administration acted in lieu of an absent native state. Had the Kurds moved to build a state under Mahmood Hafeed in 1919–20, it would have been another case of building a state-nation from above in the pre-national conditions of a fragmented, agrarian society. Their Arab neighbours, sitting at the helm in Baghdad and backed by the British, had to transform tribal shaykhs into landlords, and landlords into feudal lords ruling over the countryside in accordance with the tribal customary law, which was recognized by the 'central' government. It was a dual internal sovereignty, which allowed the state to exist. This could have been the case for the Kurds had Hafeed, who launched a campaign to unify Kurdistan, involved territories beyond the Sulaimaniya–Rawanduz axis (see Maps 1–3 on the 1920 Sèvres Treaty, above).[21] This hypothetical line of development was indeed latent; its actualization was contingent on external conditions. All the forces surrounding the Sulaimaniya Kurdish centre of would-be 'nationalism' were, in one way or another, hostile to it.[22] Sovereignty has to be generated not only from within but also from without. The native internal dynamics were also too fragile to hold. The Kurds of Iraq were segmented and fragmented in the strict sociological meaning of the term. And the Sulaimaniya centre headed by Mahmood Hafeed could not extend its influence beyond Rawanduz, and never attempted to reach out to Erbil or Duhok. The 1919 rebellion failed, as did those of 1922–3, when Hafeed placed a crown on his head as King of Kurdistan; such were also the fates of the 1927 and 1930 insurrections. In Kurdish nationalist discourse these episodes sound heroic; in British documents they look more like quixotic forays.[23]

The 'Kingdom' of Mahmood Hafeed had structural–sociological problems in its nation-building and state-formation similar to those encountered by mandated Iraq.

The well-known 1920 Sèvres Treaty – so widely cited by Kurds as the first international document in which their right to nationhood[24] was mentioned, in the spirit of the Wilsonian 14-point declaration of 1918 – was signed by the Ottoman Sultan but not ratified by his government. This document, which was soon shelved, was a draft rather than a working treaty.

The existence of a centre of power equipped with domestic legitimacy, however limited or incomplete (as Hafeed's was), is not a sufficient condition for the creation of a nation state. Back in 1919–20, or latterly in 2015–17, external recognition, regional and international, was nowhere evident. Native sovereignty cannot do without international sovereignty; they are the two legal–institutional sides of modern state-nationhood. And lack of international sovereignty is habitually the weakest point in the Kurdish edifice. One of the major Arabic blunders, by contrast, is the persistence in constructing the nation from above by coercive, monopolized, political means. Notwithstanding, a 'replica' of such an error seems to be developing in the KRG as of 2018.

For all intents and purposes, a two-party system has been in operation since at least 1991 (after the first elections in Kurdistan) and more solidly since 2005, when two successive polls – constituency elections in January and parliamentary elections in December – took place and legitimized the two ruling parties: the Barzani-led KDP and the Jalal Talabani-led Patriotic Union of Kurdistan (PUK). Peripheral parties do exist: three Islamic parties, one communist party and a few Christian outfits (Assyrian and Chaldean). Even after the Gorran (Change) splinter group left the PUK, it could not effectively challenge the presidency in Erbil. The speaker of the Kurdish Parliament, a Gorran figure, was outlawed and blacklisted in Erbil. The political schism between the KDP and the PUK is a fact of life, some electoral and political cooperation in Baghdad notwithstanding. The cleavage involves a regional–cultural–sociological break in Kurdish society. The bipolar party system bears striking similarities to the old single-party tradition so widespread in the Middle East and, of course, in Iraq under the Ba'ath regime. A single-party system provides coherent leadership at the helm but it usually prevents a comprehensive representation of all segments of society; when it does allow this, it imposes stringent controls and demands subservient loyalty in return. It also develops authoritarian tendencies, electoral freedom notwithstanding. Primordial traits, such as kinship or tribal networks, usually creep into modern ME political parties, concentrating power at the helm in fewer and fewer hands. While the single-party system may generally be a powerful engine with which to erect the foundations of nationhood (the model of nation-building from above), under specific conditions – such as 'politicized' cultural diversity and/or sociological cleavages, and ethnic multiplicity – it is counterproductive. The amalgam of party–state and party–clan is conducive to an excessive monopoly of power – which deepens fault lines and invites multiple conflicts, tearing 'national' unity apart. In short, the absence of a strong political centre in Iraq in 1919–20 worked in a similar way to the existence of an excessively powerful one in 2003–17. The historical paradox is that these two divergent modalities were/are conducive to one and the same negative outcome. Perhaps the post-referendum crisis in Kirkuk illustrates this most vividly.[25]

The pre-referendum internal crisis related to the presidency and the constitutional process. An extension of the presidency,[26] and controversy over the role of Islamic Shari'a law lay at the heart of the matter. Another factor was the constitutional debate.[27] Tensions flared as anti-KDP demonstrations in Sulaimaniya, protesting against the suspension of salary payments, ended in the killing of some demonstrators. Lastly, the latest factional split (August 2016), led by ex-KRG prime minister Barham Salih and incumbent KRG vice-president Kusret Rasool against Hero Khan, Talabani's wife and the actual leader of the PUK, spoke volumes for this overt and covert opposition to single party–family control of the levers of power.[28]

The schisms outlined above are products of the development of the authoritarian single-party system; they reveal to what extent nation-building from above is precarious when it is gradually stripped of its democratic content.

The dividing effect of authoritarianism is accentuated by another feature in the system: a mixture of rentier and command economies. The KRG's economy is basically rentierist, relying heavily on oil revenues. A command economy is still largely in place despite limited liberalism and the growth of a new business class, which has produced a few thousand multi-millionaires in both Sulaimaniya and Erbil regions. Rentierism breeds authoritarianism and enhances the power of the elite at the helm. Manufactured and controlled liberalism, on the other hand, generates a new breed of politician–businessperson; it is a mixture of crony capitalism and the politician-capitalist, wielding economic and political power in one.[29] A free-market economy, on the other hand, usually spreads a web of interconnectivity generated by economic interests and a material infrastructure bringing people and regions together; this web involves countless individuals, firms and groups in the production, circulation and exchange of commodities and services; they interact freely and directly without the mediation of the ruling power from above. Command and rentier economies, by contrast, seem to build a different type of web connecting individuals, firms and groups or entities – not among themselves, but separately to the controlling centre, i.e., the state elite. The Durkheimian, organic links associated with the market economy are thus replaced by a mechanical link, with a hegemon at the top.[30]

This command–rentier compound also acts on the party–state amalgam, investing more power in the party nomenklatura and hollowing out institutions of policy and decision making (parliament and cabinet) – an outcome that, in turn, alienates and antagonizes all groups, parties or segments outside the monopolizing centre.

Kurdish euphoria at achieving federalism in 2003–5 thrived on prospects of promoting this into an independent national entity, and such tendencies were enhanced by the spread of identity politics across Iraq. In the subsequent years, a gradual shift from identity to issue-based politics occurred, which thrived on rivalry over political and economic resources, exacerbated as it was by the emergence of a de facto single-party monopoly. This has been a pan-Iraqi phenomenon, not entirely confined to the Kurds.[31]

Lastly, cultural heterogeneity and political segmentation is again on the agenda. Pan-Kurdish nationalism theoretically involving all Kurds in Turkey, Syria, Iran, Iraq and beyond proved to be a replica of pan-Latin Americanism or pan-Arabism – that is, failed projects. Abbas Vali, an outstanding scholar of Kurdish nationalism, insists on using the term in the plural – nationalisms – to stress the *sui generis* character of each Kurdish community, acting in and reacting to the different realities of different nation states.[32] The KRG in Iraq is indeed deeply immersed in direct rivalry with a formidable contender – the PKK – not only among the Kurdish nationalist movements in Syria and Iran but also within the KRG itself.

Apart from the pan-Kurdish cleavage, the rise of the KRG – first as a de facto, autonomous statelet (1991–2003), then as a constitutionally recognized federal region – faced two different sets of cultural heterogeneity: 1. the identity politics of non-Kurdish, non-dominant communities such as Turkmen, Assyrians and Chaldeans; and 2. the Kermanji-speaking Badinan region vs the Sorani region dialect, or the Yezidi cleavages. In the words of Martin van Bruinessen, '[a]t least two different forms of this ethnic [as against pan-national] resurgence of regional-linguistic particularism ("Badinan" versus "Soran") in Iraqi Kurdistan'[33] underlie the KDP–PUK split and rivalry. The duality of the Yezidi identity, as Kurds or non-Kurds, constitutes another case in point, which could well be added.[34] The Sulaimaniya–Erbil divide has a long history. As does the tribal divide between the Barzani clan, which has provided leadership to the nationalist movement since the 1940s, and the Zibari, Herki, Sorchi, Mezori and Mezei tribes that stood against it and manned almost all mercenary groups fighting the Kurdish nationalist movement. In the official jargon, these tribes are known as Fursan Salahudin (The Knights of Salahudin); in the nationalist discourse, they are *Jash* (Donkeys). The cleavage between the two sides still lingers on today in the form of linguistic–cultural conflict. The Kermanji-speaking tribes, centred in and around Duhok Province, resisted the standardization of state-sponsored schooling and curricula on the basis of the Sorani dialect, and forced the KRG to use Kermanji-based schooling.[35]

The split between Erbil and Sulaimaniya is flagrant; that between Badinan and Soran tribes or districts was thinly concealed but ultimately resolved. Such schisms and cleavages do not in themselves hinder state-formation or nation-building; the specific approach to them does.

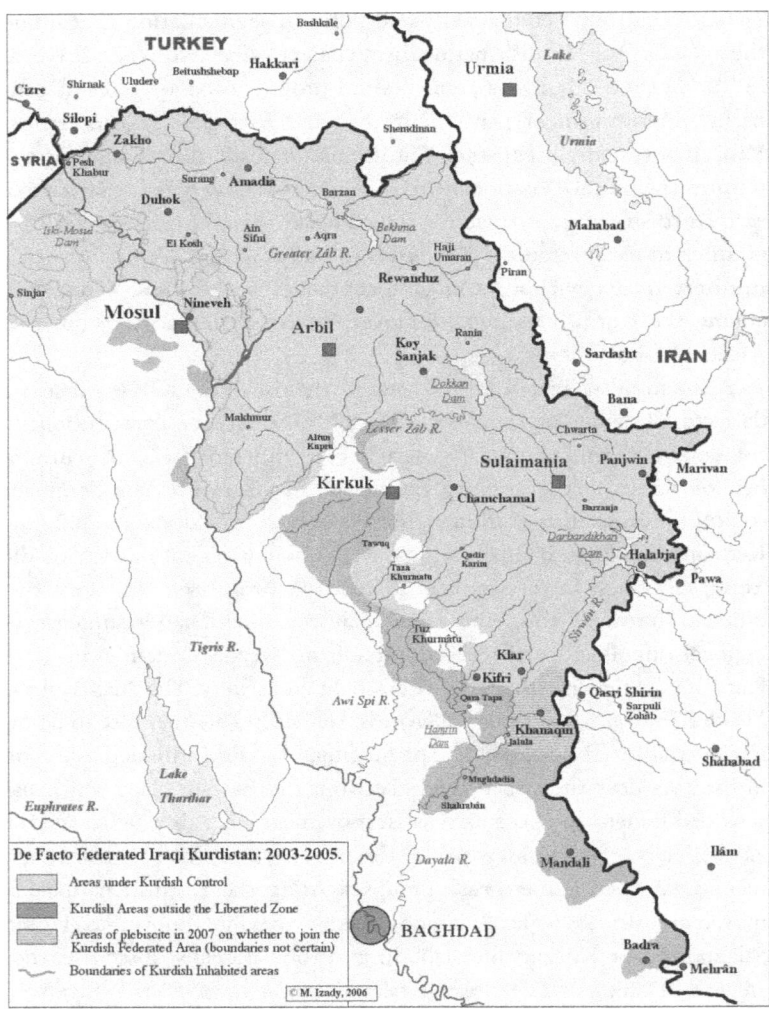

Map 1 Federated Iraqi Kurdistan 2003–5.

Conclusions

Looking at the long trajectory of state- and nation-building in Iraq by the Arabs (since 1921) or among the Kurds (since 1991), many twists and turns of success and failure stand in stark relief. We may tentatively conclude that the systems of integration required by any successful national project include a material web, flowing from a modern market economy and communications; a cultural web (lingua franca, religion, conceptions of history etc.); and a legitimately unifying political–administrative order.

A command–rentier economy; authoritarian, single-family parties; and top-down nation-building are the antithesis of any successful endeavour to construct the nationhood that the Kurds need.

Looking at the five major phases of, or approaches to, nation-building mentioned at the beginning, prospects do not improve. The bottom-up approach is definitely superior to top-down nation-building; a corollary of it is voluntary integration, which is more unifying than coercive assimilation. An open market economy is also nationally cohesive, however socially divisive (in class terms), in sharp contrast to a command economy, which is nationally and socially divisive. When negative modalities accumulate (top-down; coercion; and monopolized, command economy), they most certainly turn cultural heterogeneity into a hotbed of internal conflicts that impede the creation of nationhood in many macabre ways.

Such an outcome has the potential to shake internal sovereignty and render its corollary, that is, international sovereignty, all the more remote. Current conditions do not seem promising. Much of their negative aspects flow from eclectic policy choices; and these are not necessarily irreversible. The irony is that political options have antagonistic elements, rational and irrational at one and the same time.

References

Anderson, Benedict, *Imagined Communities* (London, Verso, 1983/1985).
Gellner, Ernest, 'Nationalism' entry, in Tom Bottomore (ed.), *Blackwell Dictionary of Social Thought in the Twentieth Century*, 3rd edition (Oxford, Blackwell, 2006), pp. 422–4.
Hobsbawm, Eric, *Nations and nationalism since 1780* (Cambridge, Cambridge University Press, 1990).
Kohn, Hans, *Nationalism, its Meaning and History* (New York, Van Nostrand 1955).
Smith, Anthony, *Theories of Nationalism* (London, Duckworth, 1971).
—— *The Ethnic Origins of Nations* (Oxford, Blackwell, 1986).
—— *National Identity* (London, Penguin, 1991).

Notes

1. In a brief digression, the disruption of nation-building mechanisms in the broader Middle East has been a catalyst, among many others, of the so-called Arab Spring. Paradoxically, the failure of this movement, culminating in civil wars (Syria, Yemen, Libya and Iraq), has brought the Kurdish quest for representation to the fore. This is one of the many factors that have created such euphoric strides in the Kurdistan region.
2. Ernest Gellner, *Nations and Nationalism* (Blackwell, Oxford, 1992 (1983)), p. 3 *passim*.
3. This relies in part on my chapter, 'Artificial and Natural Nation Building', in G.D. Koury and Nadine Meouchy, *Etats et Socieites de L' Orient Arabe 1945– 2005*, vol. II (Paris, Geuthner, 2007).
4. The history of mandatory Iraq is too well known to need recounting here. However biased their anti-Ottoman and pro-British stance, S.H. Longrigg's two books – *Four Centuries of Modern Iraq* (London, Oxford University Press, 1925) and *Iraq 1900 to 1950: a Political, Social and Economic History* (London, Oxford University Press, 1953) – are still indispensable. Philip W. Ireland, *Iraq: a Study in Political Development* (London, Cape, 1937); Majid Khadduri, *Independent Iraq 1932–1958: a Study in Iraq Politics*, 2nd revised edition (London, Oxford University Press, 1960); and Peter Sluglett, *Britain in Iraq 1914–1932* (London, Ithaca Press, 1976), are meticulous, extensive and cohesive. Hanna Batatu, *The Old Social Classes and the Revolutionary Movements of Iraq: a Study of Iraq's Old Landed and Commercial Classes and of its Communists, Ba'thists and Free Officers* (Princeton, NJ, Princeton University Press, 1978), is a masterpiece; see also Ghassan Attiyya, *Iraq 1908– 1921; a Political Study* (Beirut, Arab Institute for Research and Publishing, 1973). More recently, Charles Tripp, *A Political History of Iraq* (Cambridge, Cambridge University Press, 2000) and Toby Dodge, *Inventing Iraq: The Failure of Nation-Building and a History Denied* (New York, Columbia University Press, 2003) both breathe new life into certain aspects of this and other periods – as does Phebe Marr in the second edition of *The Modern History of Iraq* (Boulder, CO, Westview, 2004). A new addition is Gareth Stansfield, *IRAQ*, 2nd edition (Polity Press, 2016).
5. Ireland, *Iraq: a Study*, p. 273.
6. The colonial Civil Commissioner in Iraq, Sir Arnold Wilson's concept of direct colonial rule *à la* India failed. His major book on Iraq, or Mesopotamia as he called it: Wilson, Arnold T., 1930, *Loyalties Mesopotamia 1914–1917: a Personal and Historical Record* (London, Oxford University Press), is an indirect testimony to this failure.
7. Reider Visser, in his *Basra, the Failed Gulf State: Sectarianism and Nationalism in Southern Iraq* (LIT Verlag, Munster, 2005), examines centrifugal and centripetal tendencies in the Basra province in the 1920s.

    On the insurrections in Najaf and Karbala in 1916–17 and the 1920 revolution, see Sluglett, *Britain in Iraq*; Ali al-Wardi, *Lamahat ijtima'iyah min tarikh al-'Iraq al-hadith*, Vols 1–6 (Ma'arif Press, Baghdad, 1969–78).

Ghassan At-iyya, Iraq, Nash'at al-Dawla (Iraq, State formation) 1908–1921 (Dar LAM, London, 1988).
8. Cultural heterogeneity was already politicized, as was clear in the plebiscite in 1921. Attiya, ibid., examines the referendums per city-ethnic or cultural group, which showed strong rejection of the would-be kingdom by the majority of the Kurds and Turkmen, and lesser opposition in Basra. Longrigg, *Four Centuries* 1925; Longrigg, *Iraq 1900 to 1950*; and Batatu, *The Old Social Classes* offer a detailed description of this pluralism and the geographical distribution of different ethno-religious communities.
9. Muhammad Mahdi al-Baseer, *Tarikh al-Qaziya al-Iraqiya* [The Annals of the Iraq Problem], 2 volumes (Baghdad, Al-Nafeedh, 1923), v. 2, p. 192.
10. Perhaps the second issue that angered clerics was the decision of Prime Minister Muhsin Sa'doon to arrest and deport a host of clerics, including Kashani of Najaf and Khalisi of Kazimiya, to Iran. This was an unprecedented and unheard-of assault on Shi'i clerical dignities. C.J. Edmonds, in his *Kurds, Turks and Arabs. Politics, Travel and Research in North-Eastern Iraq 1919–1925* (London, Oxford University Press, 1957), chapter 23, p. 309 (Arabic edition, translation and commentary by Georgis Fat-Hulah, n.d) recalls the strong reactions in Iran and the lack of reaction in Iraq. But this is a superficial view; the incident left deep scars in Najaf, Karbala, Kazimiya and beyond.
11. Muhsin al-Mutawali, *Kurd al-'Iraq* [Kurds of Iraq] (al-Dar al-Arabiya Lil Mausu'at, Beirut, 2001), p. 111 *passim*.
12. The meeting between 'Prince' Faysal and the British high commissioner Sir Percy Cox was examined by Peter Sluglett, *Britain in Iraq* (Ithaca Press for the Middle East Centre, St Antony's College, Oxford, 1976) and re-examined in Faleh A. Jabar, 'Artificial and Natural Nation-Building, Iraq-Nation-ness and the Centrally of the State', in *États et Sociétés de l'Orient arabe en Quête d'avenir* (Paris, Guthner, 2007).
13. Abdul Razzaq al-Hasani, *Tarisk al-Wizarat al-Iraqiya* [The History of Iraqi Cabinets], vol. I (Baghdad, Afaq Arabiya, 1988), p. 317.
14. Longrigg, *Iraq 1900 to 1950*, pp. 134–5: 'The constitutional position of the territory [Iraq] was yet singularly unclear. Its elements were a Turkish sovereignty still existing, though dormant: an unratified Mandate, accepted by Great Britain but unwelcome to "Iraq itself", a constitutional monarchy with no Constitution; an intended treaty relationship with Great Britain, but as yet no treaty'.
15. This has been a recurrent theme in almost all histories and/or analysis of national (dis)integration. See Kanan Makkiya, *Republic of Fear* (Berkeley and Los Angeles, California, University of California Press, 1989); and L. Anderson and G. Stansfield, *The future of Iraq: dictatorship, democracy, or division?* (Basingstoke, Palgrave Macmillan, 2004).
16. In his major work, *The Old Social Classes*, Hanna Batatu was concerned with the formation of modern social classes and their roles in the revolutionary upheavals that shook the region: Nasser of Egypt and Qassim of Iraq, among others. Yet,

his examination of the landlord class, the social pillar of the monarchy, was never related to nation-building although this class was at the heart of it. He also failed to examine the fractured nature of the middle classes and the resultant disruption of nation-building.
17. This is the basic theme of Batatu's major work, *The Old Social Classes*; see his introduction.
18. See Faleh A. Jabar, 'Why the uprisings failed', *MERIP*, No. 176 (May–June 1992).
19. This 'French approach' was theoretically developed by the French thinker, Ernest Renan, in his 1882 lecture, 'What is a Nation?' For the 'German tradition', Johann Gottlieb Fichte is often cited. See, Fichte, 'Addresses to the German Nation', 1807–8, etc. These 'models' of interpreting the nation are in many senses antagonistic, at least in their voluntary or spontaneous application. The first has a liberal aura, the second a totalitarian touch.
20. Amatzia Baram, *Culture, History and Ideology in the Formation of of Ba'thist Iraq, 1968–89* (Oxford, St Antony's College, Oxford, 1991); Amatzia Baram, 'Mesopotamian Identity in Ba'thi Iraq', *Middle Eastern Studies*, 19(4) (October 1983), pp. 246–455; Ofra Bengio, *Saddam's Word, the Political Discourse in Iraq* (Oxford, Oxford University Press, 2002).
21. The Sèvres Treaty, section III is dedicated to Kurdish autonomy. *Treaty of Peace Between the Allied & Associated Powers and Turkey Signed at Sevres - August 10, 1920 Note: Includes Peace Treaty of Versailles 28 June, 1919* – Section III/Kurdistan/Article 62: 'A Commission sitting at Constantinople and composed of three members appointed by the British, French and Italian Governments respectively shall draft within six months from the coming into force of the present Treaty a scheme of local autonomy for the predominantly Kurdish areas lying east of the Euphrates, south of the southern boundary of Armenia as it may be hereafter determined, and north of the frontier of Turkey with Syria and Mesopotamia, as defined in Article 27, II (2) and (3). If unanimity cannot be secured on any question, it will be referred by the members of the Commission to their respective Governments. The scheme shall contain full safeguards for the protection of the Assyro-Chaldeans and other racial or religious minorities within these areas, and with this object a Commission composed of British, French, Italian, Persian and Kurdish representatives shall visit the spot to examine and decide what rectifications, if any, should be made in the Turkish frontier where, under the provisions of the present Treaty, that frontier coincides with that of Persia.'

Article 63: 'The Turkish Government hereby agrees to accept and execute the decisions of both the Commissions mentioned in Article 62 within three months from their communication to the said Government.'

Article 64: 'If within one year from the coming into force of the present Treaty the Kurdish peoples within the areas defined in Article 62 shall address themselves to the Council of the League of Nations in such a manner as to show that a majority of the population of these areas desires independence from

Turkey, and if the Council then considers that these peoples are capable of such independence and recommends that it should be granted to them, Turkey hereby agrees to execute such a recommendation, and to renounce all rights and title over these areas. The detailed provisions for such renunciation will form the subject of a separate agreement between the Principal Allied Powers and Turkey. If and when such renunciation takes place, no objection will be raised by the Principal Allied Powers to the voluntary adhesion to such an independent Kurdish State of the Kurds inhabiting that part of Kurdistan which has hitherto been included in the Mosul vilayet.'

22. See Gertrude Bell, *Review of the Civil Administration of Mesopotamia, 1914-1920* (London, H.M. Stationery Office, 1920); Arnold T. Wilson, *A Clash of Loyalties: A Personal and Historical Record* (London, Oxford University Press, 1931); and Edmonds, *Kurds, Turks and Arabs*. Later works, mostly academic, provide another, sociological, analysis: Henry Field, *The Anthropology of Iraq* (USA, Field Museum Press, May 1940), two parts; Fredrik Barth, *Principles of Social Organization in Southern Kurdistan* (Oslo, Brodrene Jorgensen A\S, 1953).

23. The British representations of these episodes are best illustrated by Bell, *Review of Civil Administration* (CMD, 1916); and Wilson, *A Clash of Loyalties*. These books are well known to the Iraqi public; Ms. Bell's text was translated by the historian, Ja'far Khayat, under the title, *Fusool min Tarisk al-'Iraq al-Qareeb* [Chapters of Iraq's Recent History] (Baghdad, Dar al-Rafidain, 1949).

24. According to the official text, Armenia was granted independence, Kurdistan a form of autonomy.

25. In my various visits to the KRG in May, August and September 2016–2017, I never came across a single leader who supported the referendum. They all had reservations one way or another, but felt unable to show what might seem a 'rejection of independence'. Statements by Dr Latif Rasheed, a PUK Political Bureau member, and similar off-the-record remarks were made by several PUK and Gorran leaders interviewed in Erbil and Sulaimaniya (July, September 2015; March 2016; and May/August–September 2017).

26. Insiders confided that KDP officials made it clear to all other parties that unless an extension of the term of presidency was offered, a *coup d'état* might follow (March 2016).

27. Interview with Shoresh Rasool, member of the constitutional committee and a leading figure in the Gorran Party, Sulaimaniya, April 2015.

28. Criticism of the 'family' control in both Erbil and Sulaimaniya is not in short supply. The 'single-party' system is tailored in such a way as to include ministers from all parties in the cabinet in exchange for their submission. Parties other than the KDP admit they have no say in economic policy; foreign policy; the military; or, according to the latest criticism (March 2016), no genuine participation in the KRG national Security Council. For monopoly of power, See, Kawa Hassan, *Kurdistan's Democracy on the Brink* (Beirut, Carnegie Middle East Center, 2015).

29. A glance at this reality can be seen in Michiel Leezenberg's chapter in this volume. An extensive examination of the new middle classes in the KRG is to appear in the coming volume on Iraqi Kurdistan.
30. Such mechanical links reveal their disintegrative impact once the command economy melts down, as in Russia in the 1990s, or the hegemon is removed, as was the case in Iraq (2003) and Libya (2012). The political consequences of the command economy and rentierism have been thus far seen to be confined to the generation of authoritarianism, but have never been examined from the standpoint of national (dis)integration.
31. See F.A. Jabar, 'The Dilemma of Political Uncertainties', in *What Can Europe Do in Iraq?*, Berlin, Heinrich Böll Stiftung, 2009), vol. 11, pp. 10–29; and F.A. Jabar, 'The Uncertainty of Identity Politics in the New Society', in Ali Paya (ed.), *Iraq, Democracy and the Future of the Muslim World* (London, Routledge, 2010).
32. Abbas Vali, 'The Kurds and their "Others"', in Faleh Jabar et al. (eds), *Ethnicity and the State, The Kurds in the Middle East* (London, Saqi, 2006), pp. 49–78.
33. Martin van Bruinessen, *Kurdish Paths to Nation* (Beirut, Iraq Studies, 2006), p. 36 *passim*.
34. It is indeed interesting to note that ethno-national identity – while conceptualized in the spirit of the old German school, Herde's *Stamme* (clan or blood-bound group) – proves situational rather than essential. Free choice of identity has never receded, among either Kurds or Arabs.
35. There are at least four Kurdish 'dialects': Sorani, Kermanji, Zaza and Luri. Surani is widespread in Erbil and Sulaimaniya; Kermanji in the region north of Arbil, Durhok, and in Kurdish regions in Syria (all written in the Arabic alphabet) and in parts of Turkey (written in the Latin alphabet). Zaza is to be found in Syria and Turkey; Luri is spoken by segments of Iranian Kurds. The implications of this linguistic diversity have been thoroughly examined by Sarbast Nabi, a professor of philosophy and Kurdologist, in an unpublished discussion paper: 'Iraq Studies Conference, The Kurdish Dilemma', December 2013. His argument may reinforce Abbas Vali's concept of fractured nationalisms, but goes beyond that into promoting cultural diversity against any coercive homogenization.

CHAPTER 2

PROBLEMS AND OUTLOOKS OF KURDISH REPRESENTATION

Renad Mansour

In modern Kurdish history, claims to represent the national Kurdistani community, however the term 'community' is understood or defined, are sundry, multifaceted and conflicting. In Iraq, Kurdish leaders have relied on several claims to legitimacy and representation when governing at home, negotiating with the central government in Baghdad and engaging in diplomacy with international actors. Drawn from Kurdish practice throughout four distinct periods of time spanning much of the twentieth century to the beginning of the millennium, this chapter investigates the leadership's varied claims and attempts to speak on behalf of their constituents.

The first period was the post-World War I era and the creation of the Iraqi state. During this time, British political officers engaged with Kurdish tribal and urban leaders to find legitimate representatives who could negotiate for the Kurds. The second period was the 1946–75 era, when Mullah Mustafa Barzani emerged as the leader of a united movement in Iraq. Barzani's movement, which relied on international support primarily from a US–Iran–Israel axis, ended in 1975 when Iran and Iraq signed the Algiers Agreement. The third period was the 1975–91 era, when the emergence of the Patriotic Union of Kurdistan (PUK), led by Jalal Talabani, presented a challenge to the Kurdistan Democratic Party (KDP) hegemony on the political scene. Finally, the fourth period is the era 1991–present, when the Kurdish political movement in Iraq was further institutionalized through the establishment of governmental bodies like the Kurdistan Regional Government (KRG) and the Kurdistan National Assembly (KNA).

The Concept

Legitimacy and representation are intricately related. A leader is legitimate when he or she can effectively claim to speak on behalf of the governed. Representation, etymologically stemming from the Latin verb *repraesentare*, means 'to make present'. In this sense, an official is tasked with acting on behalf of his or her constituents vis-à-vis national and international governmental bodies.

The literature on representation is often phrased in terms of 'principal' and 'agent'; the principal is the governed and the agent is the leadership.[1] Hanna Pitkin writes that 'there must be some connection or relationship or tie between a representative and those for whom he acts; the difficulty lies in specifying what that tie is, in trying to characterize it'.[2] However, the relationship is not static but rather a *process* of continuous interaction between the principal and the agent. Representing a constituency is problematic because the governed, unlike a single client, is not unified. As such, the leadership must find ways to make legitimate claims to represent its constituents.

In Kurdish realities, four specific types of claim to representation have emerged. Often, these claims have overlapped. Nonetheless, as the Kurdish leadership(s) endeavoured to legitimately represent the population during each period, they relied on claims to popular support, coercion, dynastic legacies of familial heritage or religious authority and international support. The leaders used these claims to justify their seat at the table as representatives of Iraq's Kurds. Below we shall examine the four types of claim as they evolved in time and space: popular mandate, coercion, dynasty and international support/recognition.

Claim One: A Popular Mandate

One approach that different leaders used to legitimize their claim to represent the Kurdish population was the 'democratic claim'. This is defined not necessarily as the procedural feature of democratic legitimacy but rather as the claim to large-scale, popular support. Each leader purported to maintain the largest following of supporters. According to the leader, this gave him the right to practise diplomacy and to negotiate local power. In these cases, the leaders communicated their popularity based on a cult of personality, which was used to amass a wide following.

Post-World War I

In the post-World War I context, several urbanized and tribal leaders sought to make this claim by raising their personal profile. For instance, Sherif Pasha, who would represent the Kurds at the Paris Peace Conference in 1919, claimed that he held a 'democratic mandate'. In 1918, he sent a communiqué to London to confirm his position as the Kurdish leader most widely supported by the masses. Then in 1919, he sent another letter to the British and unilaterally declared himself the *elected* leader of the future Kurdish state.[3] Pasha framed his diplomatic correspondence with claims to popularity in an effort to meet the British need to find a legitimate Kurdish representative and negotiating counterpart.

During this period, a number of other urban elite members employed institutions to raise their personal profile and thus to make the claim of legitimate representation. They headed popular institutions such as clubs, professional organizations, political parties and societies, and believed that the number of members gave them a strong mandate to speak on behalf of the Kurds. For instance, the Badr Khans and Abdul Qadir established the Kurdish Club to lobby for Kurdish autonomy and statehood, and to send missions of leading members to influence Kurdish tribes. The club emerged in several cities, including Diyarbakir, Mardin and Cairo. Sureya Badr Khan, who had worked with the British during the war, and Arif Pasha al-Mardini established the Kurdish Club in Cairo to lobby the British Office. In a meeting with the British Colonel French, they explicitly referred to their leadership of 'the Committee of Kurdish Independence – Egypt', to claim the support of the principal Kurdish families.[4] Qadir and the Khans were also part of the leadership of a new Kurdish Democratic Party, which was refused registration in Turkey.[5] In Constantinople, Qadir and Amin Badr Khan established the Society for the Rise and Progress of Kurdistan (*Kurdistan Ta'aliwa Taraqi Jamiyati*).[6] In short, urban leaders used their standing in various institutions to claim popular, legitimate representation of members and thus of society.

Tribal leaders, too, claimed to hold a popular mandate. They used their status to create personal profiles and make claims to popular appeal. Saiyid Taha regularly reassured British political officers that he had the support of important tribes in his geostrategic area of Rawanduz. Taha particularly emphasized support from the powerful Harki tribe, with which the British wanted to ally themselves. Shaykh Mahmood Barzinji also relied on local support in his communications with British political officers. Although barely literate, following his return in 1922, he published *Bozhi Kurdistan*, a newspaper that he established after closing down the pro-British weekly *Bangi-Kurdistan*. Shaykh Mahmood used the newspaper, which drew upon established intellectuals from Sulaimaniya, to rally popular legitimacy.[7] One issue declared, 'a great head and leader, like the King of Kurdistan, King Mahmood I., has, as if by the miracle of the Messiah, been brought to life again for us'.[8]

The target readership was the growing urban and literate generation of Kurds, and, more importantly, British and Arab readers. Like others, Shaykh Mahmood attempted to use these channels to prove his popular appeal as sole leader – or, in his words, 'King'.

Mullah Mustafa Barzani

In 1946, the Soviet Union supported the establishment of the Mahabad Republic for the Kurds. Mullah Mustafa Barzani, who had been negotiating with Iraqi Prime Minister Nouri Said in 1945, gave up on Baghdad and joined the Mahabad Republic. Although Qazi Muhammad, the Republic's leader, offered Barzani and his Iraqi Kurds sanctuary in a Kurdish state, the latter ran an independent political bloc.[9] The period from 1946 to 1975 is defined by Barzani's emergence as the sole leader who unified the Kurdish struggle in Iraq.

Barzani made claims to speak on behalf of the Kurdish people in Iraq. A US intelligence report stated that Mullah Mustafa's 'personal appeal has been stronger than any Kurdish figure of this generation'.[10] Barzani used his popular support as a tribal leader to make his claim as the sole leader of the Kurds in Iraq and in neighbouring states. Since he was better able to claim local support, he remained the KDP's president.

Barzani's hegemony as leader was at times challenged. For instance, in 1966 Jalal Talabani and Ibrahim Ahmed revived their countermovement.

In 1970, however, the opposition faction was again forced to join Barzani, who enjoyed enduring popular appeal. Abdul Rahman Ghassemlou, who was a Kurdish leader of the KDP-I (Democratic Party of Iranian Kurdistan), claimed that 'the unity of the Kurdish people became firmer still and an overwhelming majority of the Kurds in Iraqi Kurdistan united under the leadership of Mustafa Barzani'.[11]

To maintain local legitimacy, Barzani stressed unity. Rather than killing or sidelining hostile forces within the party, he employed reformist politburo members such as Ahmed and Talabani as leaders in his movement. For Barzani, unity was a tool to legitimize his claim to speak on behalf of the Kurds.

Barzani also used institutions to project his popular appeal. For instance, at its height, the Kurdish Students' Society in Europe (Komeley Xwendi karani Kurd Le Eurupa, or KSSE) had 3,000 members in 16 chapters in Germany, Sweden, Italy, Spain, France and the UK. On the front page of its newsletter, the KSSE-UK branch published a poem that began with 'to our leader Barzani we pay tribute'. The poem concluded by stating that the student organization 'respectfully greets the leader of our people General Mustafa Barzani President of the Kurdistan Democratic Party.'[12] Barzani and the KDP also used the newspaper *al-Ta'akhi* to communicate to Iraqi and Arab neighbours. The newspaper included articles that showcased Barzani's popularity in the Kurdish regions in Iraq and in neighbouring states.[13] The radio station Voice of Kurdistan, which broadcasted throughout Iraq, was used as both an account of battles and a vehicle to express Kurdish unity and the legitimacy of Barzani.[14] By using various outlets, Barzani sought to notify both the Kurds in Iraq and the government in Baghdad that he was the most legitimate authority to speak for the Kurdish population. These institutions projected his popular appeal to his diplomatic counterparts in Baghdad, the neighbourhood and in international capitals.

Post-1975

The 1975 Algiers Agreement between Iran and Iraq ended Barzani's international support and lifeline. At this point, he decided it was time to abandon the movement. Barzani's decision to halt his movement unleashed an internal schism, and the rifts that he had united under the banner of unity opened again. The reformist faction of the KDP

Politburo formed the largest splinter group. Spearheaded by Talabani, in June 1975 the group announced the formation of the Patriotic Union of Kurdistan (Yeketiy Nishtimaniy Kurdistan, or PUK), which included Nawshirwan Mustafa's Marxist–Leninist Komala (The Organization of Revolutionary Toilers of Iranian Kurdistan) and Ali Askari's Socialist Movement of Kurdistan. Talabani claimed that mistakes in 'diplomacy caused our people a tragedy in 1975'; he believed that Mullah Mustafa's trust in one power only, Washington, had spelled the KDP's ultimate downfall.[15] In 1977, the PUK moved its headquarters from Damascus to Sulaimaniya in order to establish a presence on the ground.

Despite Barzani's call to abandon the movement, his loyalists – particularly his sons Idris and Masoud and confidant Sami Abdul Rahman – announced the formation of a KDP Provisional Leadership while in Europe in August 1976. The Barzanis, who remained allied with Tehran, spent this period based mainly in Iran. Masoud was the military commander and Idris was the political negotiator. Both elements were part of the KDP's diplomatic efforts. The PUK and KDP leaderships competed in their claims to diplomatically represent the Kurdish movement.

As in past eras, the representatives wanted to prove that they were popular personalities and supported by the masses. To them, this guaranteed their position to speak on behalf of the Kurds to the international community. In 1985, Talabani told a French journalist that 'we believe that the real representatives of the Kurdish people who are directly elected by them should rule'.[16] For both the PUK and the KDP, claiming popular support on the ground was a necessary tool for diplomatic communication. In its October 1985 edition of the *Torch* newsletter, the PUK's US branch claimed that its leaders were 'most of all enjoying the support, sympathy, and embrace of the great majority of the masses of our people'.[17] The KDP made claims to popular appeal by evoking the memory of Mullah Mustafa, who was still revered by much of the population because he had come closest to providing the Kurds with autonomy in 1970.

Despite Mullah Mustafa's lasting legacy, Talabani worked to discredit the Barzanis' claims to popular legitimacy. According to him, the KDP was a 'dying trend' that could no longer relate to the 'Kurdish street'. A 1977 issue of the *Spark* featured an article criticizing the new KDP Provisional Leadership; the article stated that 'Barzani, and his KDP, do not, nor will they ever, represent the revolutionary masses of Kurdistan. They are, merely, the representatives of an outgoing and dying reactionary and puppet social class of propertied and religious feudal.'[18]

To bolster his local support, Talabani wanted to overcome the KDP's fixed attachment to the memory of Mullah Mustafa. More critically, he wanted the Kurdish population to know that he was the favoured leader.

In the hope of gaining support on the ground, each side accused the other of being controlled by foreign powers rather than mandated by the local population. In 1978, Omar Sheikhmous, who was one of the PUK's founding leaders and its spokesman in Europe, claimed that his party would 'never accept these foreign puppets [Barzani's remnants] and reactionaries [...] we shall destroy these foreign agents both politically and militarily'.[19] In 1985, Sheikhmous wrote in *Middle East* magazine that the KDP was 'under the umbrella protection of the Iranian forces', adding, 'They do not have an independent presence or bases in these areas.'[20] An article in the *Spark* claimed that 'the Kurdish revolutionary masses have totally rejected that gang of puppets and profiteers [in] human misery'.[21] The PUK wanted to discredit the KDP by painting the Barzanis as foreign puppets in order to charge them with weakness. Similarly, the KDP branded the PUK 'Ba'athists'. According to the KDP, Talabani's legitimacy came from Baghdad rather than the Kurdish street; the Ba'athists were fabricating Talabani's local legitimacy.

The leaders used demonstrations to project their popular support. Without elections or institutionalized methods of proving local support, mass rallies became the preferred empirical test of legitimacy. In 1985, Talabani claimed to a French journalist that 'from the start of the armed revolution in Iraqi Kurdistan by the PUK, demonstrations have been organized against the Iraqi government (in 1977, 1982, 1983, and 1984). At first tens of thousands and in the negotiations period hundreds of thousands. They were expressing their support only for the PUK as their representative.' Talabani also told the journalist that 'in the Newroz meeting that was called by the PUK, in Surdash, about one million people participated [...] which showed our influence among the masses of the people in Kurdistan'.[22] He wanted the foreign journalist to relay the message to Paris and other foreign capitals. Albeit on a lesser scale, the KDP also staged demonstrations during the 1980s. Organizing mass protests against the brutality of Saddam Hussein's regime allowed the KDP to parade its numbers. Both Talabani and the

Barzanis used protests to strengthen their claims as representatives. They wanted to convey their legitimacy to both their domestic audience and to foreign capitals.

1991–present

In the 1990s, the leadership still relied on showcasing its local support when claiming to speak on behalf of Iraqi Kurds. However, this time the claims to local support were institutionalized by consistent parliamentary elections, which served as an indicator of who could legitimately speak on behalf of the population. The leadership used the KRG and KNA elections to support its claim. For instance, in the Kurdistan Region's 2013 parliamentary elections, the KDP split from its electoral partnership with the PUK in order to project its exclusive, local support. When they won, KDP leaders claimed that their party should govern because it had won the most seats.[23] The leadership, therefore, believed that winning elections gave them a mandate to represent.

Claim Two: Coercion

Coercion was another way of claiming legitimate representation. According to this strategy, each leader made the case that he had the ability to control the population and was, therefore, the legitimate representative at diplomatic negotiations. This claim was different from the previous tactic, which was based merely on personal status. It hinged on claiming the power to either pacify warring Kurdish tribes (if demands were met), or to instigate instability (if demands were not met).

Post-World War I

The most prominent leader to rise by using this strategy was Shaykh Mahmood Barzinji. When he took control of the Barzinji tribe during the Ottoman era, he frequently defied Ottoman agents in Sulaimaniya. When Turkish forces departed in 1918, he became the sole leader. He positioned himself as able to coerce a number of Kurdish tribes to either take up or lay down arms. This cemented his bid to become the mandatory power's chosen leader on the ground.

To ensure internal control and further his claim to speak on behalf of the local population, Shaykh Mahmood violently eliminated potential opponents. Major Soane noted that, under Shaykh Mahmood's terror '[a] number of the most important merchants were murdered for the sake of what could be extorted from them under the pretext of vengeance. Robberies and burglary occurred in every direction. To express an opinion of even a scullion of the Shaikh was to meet death.'[24] Shaykh Mahmood wanted to expand his coercive control to other territories. In the former Mosul province, Barzinji effectively pressured most of the tribes, who had previously been antagonistic towards him, to sign a memorandum pleading for inclusion in a new state with him as its leader.[25] Mahmood used armed force to instil fear and to force the capitulation of former enemies. This coercion facilitated allegiance from the tribes in the region.

Shaykh Mahmood also used the British to further his effective hold on the region. For instance, he invited them to help him remove Turkish influence from his territory. Moreover, he made it clear to the Kurdish tribes that the British, who had selected him as the only viable leader of the Kurds, were prepared to establish his governorship by force if necessary.[26] Shaykh Mahmood used his access to the mandatory power's arsenal to posture against any leader who threatened his reign.

When Mahmood grew wary of the British political officers, however, he realigned his armed strategy to fight against the external power. To do this, he used a campaign of resistance in order to further his legitimacy among the Kurds and to signal to the British the consequences of not adhering to his demands. For example, surrounding himself with the loyal subjects who had submitted to his rule in 1919, he turned his coercive policy into explicit hostilities and he attempted to eliminate British control of Sulaimaniya. Between May and June 1919, with a force of 300 fighters from the Aoraman and Mariwan tribes on the Persian frontier, Mahmood imprisoned British political officers – including, most notably, Major F.S. Greenhouse – seized control of the treasury, raised his own flag, appointed his own retainers and disrupted the telegraph line for British messages to Kirkuk.[27] This rebellion did not last long; shortly thereafter, the British captured Mahmood in the Barzan Pass and imprisoned him. Only two years later, in October 1922, after unsuccessful attempts with alternative Kurdish leaders such as Taha, the British invited Mahmood back from imprisonment in Kuwait and made him leader of Sulaimaniya. Within a month of his return and based on his coercive abilities, the newly self-proclaimed 'King of Kurdistan' reverted to using force against the British.

According to the British political officers, Shaykh Mahmood's claim to representation was almost exclusively tied to his ability to effectively force submission from others. Civil Commissioner Arnold Wilson commented that once order was restored under Major Soane's appointment, there emerged a 'popular feeling against Shaikh Mahmood [...] many who had done so [...] out of fear because he had led them to believe that the British were ready to establish his Governorship, if necessary, by force'.[28] In short, both the local Kurdish population and international actors recognized Mahmood's legitimacy because of his ability to wield coercion in the area.

Mullah Mustafa Barzani

Similarly to Mahmood, Barzani also relied on coercion to further his claim as the representative of the Kurdish movement. In order to force his opponents to concede and to negotiate with the US and other external actors, Barzani wanted to prove his monopoly over violence to portray himself as the Kurdish strongman. During this period, the coercive apparatus was institutionalized in the peshmerga, which literally means 'those who confront death'. Barzani took control of the peshmerga when he became the minister of defence and commander of the Kurdish Army in the Mahabad Republic. He used the group of fighters to advance his rule and legitimacy in Kurdish areas after his return from the Soviet Union. He also used the peshmerga to plunder the villages of Kurdish tribes in Iraq that were reluctant to support him.[29] Unlike in the previous era, when each leader had struggled to control fighters from other tribes or groups, Barzani commanded a cross-tribal paramilitary apparatus that was accountable to him. Through his position as commander of the peshmerga, he was able to claim a monopoly over the use of violence in the territories concerned.

Barzani used coercion to silence internal dissent. As discussed, the main threat to his rule came from the Talabani and Ahmed faction. In February 1964, the faction rejected Iraqi President Abdul Salam Arif's ceasefire agreement. However, Barzani summoned his own KDP congress to endorse the agreement and then expelled the dissident faction from the area. Barzani used the strength of his forces on the ground to legitimate his leadership.[30] Between 1966 and 1970, with some help from Iranian forces, he continued to suppress the movement and killed several of its leaders.[31] According to KSSE leader Omar

Sheikhmous, Talabani and Ahmed were obliged to 'reintegrate into the main body of the Iraqi KDP'.[32] Although tensions flared at times, for most of this era intra-tribal conflict was not as great as in the previous era. Mullah Mustafa positioned himself as a leader who was not afraid to use force to subdue his opponents and maintain his rule. For him, this was an integral component of presenting a united front in order to negotiate with diplomatic counterparts. He did not want a repetition of the problems of legitimacy and disunity that had stopped the Kurds from gaining independence in the previous period.

For Barzani, effective control over the territory signalled his legitimacy to Washington and other foreign capitals. Much of his group's communication with American officials served as updates on the peshmerga's advances on territories. He sought to use successful operations to induce American support. In a 1971 letter addressed to the US Embassy in Beirut, he expressed the movement's 'full control of the mountainous strip from the Iranian border west to Rawanduz'.[33] A US intelligence report of 11 March 1974 documented how Barzani had been remarkably successful in gaining followers. According to the source, 'the provincial governors, their staffs, and 5000 policemen have joined him. He now claims to have 250 000 new refugees to maintain.'[34] For Barzani, presenting the KDP peshmerga as an effective fighting force commanding vast territory provided another channel by which to successfully make his claim to representation.

Post-1975

During this period, the KDP and PUK both made claims to legitimacy based on coercion control. By presenting themselves as the strongest and most effective force, each hoped to strengthen its claim to representation.

To project power and effective control and to weaken the other side, the two parties often clashed with each other. When the PUK first emerged, KDP allies loyal to Mullah Mustafa's legacy attempted to violently stifle Talabani's group. They staged ambushes and murderous campaigns. For example, between July 1976 and January 1977, almost 50 PUK members were killed while crossing the Turkish–Iraqi border, which was still dominated by KDP allies. Sami Abdul Rahman, a Barzani loyalist, used networks and bases inside Turkey and along the border to launch several senior-level assassinations. Most notably, long-time Kurdish leader and PUK member Ali Askari was killed on the border in 1978.[35] In the years directly following its founding, the PUK faced a strong challenge from KDP leaders, who wanted to ensure that Talabani did not emerge as a viable leader. As such, the KDP was initially bolder in its claim to coercive power.

However, in the 1980s the reality changed. The PUK began to present itself as the more formidable fighting force on the ground. It sought to discredit the KDP and its allies. The 1985 edition of the *Torch* claimed, 'the leaders of Iraqi Kurdistan Democratic Party, for instance, [are] still daydreaming about their glorious days in the 60s and early 70s when they had the grip of the Kurdish revolution in their hands. But these days they have nightmares about their political and military defeat in front of PUK forces, and wonder why and how things changed so quickly in the last 10 years after their abandoning.'[36] The PUK also proved its fighting capability against other opposition groups in the region, including the KDP-allied Iraqi Communist Party (ICP) and the Socialist Party of Kurdistan. In May 1983, the PUK killed 150 ICP cadres and central committee members in Pasht Ashan.[37]

To diplomatic counterparts, both the PUK and the KDP sought to show their control of land in order to claim legitimacy. A US State Department memo from August 1987 reported that 'the fighters of the Patriotic Union of Kurdistan, who have become the predominant factor within Kurd resistance movements, and the Kurd Democratic Party have succeeded in extending their area of control which mainly covers the mountainous border region east of the line Arbil-Kirkuk-Sulaimaniya and north of al Amadiyah-Duhok'.[38]

The KDP used the media to communicate its control of territory. In August 1988, its leadership secured an interview with the *Financial Times*, which then reported that 'the Kurdish Democratic Party says it has 15 000 peshmergas – guerrilla fighters – and 30 000 militiamen under arms and control about 4 000 square miles of northern Iraq'.[39] The KDP wanted to use foreign media outlets to boast of its control over both territory and population. This was part of its claim to be the true representative of Kurdish interests.

However, the PUK argued that the Iran-based KDP were minimally present in the Kurdish areas of Iraq. According to Talabani, the small territory that the KDP controlled was only due to external actors, namely Iran. In 1985, Omar Sheikhmous wrote a letter to *Middle East* magazine claiming that 'the KDP has no presence in any other part of Iraqi Kurdistan (e.g., Kirkuk, Sulaimaniyya, and Arbil provinces) except in those pockets that are occupied by the Iranian forces in Penjamin and Haj Oman areas'.[40]

Talabani's group used its military control on the ground to showcase its legitimacy. The PUK's diplomats stressed to Western outlets that 'PUK forces are the only resistance movement that are active and dominant in the provinces of Arbil, Kirkuk, and Sulaimaniyya'.[41] Therefore, they felt that they were in a stronger position to speak on behalf of events occurring in Iraqi Kurdistan. The PUK had several organizations based in various Kurdish cities in Iraq. To claim to represent Iraq's Kurds, Talabani wished to demonstrate his control of land to foreign capitals. At times, he used international organizations and the media to relay this message.

In the 1980s, the newly established Kurdistan Workers' Party (PKK), a Kurdish group fighting against the Turkish state, began taking control of traditionally KDP-held areas along the Iraq–Turkey border. An October 1988 State Department memo claimed that Talabani had established relations with PKK leader Abdullah Öcalan through Syrian intermediation and impetus.[42] For the PUK, a relationship with the PKK would further discredit the KDP's claims to effective control on the ground.

In February 1988, the US Ambassador to Iraq complained of 'Masoud's increasing lack of control which allows the PKK to use bases in KDP territory despite enmity with Masoud'.[43] For the Kurdish representatives, the ability to control territory signalled the party's strength and therefore its right to have a voice on the international stage. By arguing that the KDP was weak by the 1980s, Talabani sought to project his legitimacy to the international community.

1991–present

After 1991, coercion was still necessary for internal legitimacy. Both the KDP and PUK used their peshmerga forces to control their respective areas and bolster their claims to speak on behalf of the residents. This period is still defined by intra-Kurdish fighting, as each faction sought to gain complete legitimacy. It was marked by the outbreak of civil war in 1994, lasting until 1998, and continued tensions as each side used its security forces to maintain legitimacy. When Gorran emerged as an opposition party after 2009, its leadership still faced difficulties making certain claims because it did not have a peshmerga force and could not provide security. However, the PUK endured despite its losses in popular legitimacy partly because it could still claim to enjoy coercive control. To further its claims to representation, the Region's leadership wanted to showcase its ability to provide stability and security in the precarious neighbourhood. Ultimately, the domestic audience put more faith in the government because the leadership claimed to secure the sub-state. International actors also recognized the power of the peshmerga, which they supported in the fight against the self-proclaimed Islamic State.

Claim Three: Dynasty

Another way of claiming the right to represent was by relying on dynastic legacy. Certain family names sat atop the Kurdish tribal structure. Leaders that came from prominent families, based on tribe or religion, were better able gain a following among the masses and thus represent the Kurdish street.

Post World War I

During this period, the Badr Khan family, including Amin and Abdul Rizaq in Constantinople and Sureya in Cairo, was responsible for much of the urbanized Kurdish nationalist movement at this time. They all rose to prominence in part due to their family history. Tribal legacies served as crucial claims to representation. In addition, the Baban dynasty was one of the most renowned families in the region. It had for several centuries claimed representation over the territory. Sherif Pasha was a descendent of the Babans. Moreover, in 1919, the British sought to make Hamdi Beg Baban the leader of Sulaimaniya.[44]

Shaykh Mahmood Barzinji also based part of his claim to representation on dynastic legacy. His great-grandfather, Said, was a revered Kurdish religious leader whose shrine in Sulaimaniya attracted scores of pilgrims. According to British political officers, Mahmood made a claim to representation based on his family's religious authority. David McDowall argues that, rather than nationalism, Mahmood's first revolt against British rule evoked a religious jihadist struggle.[45] Although Mahmood employed Christians such as Karim Alaka in his administration, he nonetheless instrumentalized religion at times to command greater legitimacy. The religious dynasty allowed many of the tribes that Mahmood claimed to represent – including the Hawrami and Marivi tribes, as well as several groups from Hawraman – to remain staunch allies. Mahmood was known to carry a Qur'an on his person, strapped to his arm at all times.[46] This set him apart from the other major dynasties such as the Badr Khans, who lacked the same religious background and legitimacy.

During this era, a majority of the Kurdish leadership used claims to tribal names in order to propose their bids for legitimacy. They sought to convince the British that they claimed a strong mandate from the tribes in the region and were therefore fit to become negotiating and diplomatic partners. For example, Saiyid Taha claimed that he was the head of the Nihri, a large and revered tribe near Rawanduz. This strategy of legitimization was taken seriously by the British, who initially knew very little of the personalities in the region. However, the British soon began to sense that many of the actors who made the dynastic claim, such as Mahmood or Taha, enjoyed limited popularity outside their tribal structures or towns. Again, the foreign power was disappointed in its search for legitimate representatives.

Mullah Mustafa Barzani

As a consequence of Barzani's popular appeal and unification, the dynastic-legacy card did not feature prominently during this period. It pertained mainly to the legitimacy of the Barzanis and specifically to Mullah Mustafa, who based his claim on his status as a tribal chief and Naqshbandi shaykh.[47] Nonetheless, other familial or religious dynasties yielded to Barzani.

Post-1975

The PUK also wanted to move away from the dynastic claims to representation that had featured in previous Kurdish movements. Talabani wanted to use dynasties as a way to *delegitimize* his KDP opponents, who relied on the Barzani legacy. Iranian Kurdish leader Ghassemlou, an ally of Talabani, ridiculed Masoud Barzani and the idea that the KDP was ever 'a real party'. To Ghassemlou, the KDP was 'merely a tribe.'[48] Talabani constructed a dichotomy between the exclusivity of the Barzanis and the openness of the PUK, which was based on egalitarianism rather than family rule or privilege. The PUK, which sought to justify its case to a US audience, used the *Spark* to delegitimize the 'Barzani-KDP clique'. In front of international actors, Talabani wanted to juxtapose his widespread local support with the KDP's waning claims based on tribes and dynasties. For him, this would solidify his bid as Iraqi Kurdistan's external representative.

1991–present

The dynasty card continued to play a role following the institutionalization of Kurdish politics after 1991. For example, the Barzanis remained highly relevant on the political scene. They made claims to representation based on the memory of Mullah Mustafa Barzani. As such, the president was Mullah Mustafa's son, Masoud Barzani, and the prime minister and the leader of the National Security Council were both grandsons of his – Nechirvan and Masrour Barzani, respectively.

The Talabanis also remained very influential. For instance, the KRG's deputy prime minister was Jalal Talabani's son, Qubad Talabani.

Claim Four: International Support

Claiming to be an external power's chosen actor was the final way in which Kurdish leaders sought to solidify their positions as representatives. They believed that the Kurdish masses would support the leader who was backed by international actors.

Post-World War I

During this period, striving Kurdish representatives also claimed to be the foreign powers' chosen actor. This primarily meant a claim to represent the British to the Kurds and the Kurds to the British. At one point or another, each leader sought friendly relations with the mandatory power. Material and political reasons shaped the need for international support. At some point, each Kurdish leader needed British or Turkish political backing to claim legitimate representation. An individual who presented himself as 'chosen' by external actors could more easily co-opt Kurdish tribes. However, in Mosul, the success and regional influence of the British over the withering Ottomans meant that those who counterbalanced by turning to Turkey jeopardized their claims to representation and their chances of ruling a Kurdish state from the province of Mosul.

Part of the policy was to recognize and cater to British regional interests, which included ensuring stability while the fate of Mosul was being negotiated; minimizing Turkish influence; and protecting minorities, particularly the Christian (Assyrian, Chaldean and Armenian) population. When not on good terms with the British, Kurdish leaders used other foreign actors – namely, Turkey – as a counterbalance.

The urbanized elite understood the significance of international support. Pasha attempted to appeal to the British by stressing the importance of modernizing the Kurdish tribes and preparing Kurdistan for the Westphalian system of states. Moreover, on 7 October 1919, leaders from the Turkey-based Kurdish Democratic Party wrote a letter to the UK High Commission claiming that the Kurds 'can become a factor for the peace in the world only when they can live within such boundaries and under the flag of an autonomous Kurdistan [...] an oppressed people that puts all of its hopes in England'.[49]

Shaykh Mahmood also made it clear that he wanted British support. He telegraphed the High Commissioner and offered himself as the only lifeline against the Turks in the north. Mahmood eventually received British support because of his ability to limit Turkish influence. At this point, even the urban elite, including Qadir and the Khans, capitulated to his administration. Wilson claimed that Mahmood had a 'desire to form a unitary autonomous state of which he was to be the head under British protection'.[50] His initial diplomatic strategy was to appease British political officers. He then wished to use the resulting political support to solidify his reign. Twice in May 1918, he sent representatives with letters to Baghdad calling for the British to support his political control of Sulaimaniya.[51] His representatives were usually well-trusted blood relatives of his tribe. Arnold Wilson convened a meeting of Kurdish shaykhs in Sulaimaniya in December 1918. At this time, Shaykh Mahmood handed Wilson a document, which included signatures from 40 Kurdish leaders (*aghas*), calling on Britain to 'send a representative with the necessary assistance to enable the Kurdish people under British auspices to progress peacefully on civilised lines'.[52]

Mahmood enjoyed greater legitimacy among the Kurdish tribes after he was promoted to become the British choice for leader in Kurdistan. To attract attention from the region's tribes, he worked actively to publicize his dealings with the British. Owing to this strategy, Kurds beyond Sulaimaniya began to recognize Shaykh Mahmood as their leader. Past enemies, like the Talabanis, submitted to his rule.

To the British, Taha posed as a champion against the Turks, who were employing anti-British propaganda in the region. For instance, he notified them of a letter sent by Abdul Rahman, chief of the Shernakh Kurds, to the five main Kurdish chiefs. In the letter, Rahman claimed that Kurds who were cooperating with the British 'shall lose our religion and become Kafirs like them.'[53] Moreover, although he had invoked anti-Christian sentiments in the past, Taha increasingly expressed remorse for the Christian problem, which was a priority for the British. According to the mandatory power, Taha ultimately wanted to gain legitimacy by becoming its choice from a pool of untrusted leaders. This would grant him a louder voice as a Kurdish diplomat.

Kurdish leaders used Turkish support to counterbalance the British and to pursue the goal of becoming the Kurds' representatives. To the British, Shaykh Mahmood was known to hedge his bets between the two powers. He betrayed his promises to the British and established contact with Euz Demir, the Turkish commander in the region. His policy was to play one power off the other so that over-reliance would not result in imprisonment.

In the later years of this period, Taha also pursued a policy of balancing the British against the Turks. For example, when he received word that his rival, Qadir, was returning to Kurdistan with British support, Taha turned to the Turks for insurance. The British then evacuated Rawanduz and ended Taha's short-lived dream of being *hukumdar* (governor) of a Kurdish entity.[54] He remained a British aide. However, in April 1923, he attempted to use international support in a campaign to gain fealty from other Kurdish tribes.

Mullah Mustafa Barzani

Similarly, Barzani knew that he needed international support to solidify his bid for the leadership. His aim was twofold: to seek political legitimacy by having strong state partners, and to pursue financial support and military training that could strengthen the movement.

Unlike in the previous era, the KDP stationed representatives who could spread its agenda in the US. For example, it employed Chafiq Qazzaz, who had been resident in Washington, DC since 1959, to lobby the US to support Barzani's movement. Qazzaz became a KDP representative in the United States. In 1972, he negotiated arrangements for US financial support, which began with a $3 million subsidy.[55] For Barzani, Mohammed Dosky was another key representative in Washington. He regularly visited Congress and the State Department to lobby on behalf of the KDP. Dosky developed close contacts with Senator Henry Jackson and his assistant, Richard Perle, and Ernest Lee, head of the Foreign Department of the American Federation of Labor and Congress of Industrial Organizations (AFL-CIO).[56] Moreover, Dosky enjoyed a personal relationship with Justice William Douglas and several heads of Zionist organizations, which offered another front for the KDP's lobbying efforts.[57] K.A. Badr Khan, who had initially intended to be in New York for only two weeks, became another permanent representative in the USA. He was tasked with improving relations and increasing contacts with influential circles. These officials served crucial purposes for the KDP's pursuit of financial and political support from Washington. This then facilitated Barzani's claim to represent the movement.

To increase international support, Barzani knew that he had to work with the Shah of Iran, who was a strong American ally. Iranian aid averaged $74 million per year.[58] Beyond the aid, however, Barzani viewed the relationship with Iran as important for both increasing his international profile and for using Tehran to make legitimate appeals to Washington. In a letter he wrote, 'We wish to make it clear that your Imperial Majesty may speak on our behalf in the United States or anywhere else you might consider expedient. We are prepared to make whatever commitments may be required of us in return for assistance.'[59] Following persistent petitioning, Tehran informed US Secretary of State Henry Kissinger that 'the Shah believes you should talk personally with two Kurdish representatives of Mullah Mustafa Barzani who will be travelling to the US shortly [...] Given current Iraqi policies, the Shah believes the Kurds should be protected from Communist influence.'[60] With Iran's political and financial support, the KDP was better able to stand as the body representing Iraq's Kurds in Washington and other foreign capitals.

By constantly choosing to talk to him, Baghdad's leadership solidified Barzani's claim to representation. Rather than using negotiating partners already on the ground, such as members of the KDP Politburo, in 1958, Iraqi Prime Minister Abdulkarim Qassim invited Barzani back from the Soviet Union to negotiate. Throughout this era of diplomacy, centre–periphery negotiations usually included Mullah Mustafa. Talabani was not as successful in his relations with Baghdad. Although he worked with the Ba'ath Party in the mid-1960s, he failed to reach any settlement. This hindered his claim to representation. On the contrary, the 1970 Autonomy Agreement, which Barzani signed with Saddam Hussein, elevated Mullah Mustafa's status as chief Kurdish negotiator. The agreement was the closest the Kurds had ever been to autonomous rule (*mafixudmuxtari* in Kurdish and *hukumdhati* in Arabic). Realizing that Barzani was the only legitimate means of negotiating self-determination with the central government, the reformist faction of the KDP Politburo was forced to capitulate in his favour.

Post-1975

Despite Washington's betrayal, international support continued to serve as a legitimizing force during this era. In 1988, Assistant Secretary of State for Intelligence and Research Morton Abramowitz reported that Iraq's Kurds still valued diplomatic relations and were thus 'unlikely to resort to terrorist acts against Iraqi diplomats abroad in order to keep their cause alive.'[61] Diplomacy and international support remained an important lifeline for a landlocked Iraqi Kurdistan.

Nonetheless, external alliances became heavily politicized during this period. Remembering the betrayal of 1975, the PUK leadership was critical of the 'imperialist interests' of the USA and its allies. In the September 1978 edition of the *Spark*, it claimed that 'all the operations, publications and functionaries of Provisional KDP are supported by Barzani's personal accounts, by CIA, by SAVAK, by MIT, and by Israeli intelligence'.[62] The PUK used the memory of betrayal to criticize the KDP's choice of international supporters. Talabani publicly mocked the KDP leadership for persistently attempting to win back American support. By criticizing the KDP's choice of allies, the PUK wanted to garner further support on the ground for its own group of international supporters.

Despite the politicization of international support, the parties still relied on it. Material support remained crucial for effective claims to representation. In September 1988, Abramowitz reported that 'in addition to offering training and equipment, Guard [Iran's Islamic Revolutionary Guard Corps, the IRGC] Commandos joined the Kurdish rebels in actions against the Kirkuk refinery in 1987 and in the Halacheh and Darband-i Khan Areas in 1988.'[63] The KDP used the Iran–Iraq War to position itself as a fifth column; after 1985, the PUK pursued the same line. Both parties received military support and training from Iran to fight Saddam's regime. For example, the PUK relied on Iranian forces and support to reclaim Halabja in March 1988. US State Department Official Philip Remler claimed that 'Jalal Talabani and the PUK were more pragmatic, using both the threat and reality of Iranian support to wring concessions out of Baghdad.'[64] With material support from international actors, the KDP and PUK were better able to establish influence and thus speak on behalf of the population.

Beyond material assistance, political support from international actors also legitimized the parties. As in previous eras, the leader with whom external actors chose to interact was granted a stronger claim to speak on behalf of the movement. In 1983, Jalal Talabani chose to negotiate with Saddam Hussein. In part, Talabani believed that going to Baghdad would elevate his status as the Iraqi Kurds' spokesperson, just as it had elevated Mullah Mustafa's status once in 1958 and again in 1970. For Talabani, this might subdue the Barzanis' historical claim. To gain legitimacy, Talabani sought to showcase the PUK as the new party negotiating with the central government.

Syrian political support was also crucial for PUK legitimacy. Talabani stated that since 1975, 'we maintain a special relationship with Syria'.[65] As we have seen, in the 1980s Damascus used its political clout to help Talabani establish relations with PKK leader Abdullah Öcalan. The PUK sought ties with the PKK to further its pan-Kurdish appeal. US Ambassador Newton claimed that 'Talabani is seeking greater status as "the pre-eminent Kurdish leader" and thus wants the PKK as an ally, but only if the PKK behaves itself.'[66] More critically, the PUK wanted to ally with the PKK in order to weaken the KDP.

Talabani occasionally used other Kurdish leaders, such as the Iranian Abdul Rahman Ghassemlou, as quasi-diplomats to relay legitimacy to the USA. In 1988, Ghassemlou, who shared strong relations with Washington, reported to the US State Department that because of the PUK, 'the situation for the Baghdad regime in Iraqi Kurdistan has deteriorated so sharply over the past three years.'[67] Talabani viewed all international supporters, including Kurdish neighbours, as opportunities to develop his standing as leader.

Each Iraqi Kurd leader wanted to be seen as the international community's chosen one. In February 1977, the KDP sent a letter to the US Senate and House of Representatives to assert that 'President Carter can use his influence, either directly or indirectly, to bring pressure upon the Iraqi Government to fully implement the 11 March 1970 Agreement.'[68] Although the US had recently betrayed Barzani's movement, the KDP still wanted to use an international figure such as the US president to bolster its status vis-à-vis Baghdad and internal Kurdish groups. The PUK similarly highlighted its diplomatic communications with international actors. A June 1977 edition of the *Spark* featured a report that 'the United Nations has responded positively to the "Memorandum on the Situation of the Kurdish People in Iraq" presented by PUK in March, 1977'.[69] For the KDP and PUK, it was important to let foreign actors know that they were supported by recognized international individuals and groups.

In the late 1980s, the PUK became the strongest representative of Iraq's Kurds. A US State Department note argued that 'owing to Syrian and Iranian support and the weakness of Barzani leadership, Talabani was recently elected leader and spokesman of the Iraqi Kurdistan Front, an Iranian-backed Kurdish umbrella group'.[70] Talabani used his relations with international actors to strengthen his claim to speak on behalf of the Kurdish movement.

1991–present

The sub-state's leadership continued to use international support to strengthen its claim. It wanted to boast about the sub-state's relations with senior officials in Washington and other foreign capitals. For example, in 2010, Qubad Talabani tweeted, 'US VP Calls Kurdistan Region President Barzani.'[71] Falah Mustafa claimed that his government was now a major regional player because his president was being invited to meet with heads of states and to participate in international forums such as Davos.[72] At times, the leadership exaggerated this claim in order to boost its status, but it formed a significant part of the leadership's legitimacy. The sub-state's representatives used their diplomatic engagements – including visits by important officials like the US Secretary of State, the French President or the UN Secretary General to Erbil – to seek legitimacy from their citizens, who were happy to see their leaders on the world stage. The KRG's official website, www.krg.gov (now, cabinet.gov.kd), primarily published press releases on the leadership's diplomatic engagements with external officials. The leaders played this card to maintain their position as representatives.

Blurred Representation

Even with the government as the agent and the people as the principal, Kurdish representation has not been clear. This was a consequence of being a sub-state; the government was not yet defined in a *de jure* way and the new institutions remained weak and susceptible to different strategies. Although much of this chapter has identified how the leadership made claims to represent its constituency in various contexts, it is also noteworthy to analyze what the leaders were representing.

For the Kurdistan Region, representation was a complex web of intersecting claims, identities and principals, which were influenced by its sub-state status. The leaders *officially* claimed to represent all citizens inside the three provinces of Erbil, Sulaimaniya and Duhok. However, on other occasions they claimed to represent a 'Kurdish house' (*MalyKurdi* or *BeitKurdi*) and pursued policies of representing Kurds beyond the three provinces; they claimed to represent Kurds who lived in the other 15 Iraqi provinces. Lacking clearly demarcated boundaries, the sub-state also at times claimed to govern the 'contested territories'. These areas included Kirkuk, which some of the leadership considered to be the 'Kurdish Jerusalem',[73] and parts of the Nineveh province. More importantly, the leadership referred to non-KRG governed areas that it claimed as 'contested' when speaking to a certain audience and 'occupied' when speaking to another. At times, the representatives themselves expressed confusion over what they represented.

This confusion was a consequence of being a sub-state that was still negotiating its territory. Without defined boundaries, the Region's diplomats believed that they could benefit by keeping their claims to representation vague and extensive. Following Islamic State's 2014 invasion of these areas, the Kurdistan Region's peshmerga re-took control of Kirkuk. Immediately following this, they announced that the province was now part of their territory.[74] The representatives, therefore, believed that the best practice was to tactfully use different claims in diplomatic communication and in negotiation to circumvent the asymmetrical relationship with a *de jure* state. Flexibility in claims to representation allowed the sub-state's diplomats to overcome power asymmetries and strengthen the KRG's diplomacy.

Conclusion

In sum, throughout the various time periods assessed, Kurdish leaders relied on a 'toolbox' of claims – which were based on local popularity, effective control, dynasty and international support – to the domestic and international audience to prove their legitimacy as representatives. Representation and legitimacy remained the cornerstones of the nationalist programme, and many of the claims remain as part of the movement today.

Notes

1. See Hanna Pitkin, *The Concept of Representation* (Berkeley, CA: University of California Press, 1972); David Runciman and Monica Brito Vieira, *Representation* (Cambridge: Polity Press, 2008).
2. Pitkin, *Concept of Representation*, p. 114.
3. India Office Records (IOR), Mesopotamia: British Relations with Kurdistan, IOR/L/PS/18/B332, 27 August 1919.
4. Foreign Office (FO), InterDepartmental Conference on Middle Eastern Affairs, FO 371/4192, September 1919.
5. This Kurdish Democratic Party is not linked to the Kurdistan Democratic Party (KDP), formed in 1946.
6. FO, General Correspondence from 1906–1966, FO 371/4192, 1919.
7. For an account, see C.J. Edmonds, 'A Kurdish Newspaper: Rozh-i Kurdistan', *Journal of the Royal Central Asian Society (JRCAS)* (1925).
8. Ibid.
9. William Eagleton, *The Kurdish Republic of 1946* (London: Oxford University Press, 1963), p. 76.
10. Charlotte Morehouse, 'The Kurds of Iraq: Renewed Insurgency?' US Department of State Bureau of Intelligence and Research, 1972.
11. Abdul Rahman Ghassemlou, *Kurdistan and the Kurds* (Prague: Publication House of the Czechoslovak Academy of Sciences, 1965), p. 226.
12. Kurdish Students Society in Europe United Kingdom Branch, '11th September', May 1974.
13. *Al-Ta'akkhi* (Baghdad, daily), 15, 21 November 1972, quoted in Ofra Bengio, *The Kurds of Iraq: Building a State within a State* (London: Lynne Rienner Publishers, 2012), p. 92.

14. US Department of State (DoS), Telegram From the Interests Section in Baghdad to the Department of State, 11 April 1974.
15. The Patriotic Union of Kurdistan (PUK) in North America, 'Editorial', October 1985, Omar Sheikhmous' Collection (OSC).
16. Jalal Talabani, 'Excerpt of an interview', September 1985, OSC.
17. PUK in North America, 'Editorial', *Torch* 3, October 1985, OSC.
18. PUK, 'Kurdish Reaction Looks to U.S. Imperialism for Salvation', *Spark* 1, June/July 1977, OSC.
19. Omar Sheikhmous, Statement, 2 June 1978, OSC.
20. Sheikhmous, Letter to *Middle East* magazine, 1985.
21. PUK, 'Kurdish Reaction', *Spark* 1, June/July 1977, OSC.
22. Talabani, Excerpt from interview with Jalal Talabani, September 1985, OSC.
23. Interview with Ahmed Kany in Erbil, December 2014.
24. E.B. Soane, *To Mesopotamia and Kurdistan in Disguise* (London: J. Murray, 1912), p. 192.
25. Shaykh Mahmood never insisted on the inclusion of Kirkuk or Kifri, because of his inability to effectively control these areas. Arnold T. Wilson, *A Clash of Loyalties: A Personal and Historical Record* (London: Oxford University Press, 1931), p. 130.
26. Ibid., p. 135.
27. IOR, Personalities, Mosul, Arbil, Kirkuk, Sulaimani and frontiers. Note on Mosul Town, IRO/L/PS/20/C226, 1923.
28. Wilson, *A Clash of Loyalties*, p. 135.
29. David McDowall, *A Modern History of the Kurds* (London: I.B.Tauris, 1996), p. 311.
30. Charles Tripp, *A Political History of Iraq* (Cambridge, Cambridge University Press, 2000), p. 172.
31. Omar Sheikhmous, 'Intra-Kurdish Relations of Kurds of Iraq with Kurds of Other Parts of Kurdistan', paper presented at conference Irakisch-Kurdistan: Status und Perspektiven. Ergebnisse einer internationalen, Berlin, 10 April 1999.
32. Ibid.
33. DoS, Request from Mustafa Barzani for Clandestine Contact with US Government, 16 July 1971.
34. DoS, Intelligence Update: Iraqi Decree Gaining Limited Autonomy to the Kurdish Areas, 11 March 1974.
35. McDowall, *A Modern* History, p. 345.
36. PUK in North America, 'Editorial', *Torch* 3, October 1985, OSC.
37. Tareq Ismael, *The Rise and Fall of the Communist Party of Iraq* (Cambridge: University of Cambridge Press, 2008), p. 201.
38. US Joint Chiefs of Staff, IIR [Excised] the Internal Situation in Iraq, 1987.
39. Foreign Staff, 'Kurds Urge Turkey to Let in Victims of Iraqi Gas', *Financial Times*, OSC, 30 August 1988.
40. Sheikhmous, Letter to *Middle East* magazine.

41. Omar Sheikhmous, Letter to the Editor of *Middle East* magazine, 13 September 1985, OSC.
42. Ibid.
43. David Newton, 'Kurdish Insurgency in Iraq and Turkey', DoS, 28 February 1988.
44. Martin van Bruinessen, 'Kurdish Paths to Nation,' in Faleh A. Jabar and Hosham Dawod (eds), *The Kurds: Nationalism and Politics* (London: Saqi, 2006), p. 93.
45. McDowall, *A Modern History*, p. 158.
46. Wilson, *A Clash of Loyalties*, p. 139.
47. Tripp, *A Political History*, p. 154.
48. David Newton, 'Views of Iranian Kurdish Leader Qassemlu', DoS, 16 February 1988.
49. IOR, Kurdistan: Situation, IOR/L/PS/10/781, 1918–1920.
50. Wilson, *A Clash of Loyalties*, p. 130.
51. IOR, Personalities, Mosul, Arbil, Kirkuk, Sulaimani and frontiers. Note on Mosul Town, IRO/L/PS/20/C226, 1923.
52. IOR, Mesopotamia: British Relations with Kurdistan, IOR/L/PS/18/B332, 1919.
53. Ibid.
54. McDowall, *A Modern History*, p. 217.
55. DoS, Memorandum from Director of Central Intelligence Colby to the President's Assistant for National Security Affairs, 7 August 1973.
56. David Korn, 'The Last Years of Mustafa Barzani', *Middle East Quarterly* 2 (1994), p. 20.
57. US Department of State Bureau of Intelligence and Research, 'The Kurds of Iraq', 31 May 1972.
58. DoS, Memorandum Director of Central Intelligence Colby to the President's Assistant for National Security Affairs (Kissinger), 2 November 1974.
59. DoS, Memorandum from Acting Director of Central Intelligence Walters to the President's Assistant for National Security Affairs (Kissinger), 7 October 1974.
60. Most meetings with the Shah were also covert and restricted to oral conversations. DoS, Memorandum from Harold Saunders of the National Security Staff to the President's Assistant for National Security Affairs (Kissinger), 7 June 1972.
61. Morton Abramowitz, Information Memo: Swan Song for Iraq's Kurds, DoS, September 1988.
62. PUK, 'Barzani's Carousel and Israel', *Spark*, May 1978, OSC.
63. Abramowitz, Information Memo.
64. Philip Remler, 'The US and the Kurds: Some Policy Considerations', DoS, 24 October 1988.
65. Bengio, *Kurds of Iraq*, p. 221.
66. Newton, 'Kurdish Insurgency'.
67. Newton, 'Views of Qassemlu'.

68. PUK, 'Kurdish Reaction'.
69. PUK, 'Positive UN Response to PUK Memorandum', *Spark*, June/July 1977, OSC.
70. Defense Intelligence Agency, 'Kurdistan Resistance Forces at Peril', cable from the Defense Intelligence Agency, 24 October 1988; reproduced as 00683 in National Security Archive.
71. Qubad Talabani, Twitter post, 17 December 2010, 8:39 am. Available at https://twitter.com/qubadjt/status/15808405142765568 (accessed February 2018).
72. Interview with Falah Mustafa in Erbil, January 2014.
73. A phrase famously used by Jalal Talabani.
74. Al Hayat, 'بارزاني يؤكد أن سيطرة الأكراد على كركوك ومناطق أخرى متنازع عليها نهائي', 27 June 2014. Available at http://alhayat.com/Articles (accessed February 2018).

CHAPTER 3

SEGMENTATION OF POLITICAL PARTIES IN UNDERDEVELOPED CONTEXTS – THE CASE OF THE KURDS

Gareth Stansfield

The Kurds have become synonymous with notions of segmentation, fragmentation and factionalism in their social and political life. Indeed, their lack of political unity at a range of scales is now taken for granted by academic observers, and often used by detractors of the Kurds as evidence as to why they can never become greater than the sum of their parts and venture beyond their non-stateness into the realms of 'stateness'. This view is grounded on firm empirical evidence. At whatever level on which Kurdish political life is considered, segmentation, fragmentation and factionalism is evident. And the divisions are complex in their nature and many in their typology – with Kurdish political differences being structured according to territory and space (spatial segmentation), ideological and confessional belief structures (ideological segmentation), socio-economic differences (socio-economic segmentation) and considerations that emanate from the often different political views held by older generations compared to more recent ones, depending upon their relative experiences and aspirations (generational segmentation).

This has resulted in a highly variegated and multiply bifurcated party-political landscape, with there being many political parties in each part of the Kurdish-populated areas of the Middle East and with virtually all of these parties exhibiting some form of segmentation and factionalism within their ranks. But how unusual is this phenomenon? When considering factionalism in established democracies, Françoise Boucek notes that '[p]olitical parties are not monolithic structures but collective entities in which competition, divided opinions and dissent create internal pressures. In turn, these pressures often trigger the formation of factions that render the unitary actor assumption highly questionable.'[1] This is arguably even more true for political parties that exist in what this chapter refers to as 'underdeveloped' contexts, but which might be more accurately considered 'transitional' – from an authoritarian to a democratic system; from the 'conflict' to the 'post-conflict' environment; and, in the case of the Kurds, from the politically marginal to the politically central.

In considering segmentation and factionalism among the Kurds, there is a strong tendency to regard these characteristics as inherently negative since they generate or exemplify disunity, further the ambitions of political entrepreneurs who take advantage of a particular issue and thus continue and deepen the suffering of those Kurds whose interests are represented by the segmented parties of a broken system. This may be a fairly accurate picture of the situation, at least for some of the time in some of the spaces of Kurdistan. But it is interesting to pursue a counter-intuitive argument as well – one of segmentation and factionalism not being static features of the political landscape, most appropriately viewed through a spatial lens or via tribal or confessional models that would be unchanging over time, but of them being dynamic and relative features, constantly changing according to endogenous and exogenous pressures. Furthermore, it is also challenging to view segmentation and factionalism as not being inherently 'bad' characteristics – which is often the conclusion that a more traditional approach to the subject may reach – but that they may have benefits. Boucek, again, notes that 'factionalism is a multi-faceted phenomenon which can transform itself over time in response to incentives [...] the benefits of factions are often overlooked, and [...] factionalism can acquire different faces at different times under specific conditions'.[2] This brief chapter attempts to provide the beginnings of an understanding of the different facets of Kurdish segmentation and factionalism.

Segmentation and Fragmentation in Ethno-Political Movements

The impact of fragmentation is an increasingly important area of research, and – particularly with reference to the Middle East – has a great deal of application. As the international community struggles with the question of how to understand the complex world of political mobilization in Syria and Iraq, within this theatre, the Kurds are perhaps *primus inter pares* in terms of their combined political importance, and their internal segmentation. The Kurds are not unique in their internal fissiparousness. Indeed, other examples abound from around the globe – albeit, particularly in the Middle East. But while few other examples of splits among ethno-political groups can match the Kurds in terms of their spatial scale, ideological complexities and exogenous drivers (emanating from a range of state interests rather than merely one), reference as to why the Kurds display a profound – perhaps even pathological – propensity to fragment is somewhat lacking in what is an increasingly active and insightful body of research into this subject.

Within the growing literature provided by political scientists, several predominant ways of viewing fragmentation are presented. In terms of the causative factors of fragmentation, Seymour et al. present an argument that focuses upon 'the competition that exists within ethno political movements and between those movements and the states whose authority they contest'.[3] The role of the State and its ability to fragment 'separatists' is also a key area of interest, with some states seeking to divide their non-state opponents by offering differential concessions, but then finding that the success of making concessions to a fragmented movement may see conflict recommence more sooner than if dealing with a unified movement.[4]

'Competition' – a key element in this fragmentation – creates a 'dual contest'; ethnic groups engage in conflict with their host state(s) and also with co-ethnic factions.[5] The complex and sometimes unexpected outcomes of fragmentation include weaker entities becoming more willing to negotiate agreements with the hosting state in order to end conflict.[6] But which causative forces generate the rifts within ethno-political movements that grow into cracks that divide them? The power of the host state, after all, would struggle to generate disunity among a movement unless there were weaknesses there from the outset.

Asal et al.[7] employ organization theory to show that those movements with an already 'factional' leadership are more likely to break up. But from where do these factional leaders come? In the case of the Kurds, the recent advances made in political-science literature have shed considerable analytical light on the complex political environments in which they are placed, and inform us as to how their factionalism and fragmentation may or may not feed into the future progression of their 'dual contest', or inter- and intra-community contestation. But these modern manifestations of fragmentation are built upon an older history of sociological segmentation – one that, in turn, rests upon the legacies of tribalism and the interaction of social organization with geography and topography.[8]

The Origins of Kurdish Political Segmentation

While the Kurds are generally acknowledged to exhibit considerable political disunity, almost to the point of it being a truism, the reasons and origins of this defining characteristic are less clearly stated. For some, the very fact that the Kurds inhabit a largely mountainous environment replete with deep valleys and lofty peaks that serve to create small, tightly organized familial and tribal groupings is a strong causative factor that explains the penchant of Kurds to seek to organize themselves in the modern world in small, niche interest groups. This model would also explain the highly fractious nature of political life in Afghanistan and Yemen, and present 'the peoples of the mountains' as being a product of environmental determinism – with the legacies of this relationship with the physical world reaching into the present.

Kurdish tribalism remained a powerful dynamic, even in the twentieth century. The Kurds exhibit a different model of tribal organization to that of their Arab neighbours in particular – one that is very firmly rooted in the physical environment, with bloodlines and kinship being a secondary concern. A further element in Kurdish segmentation – again shared with the Afghan experience, if not the Yemeni – is the lack of a unified and unifying linguistic core.[9] 'Kurdish' is, of course, spoken by the Kurds, but not all Kurds speak the same sort of Kurdish, with the language group being divided into the two distinctive dialects (which some experts refer to as different languages) of

Sorani (in the south-east of the Kurdish-inhabited regions, from Erbil to the Kurdish areas of Iran) and Kurmanji (in Turkey, north-west Iran, Syria, and north and western Kurdistan in Iraq). And even within these principal dialect groupings, there exists a range of sub-dialects and even a smattering of distinctive languages. These have, for some, either militated against the emergence of a unified Kurdish political milieu that would then give rise to a more ordered political culture and structures, or have been used as indicators of difference by Kurds once they have become political ordered.

The Kurds' political fractiousness has undeniably been advanced by their geographical location at the peripheries of established states. These mountainous peripheries were not only far removed from the imperial centres of the Middle Eastern empires that constituted the state structure before World War I but they were also isolated, physically impenetrable and difficult to control through regular administrative means or via the deployment of military force. For the pre-World War I empires – and especially the Ottoman and Qajar empires – the response was elegant: to allow for a range of semi-autonomous Kurdish emirates across the borderlands of the empires.[10] These emirates would give their allegiance to either one of the empires in return for being able to live in relative autonomy from the imperial centre, and also in return for doing the empire's bidding in times of war and conflict. However, being so far away from Tehran and Istanbul, and being locally powerful, they also were attractive propositions to be used as proxies against their nominal overlords. They thus imbued the Kurdish political elites with the experience of moving their alliances quickly, according to the prevailing geopolitical currents, but also of being susceptible to internal division as the imperial centres mobilized their own resources to ensure that their interests were maintained in the delicate borderlands.

Ethnic Segmentation, Territorial Partition and Political Fragmentation

This territorial partition created semi-autonomous principalities in the pre-modern period – a period that in Europe saw the foundations of early notions of nationalism, and which also saw the consolidating of state structures and competences.

For the Kurds, however, the seeds of an overarching nationalist project were slow to germinate in an environment that had remained structured around the exclusivist social organization of the tribe and their greater confederations, and around the politically subordinated relationship of the semi-autonomous principality with the Ottoman and, to a lesser extent, the Safavid and Qajar empires.[11] Kurdish notables and intellectuals were, from the mid-nineteenth century onwards, exposed to the European ideas of nationalism and broader political imaginations that were beginning to permeate the Ottoman Empire in particular, and some moved to establish newspapers and journals in order to further discussion about the condition of the Kurds. The Bedirkhan family was particularly noteworthy in this regard, publishing the first Kurdish newspaper, *Kurdistan*, at the very end of the century – but in Istanbul, not in 'Kurdistan' itself.[12] Yet, aside from the activities of such notable families working to bring the situation of the Kurds to the attention of the imperial elites, the Kurds as a whole remained inherently segmentalized, inwardly focused upon tribal concerns and wholly unprepared for the new reality of the state system that was to be imposed upon them. As such, the Kurds themselves were at least partly responsible for the non-appearance of a Kurdish state in the aftermath of World War I.[13] With only a limitedly held notion of national cohesion and distinctiveness, there was also very little to suggest that an aspiration to independence existed beyond the actions of some prominent figures such as Shaykh Mahmood Barzinji of Sulaimaniya. However, even this self-proclaimed 'King of Kurdistan' failed to persuade the British forces occupying this part of Kurdistan in World War I that he represented the Kurdish people en masse. Rather, he, along with others, was seen as exploiting the instability generated by the collapsing Ottoman Empire for his own parochial gains. The attempts by Sherif Pasha and Emin Ali Bedirkhan to engage with the Paris Peace Conference in 1919 were perhaps seen in a more serious light; however, even at this most crucial of venues the members of the Kurdish delegation could not agree upon a common negotiating position, thus weakening their ability to stake their claim in the new state system that was beginning to unfold.[14]

Contrary to the perception commonly held by commentators of the Kurds' statelessness, their current predicament of being partitioned and incorporated as minorities into the host states of Iraq, Turkey, Iran and

Syria did not happen according to the Sykes – Picot Agreement of 1916. It is true, of course, that this agreement envisaged the partition of Kurdistan, and the territory of the Ottoman Empire in general, but it was never implemented. Instead, the post-World War I state system developed through a range of agreements and treaties – some secret, some not – that took place throughout World War I and in the years afterwards, culminating with the League of Nations' arbitration between Iraq and Turkey that led to the signing of the Frontier Agreement in 1926, thus finally partitioning the Kurds of Iraq and Turkey.[15]

This partition of the Kurds by the hardened boundaries of the modern state system introduced a new and powerful barrier that physically hindered the ability of Kurds to interact socially, politically and economically with each other, and also moved them into a position of actors, pawns and proxies in the politics of their host states. This new reality would condition Kurdish political and social life for the remainder of the twentieth century, with three distinct Kurdish nationalist movements developing in Iran, Turkey and Iraq. Perhaps due to the Kurdish population in Syria being fewer in number, or maybe due to the highly provincialized nature of their existence in Syria, the nationalist project there was very limited in its nature and scope and was largely dominated by the competing agendas, in the latter part of the twentieth century, of the Kurdish political organizations that had emerged in Turkey and Iraq – mainly the PKK, KDP and PUK.[16]

Each of these Kurdish nationalist movements operated within the settings of their host countries. They sometimes engaged within their host states in negotiations over autonomous rights, which at times, such as in the 1970s in Iraq, were far-reaching.[17] They more often engaged in conflict with their host states, as they rebelled against the central authorities with varying degrees of success. The relationship between the Kurds and the states was not, however, a straightforward one of those in Iraq striving for their rights, while their kin people in Turkey and Iran did the same. Iran and Iraq were adept at using each other's Kurds as proxies in their own conflicts, with Iran in particular being able to provide support for Kurdish allies in Iraq as Tehran and Baghdad engaged in the territorial contestation that would ultimately lead to the Iran–Iraq War of 1980–8. Iraq, too, would recruit pliant Kurdish organizations in a bid to counter the strategy of Iran, thus pitting Kurds against Kurds in a confused and debilitating series of conflicts throughout the second half of the twentieth century.

The history of the Kurdistan Democratic Party–Patriotic Union of Kurdistan (KDP–PUK) conflict in Iraq is, of course, related to the internal contestation that exists between two entities' powerful leaderships, which are ideologically very different and which appeal to different social groups in Iraq. But it is equally a product of state competition and of the Kurds being used as proxies in the conflict between Iran and Iraq. Turkey, too, was not immune to the problem of Kurds being used against the state by its neighbours, nor was it innocent in employing this tactic. The Kurdistan Workers' Party (PKK) was initially focused on establishing a pan-Kurdish entity, but its Turkish focus made it an ideal recipient of support and sponsorship from the opponents of Turkey – including Syria and Iran. The relative closeness of the Iraqi Kurdish KDP with Turkey, from the 1990s onwards, then saw Turkey use the KDP as a proxy against the PKK in an attempt to limit the operations of the PKK from their bases on the Turkey–Iraq border.[18] But this alliance then saw the Iraqi Kurdish PUK brought into the fray against the KDP, with support from Iran. While the details of each of these engagements would need several articles or even books to adequately uncover and analyze, the story develops of a lack of a unified Kurdish project at the beginning of the twentieth century that translates into the Kurds not only being politically segmented (which is in itself innocuous), but of being territorially partitioned by the imposition of the state system following the demise of the Ottoman Empire. They were then politically fragmented and factionalized by the borders that divided them, and also within themselves in the territories that now contained them.

Ideational and Organizational Segmentation

The Kurds were thus divided by the state system of the twentieth century, but this partition only partially explains the politicization of the social segmentation that had been developing since earlier centuries. As discussed earlier, the population of this high, mountainous, isolated region had already been significantly conditioned by the physical environment.

Kurdistan was already socially and politically complex even before the end of the Ottoman Empire, with distinctive regionalisms emerging that promoted contrary political allegiances, ideational viewpoints, elite assemblages and nationalist trajectories.

One of the earliest ideational conflicts, or transitions, to take place was the move away from the focus on narrow tribal interests towards embracing a nationalist project. In Iraqi Kurdistan in particular, this tension was further mirrored in the regionalism that made Sulaimaniya distinctive as a centre of urban intellectualism and leftist thought compared to the more inward-looking interests of prominent tribes, and especially the Barzanis, who were traditional holders of power in the more conservative parts of Iraqi Kurdistan.[19] This dialectic between what can best be described as structures emanating from the traditional legacies of Kurdish political and social organization, and the modernist notions of socialism and nationalism, remains a driver in the contemporary politics of the Kurds of Iraq in particular. The legacies of this ideational cleavage remain in place today since the Kurdish political space in Iraq remains dominated by the KDP on the one side and the PUK and Gorran Movement on the other, in the space originally carved out in the 1960s and 1970s by those leaders opposed to what they considered to be the dominance of political life by socially conservative forces.

While it is clear where the social conservativism of today's KDP originates – as an organic development of traditional Kurdish organization – the emergence of the leftist tendencies of the PUK and Gorran, and also of the progressive elements within the KDP, is less obvious. Of course, they did not appear suddenly from inside Kurdistan, and we need to place the emergence of leftist and nationalist ideational trends in Kurdistan in the wider setting of the twentieth-century Middle East exposed to a variety of global, political currents – from state-led nationalist discourses from the nineteenth century onwards through to the stark reality of the Kurds existing in states dominated by the nationalist projects of other peoples, in which they existed as a mere minority, sometimes subjected to the homogenizing strategies of the dominant nation in power.

The region was also exposed to the powerful rhetoric of the revolutionary left – with Marxism, Leninism and Maoism all having a powerful effect upon emerging groups of largely urban-based intellectuals and activists that were as much opposed to their conservative-minded ethnic counterparts as they were to the states in which they lived. Indeed, as committed leftists, they were perhaps more opposed to the old, landed, conservative and tribal authority structures, which they saw as ossified legacies of a bygone age that needed to be swept away for the greater good. These leftist groups were also linked across the region, with the Iranian Tudeh (i.e., communist party) being a particularly powerful influence on the thinking of many Iranian and Iraqi Kurds who would go on to form leftist political groups as they hived off from their established parties.[20] In Iran, the challenge to the KDP-I came from such leftist groups, with organizations such as Komala emerging that challenged what was seen to be the more conservative KDP-I.[21]

In Iraq, the KDP struggled to maintain some form of cohesion between a 'tribal' wing loyal to Mullah Mustafa Barzani and a 'progressive' wing under the control of Ibrahim Ahmed and his protégé, Jalal Talabani – with this balancing act collapsing from the mid-1960s onwards. From this time, new groupings of radically minded students and non-tribally affiliated Kurds began to form under the guidance of Talabani and his lieutenants, including Marxist-Leninist Komala and other organizations designed to attract adherents from different social strata and age cohorts. With the collapse of the Kurdish rebellion against Iraq in 1975, these groups came together under the banner of the PUK, thus setting in place the near-binary model of political life dominated by the KDP and the PUK that still largely exists to the present day.

Meanwhile, in Turkey, the same anti-traditional mindset had taken hold among the urban youth and leftist-inspired activists. Kurdish activism had been eradicated in Turkey following the suppression of three armed uprisings, in 1925, 1930 and 1938. All had been tribally led, and all were quickly ended by the military forces of the new Turkish state.[22] The relative lack of Kurdish activism lasted until the 1960s. Following the *coup d'état* of 1960, a new leftist party, the Workers' Party of Turkey (TIP), formed from which the Kurdistan Workers' Party (PKK) would emerge some ten years later, following splits within the TIP. Interestingly, the initial identity of the organization founded by Abdullah Öcalan in the early 1970s was as much 'Turkish' as it was 'Kurdish', but the overall Kurdish identity was in effect thrust on the movement by its members who had been inspired by the successes of Barzani's KDP in Iraq. This tension in the ambition of the PKK would be a common feature under Öcalan's leadership, illustrating the ideational pulls of non-national specific leftism on the leadership and the nationalist desires of many of the Kurds in the ranks of the PKK.

Whatever the tensions were within the PKK, it was and remains resolutely opposed to what are seen as outdated and discredited mechanisms of social, economic and political organization – and in particular any notion of tribal legitimacy. As a social-democratic, leftist organization, the PKK found common cause with other like-minded parties – and especially the PUK in Iraq – and so, as the twentieth century progressed, a further cross-boundary schism began to crystallize. On the one side where those parties that represented the more traditional, established side of Kurdish society, perhaps tied to a somewhat older generation or with stronger roots back into the traditional mores of Kurdish social life. These parties – including the KDP in Iraq, the KDP-I in Iran and the KDP-S of Syria – contrast starkly with the other side of the political divide, which includes the PUK of Iraq; the PKK of Turkey; the PYD and its military wing, the YPG of Syria; and PJAK (Free Life Party of Kurdistan) of Iran.[23] While the PUK is in itself a distinct political party, the linkage between the PKK, PYD, YPG and PJAK is much closer, with the PKK often being described as the underlying organization behind the setting up of sister organizations in Syria and Iran.

The Third Schism

While it is tempting to discuss the segmentation and factionalism of Kurdish political life into the traditional and progressive, the conservative and the left, or into different regions such as Sulaimaniya and Bahdinan, one final lens needs to be employed in order to give a fuller picture of the complexities of the Kurdish political world. This is the lens of religion. While it remains the case that political Islam is a 'third force' in Kurdish political life, it is nonetheless a powerful force in society at large and has at times risen to challenge the more established political parties. Political Islamism in Kurdistan has manifested in different ways, as can be seen particularly when Turkey and Iraq are compared in recent years.

In Iraq, Islamist parties have had a prominent place on the landscape, with the Islamic Movement of Kurdistan (IMK) emerging as a powerful political and military force in the 1980s and into the 1990s. Indeed, its influence in the 1990s was so significant that it was able to engage in military conflict with the PUK in the middle years of that decade, and it effectively controlled the districts around the town of Halabja, in the east of the Kurdistan Region, until 2003. As with other Kurdish parties, the IMK was not immune to its own internal factionalism, and more radical groups splintered away from it in the late 1990s, forming Jund al-Islam and then Ansar al-Islam, with returning Kurdish fighters from Afghanistan aligning their groups with Al Qaeda. These radical groups would later go on to form part of the Al Qaeda Iraq (AQI) group led by Abu Musab al-Zarqawi, and were also present at the formation of the Islamic State of Iraq and al-Sham (ISIS) that began to emerge from 2011 onwards.[24]

In contrast to these violent salafi groupings, there is also the Kurdistan Islamic Union (KIU). A non-military political party affiliated with the Muslim Brotherhood, the KIU has often benefitted from being an opposition party unaligned with either the KDP or the PUK. However, in recent years, and since the emergence of the Gorran Movement, it has been in relatively decline.

The manner in which Islamism has expressed itself in Turkey is very different. In Iraqi Kurdistan, the Islamist parties are still inherently 'Kurdish' even if they are radical jihadist and now fight for the establishment of the Islamic State rather than for the Republic of Kurdistan. With most of the Kurdish-populated region of Turkey being socio-economically poorer than other parts of the country, and with many of the people of these areas being socially conservative and religiously orientated, it is not always the case that they constitute natural support bases for the PKK or are willing to support the pro-democracy causes of Kurdish-associated parties such as the People's Democratic Party (HDP) of Selehattin Demirtas. Rather, many Kurds of a more conservative nature have expressed their political views by voting for the AK Party of Recep Tayyip Erdoğan, thus exposing again the interesting tension that exists in Kurdish political mobilization in Turkey – of being divided between a Kurdish nationalist agenda and a broader agenda that protects rights across the Turkish state.

Conclusion

Kurdish political segmentation has a long history that predates the establishment of the twentieth-century state system. This segmentation can be discussed in a variety of ways – as linguistic, religious, regional and tribal – but it would seem reasonable to argue that it is primarily as much to do with the impact of topography upon group cohesion, coherent intellectual development and shared political aspirations as any other causative factor. Indeed, it was the existence of a segmented Kurdish political landscape that governed the manner in which the Ottoman, Safavid and Qajar empires administered the Kurdish border territories, and which made it less likely that the Kurds would succeed in gaining some form of territorial control after World War I. This segmentation also provided cleavages between groups that could be exploited by the new states of the twentieth century, as they moved to use Kurds as proxies. But the Kurds have also had to deal with their own internal fractiousness – a fractiousness that cannot wholly be laid at the door of environmental determinism, but one that represents the many Kurdish reactions to global intellectual trends. As the long twentieth century unfolded, the Kurds have been affected by the combined currents of nationalism, socialism, democratization, Islamism, and regional and global geopolitics – perhaps more so than any other people. Indeed, it is difficult to imagine who can make a greater claim to this unhappy title. The legacies of the segmentation and factionalism of the twentieth century have continued into the twenty-first, and the Kurds remain at the mercy of exogenous influences as much as they are conditioned by endogenous dynamics. But the long twentieth century is perhaps coming to an end, and the state-building process, which began in the aftermath of World War I, appears as though it may be entering a second phase exactly a century later. The question for the Kurds, and their regional allies and enemies, is whether history will repeat itself or whether the Kurds will rise above their internal differences to be, for the first time in their history, at least the sum of their parts, if not greater.

References

Ahmadzadeh, Hashem and Gareth Stansfield, 'The Political, Cultural, and Military ReAwakening of the Kurdish Nationalist Movement in Iran', *Middle East Journal*, 64(1) (2010), pp. 11–27.

Allsopp, Harriet, *The Kurds of Syria: Political Parties and Identity in the Middle East* (London: I.B.Tauris, 2014).

Asal, Victor, Mitchell Brown and Angela Dalton, 'Why Split? Organizational Splits Among Ethnopolitical Organizations in the Middle East', *Journal of Conflict Resolution*, 56(1) (2012), pp. 94–117.
Ateş, Sabri, *The Ottoman-Iranian Borderlands: Making a Boundary, 1843–1914* (Cambridge: Cambridge University Press, 2013).
Aykan, Mahmut Bali, 'Turkey's Policy in Northern Iraq, 1991–95', *Middle Eastern Studies*, 32(4) (1996), pp. 343–66.
Bakke, Kristin M., *Decentralization and Intrastate Struggles: Chechnya, Punjab, and Québec* (Cambridge: Cambridge University Press, 2015).
Bakke, Kristin M., Kathleen Gallagher Cunningham, and Lee J.M. Seymour, 'A Plague of Initials: Fragmentation, Cohesion, and Infighting in Civil Wars', *Perspectives on Politics*, 10(2) (2012), pp. 265–83.
Barr, James, *A Line in the Sand: Britain, France and the Struggle that Shaped the Middle East* (London: Simon & Schuster, 2011).
Bengio, Ofra, *The Kurds of Iraq: Building a State Within a State* (Boulder, CO: Lynne Rienner, 2012).
Boucek, Françoise, 'Rethinking Factionalism: Typologies, Intra-Party Dynamics and Three Faces of Factionalism', *Party Politics*, 15(4) (2009), pp. 455–85.
Brubaker, Rogers, *Nationalism Reframed: Nationhood and the National Question in the New Europe* (Cambridge: Cambridge University Press, 1996).
Bruinessen, Martin van, *Agha, Shaikh and State: The Social and Political Structures of Kurdistan* (London: Zed Books, 1992).
Černy, Hannes, 'Ethnic Alliances Deconstructed: The PKK Sanctuary in Iraqi Kurdistan and the Internationalization of Ethnic Conflict Revisited', *Ethnopolitics*, 13(4) (2014), pp. 328–54.
Cunningham, Kathleen Gallagher, 'Divide and Conquer or Divide and Concede: How Do States Respond to Internally Divided Separatists', *American Political Science Review*, 105(2) (2011), pp. 275–97.
———— 'Actor Fragmentation and Civil War Bargaining: How Internal Divisions Generate Civil Conflict', *American Journal of Political Science*, 57(3) (2013), pp. 659–72.
Cunningham, Kathleen Gallagher, Kristin M. Bakke and Lee J.M. Seymour, 'Shirts Today, Skins Tomorrow: Dual Contests and the Effects of Fragmentation in Self-Determination Disputes', *Journal of Conflict Resolution*, 56(1) (2012), pp. 67–93.
Dowd, Caitriona, 'Actor Proliferation and the Fragmentation of Violent Groups in Conflict', *Research and Politics* (October–December 2015), pp. 1–7.
Eskander, Saad, 'Britain's Policy in Southern Kurdistan: The Formation and Termination of the First Kurdish Government, 1918–1919', *British Journal of Middle Eastern Studies*, 27(2) (2000), pp. 139–63.
———— 'Southern Kurdistan Under Britain's Mesopotamian Mandate: From Separation to Incorporation, 1920–1923', *Middle Eastern Studies*, 37(2) (2001), pp. 153–80.
Fromkin, David, *A Peace to End All Peace: The Fall of the Ottoman Empire and the Creation of the Modern Middle East* (New York: Henry Holt, 1989).
Ghods, M. Reza, 'The Iranian Communist Movement Under Reza Shah', *Middle Eastern Studies*, 26(4) (1990), pp. 506–13.
Gunter, Michael, *Out of Nowhere: The Kurds of Syria in Peace and War* (London: Hurst & Co., 2014).

Findley, Michael and Peter Rudloff, 'Combatant Fragmentation and the Dynamics of Civil War', *British Journal of Political Science*, 42(4) (2012), pp. 879–901.

Halliday, Fred, 'The Tudeh Party in Iranian Politics: Background Notes', *MERIP Reports*, 86, *The Left Forces in Iran* (1980), pp. 22–3.

Hassanpour, Amir, *Nationalism and Language in Kurdistan 1918–1985* (New York: Edwin Mellen Press, 1992).

Jwaideh, Wadie, *The Kurdish National Movement: Its Origins and Development* (Syracuse, NY: Syracuse University Press, 2006).

Keith, A. Berriedale, 'The League of Nations and Mosul', *Journal of Comparative Legislation and International Law*, 8(1) (1926), pp. 38–49.

Leezenberg, Michiel, 'Political Islam Among the Kurds', paper prepared for the International Conference 'Kurdistan: The Unwanted State', 29–31 March 2001, Jagiellonian University/Polish-Kurdish Society, Kraków, Poland.

Midlarsky, Manus I. and Elizabeth R. Midlarsky, 'When the Weak Roar: Understanding Protracted Intrastate Conflict', *Peace Economics, Peace Science and Public Policy*, 19(3) (2013), pp. 321–31.

Natali, Denise, *The Kurds and the State: Evolving National Identity in Iraq, Turkey, and Iran* (Syracuse, NY: Syracuse University Press, 2005).

Newman, Edward, *Understanding Civil Wars: Continuity and Change in Intrastate Conflict* (London: Routledge, 2014).

Özcan, Ali Kamal, *Turkey's Kurds: A Theoretical Analysis of the PKK and Abdullah Öcalan* (London: Routledge, 2006).

Özkırımlı, Umut, *Theories of Nationalism: A Critical Introduction* (New York: Palgrave, 2011).

Özoğlu, Hakan, *Kurdish Notables and the Ottoman State: Evolving Identities, Competing Loyalties, and Shifting Boundaries* (New York: State University of New York [SUNY] Press, 2004).

Pearlman, Wendy and Kathleen Gallagher Cunningham, 'Nonstate Actors, Fragmentation, and Conflict Processes', *Journal of Conflict Resolution*, 56(1) (2012), pp. 3–15.

Rae, Heather, *State Identities and the Homogenisation of Peoples* (Cambridge: Cambridge University Press, 2002).

Romano, David, *The Kurdish Nationalist Movement: Opportunity, Mobilization and Identity* (Cambridge: Cambridge University Press, 2006).

Rudloff, Peter and Michael G. Findley, 'The Downstream Effects of Combatant Fragmentation on Civil War Recurrence', *Journal of Peace Research*, 53(1) (2016), pp. 19–32.

Savelsberg, Eva, 'The Syrian-Kurdish Movements: Obstacles Rather than Driving Forces for Democratization', in David Romano and Mehmet Gurses (eds), *Conflict, Democratization, and the Kurds in the Middle East: Turkey, Iran, Iraq, and Syria* (New York: Palgrave, 2014), pp. 85–110.

Seymour, Lee J.M., Kristin M. Bakke and Kathleen Gallagher Cunningham, 'E Pluribus Unum Ex Uno Plures: Competition, Violence, and Fragmentation in Ethnopolitical Movements', *Journal of Peace Research*, 53(1) (2016), pp. 3–18.

Staniland, Paul, 'Between a Rock and a Hard Place: Insurgent Fratricide, Ethnic Defection, and the Rise of Pro-State Paramilitaries', *Journal of Conflict Research*, 56(1) (2012), pp. 16–40.

Stansfield, Gareth R.V., *Iraqi Kurdistan: Political Development and Emergent Democracy* (London: RoutledgeCurzon, 2003).

———— 'The Kurdish dilemma: the golden era threatened', *Adelphi Papers* (2003), pp. 131–48.

Vali, Abbas, *Kurds and the State in Iran: The Making of Kurdish Identity* (London: I.B.Tauris, 2011).

Warren, T. Camber and Kevin K. Troy, 'Explaining Violent Intra-Ethnic Conflict: Group Fragmentation in the Shadow of State Power', *Journal of Conflict Resolution*, 59(3) (2015), pp. 484–509.

Wimmer, Andreas, *Nationalist Exclusion and Ethnic Conflict: Shadows of Modernity* (Cambridge: Cambridge University Press, 2002.

Notes

1. Françoise Boucek, 'Rethinking Factionalism: Typologies, Intra-Party Dynamics and Three Faces of Factionalism', *Party Politics*, 15(4) (2009), pp. 455–6.
2. Ibid., p. 456.
3. Lee J.M. Seymour, Kristin M. Bakke and Kathleen Gallagher Cunningham, 'E Pluribus Unum Ex Uno Plures: Competition, Violence, and Fragmentation in Ethnopolitical Movements', *Journal of Peace Research*, 53(1) (2016), p. 4.
4. Kathleen Gallagher Cunningham, 'Divide and Conquer or Divide and Concede: How Do States Respond to Internally Divided Separatists?' *American Political Science Review*, 105(2) (2011), p. 276.
5. Kathleen Gallagher Cunningham, Kristin M. Bakke and Lee J.M. Seymour, 'Shirts Today, Skins Tomorrow: Dual Contests and the Effects of Fragmentation in Self-Determination Disputes', *Journal of Conflict Resolution*, 56(1) (2012), p. 67; Warren, T. Camber, and Kevin K. Troy, 'Explaining Violent Intra-Ethnic Conflict: Group Fragmentation in the Shadow of State Power', *Journal of Conflict Resolution*, 59(3) (2015), pp. 484–509.
6. Michael Findley and Peter Rudloff, 'Combatant Fragmentation and the Dynamics of Civil War', *British Journal of Political Science*, 42(4) (2012), pp. 879–901.
7. Victor Asal, Mitchell Brown and Angela Dalton, 'Why Split? Organizational Splits Among Ethno political Organizations in the Middle East', *Journal of Conflict Resolution*, 56(1) (2012), pp. 94–117.
8. Martin van Bruinessen, *Agha, Shaikh and State: The Social and Political Structures of Kurdistan* (London: Zed Books, 1992); Wadie Jwaideh, *The Kurdish National Movement: Its Origins and Development* (Syracuse, NY: Syracuse University Press, 2006). For linguistic and cultural differences, see Amir Hassanpour, *Nationalism and Language in Kurdistan 1918–1985* (New York: The Edwin Mellen Press, 1992). For the impact of modern conceptions of nationalism, see Rogers Brubaker, *Nationalism Reframed: Nationhood and the National Question in the New Europe* (Cambridge: Cambridge University Press, 1996); and Umut Özkırımlı, *Theories of Nationalism: A Critical Introduction* (New York: Palgrave, 2000). For the imposition of narratives of dominant nationhood, see Andreas Wimmer, *Nationalist Exclusion and Ethnic Conflict: Shadows of Modernity* (Cambridge: Cambridge University Press, 2002); and Heather Rae, *State Identities and the*

Homogenisation of Peoples (Cambridge: Cambridge University Press, 2002). For subsequent engagement/contestation with the host states of the twentieth century, see Stansfield, 2003 [Denise Natali], *The Kurds and the State: Evolving National Identity in Iraq, Turkey, and Iran* (Syracuse, NY: Syracuse University Press, 2005); David Romano, *The Kurdish Nationalist Movement: Opportunity, Mobilization and Identity* (Cambridge: Cambridge University Press, 2006); Abbas Vali, *Kurds and the State in Iran: The Making of Kurdish Identity* (London: I.B.Tauris, 2011); Ofra Bengio, *The Kurds of Iraq: Building a State Within a State* (Boulder, CO: Lynne Rienner, 2012); and Harriet Allsopp, *The Kurds of Syria: Political Parties and Identity in the Middle East* (London: I.B.Tauris, 2014).

9. See Hassanpour 1985 for what remains one of the most comprehensive analyses and assessments of the emergence and development of Kurdish language groups.
10. Hakan Özoğlu, *Kurdish Notables and the Ottoman State: Evolving Identities, Competing Loyalties, and Shifting Boundaries* (New York: State University of New York [SUNY] Press, 2004); Sabri Ateş, *The Ottoman-Iranian Borderlands: Making a Boundary, 1843–1914* (Cambridge: Cambridge University Press, 2013).
11. See Bruinessen, *Agha, Shaikh and State* for what remains an unparalleled account of Kurdish tribal structures and the interaction of these structures with their religious and state counterparts.
12. Özoğlu, *Kurdish Notables and the Ottoman State*, p. 35.
13. There is a voluminous literature on the negotiations that took place at the end of World War I. For accessible yet detailed work on this subject, see the magisterial book by David Fromkin: *A Peace to End All Peace: The Fall of the Ottoman Empire and the Creation of the Modern Middle East* (New York: Henry Holt, 1989); and James Barr, *A Line in the Sand: Britain, France and the Struggle that Shaped the Middle East* (London: Simon & Schuster, 2011). For a specifically Kurdish focus, see Said Eskander, 'Britain's Policy in Southern Kurdistan: The Formation and Termination of the First Kurdish Government, 1918–1919', *British Journal of Middle Eastern Studies*, 27(2) (2000), pp. 139–63; and Said Eskander, 'Southern Kurdistan Under Britain's Mesopotamian Mandate: From Separation to Incorporation, 1920–1923', *Middle Eastern Studies*, 37(2) (2001), pp. 153–80.
14. Özoglu, *Kurdish Notables and the Ottoman State*.
15. For a contemporary account of the League of Nations arbitration over the Mosul *vilayet*, which continues to be essential reading today, see A. Berriedale Keith, 'The League of Nations and Mosul', *Journal of Comparative Legislation and International Law*, 8(1) (1926), pp. 38–49.
16. See Allsopp, *The Kurds of Syria*; Eva Savelsberg, 'The Syrian-Kurdish Movements: Obstacles Rather than Driving Forces for Democratization', in David Romano and Mehmet Gurses (eds), *Conflict, Democratization, and the Kurds in the Middle East: Turkey, Iran, Iraq, and Syria* (New York: Palgrave Macmillan, 2014).

17. See Stansfield, 2003.
18. Mahmut Bali Aykan, 'Turkey's Policy in Northern Iraq, 1991–95', *Middle Eastern Studies*, 32(4) (1996), pp. 343–66.
19. See Stansfield, 2003; Bengio, *The Kurds of Iraq*.
20. For an account of the Tudeh Party, see Fred Halliday, 'The Tudeh Party in Iranian Politics: Background Notes', *MERIP Reports*, 86, *The Left Forces in Iran* (1980), pp. 22–3; and M. Reza Ghods, 'The Iranian Communist Movement Under Reza Shah', *Middle Eastern Studies*, 26(4) (1990), pp. 506–13.
21. See Hashem Ahmadzadeh and Gareth Stansfield, 'The Political, Cultural, and Military ReAwakening of the Kurdish Nationalist Movement in Iran', *Middle East Journal*, 64(1) (2010), pp. 11–27.
22. Ali Kamal Özcan, *Turkey's Kurds: A Theoretical Analysis of the PKK and Abdullah Öcalan* (London: Routledge, 2006), p. 84.
23. For analyses of Kurdish political parties in Syria, see Allsopp, *The Kurds of Syria*; Michael Gunter, *Out of Nowhere: The Kurds of Syria in Peace and War* (London: Hurst & Co., 2014); and Savelsberg, 'The Syrian-Kurdish Movements'.
24. See Michiel Leezenberg, 'Political Islam Among the Kurds', paper prepared for the International Conference 'Kurdistan: The Unwanted State', 29–31 March 2001, Jagiellonian University/Polish-Kurdish Society, Kraków, Poland; Gareth Stansfield, 'The Kurdish dilemma: the golden era threatened', *Adelphi Papers* (2003), pp. 131–48.

CHAPTER 4

THE RISE OF THE WHITE KURDS – AN ESSAY IN REGIONAL POLITICAL ECONOMY

Michiel Leezenberg

The so-called Arab Spring, that is, the wave of popular protests against corruption and authoritarianism that swept across the Arab world in the spring of 2011, has had very different effects on the non-Arab population groups living in the region – foremost among them, the Kurds. Indeed, the very term 'Arab Spring' suggests a problematic Arab-nationalist bias. In Syria, Kurds were reluctant to join the opposition; subsequently, the Democratic Union Party (PYD), a Kurdish party with an ambivalent relationship with the Assad regime, carved out a territory for itself that has become known as Rojava. In Iraq, popular protest against the Shi'a-dominated Baghdad government was concentrated in the Sunni Arab areas; in the Kurdistan region, there were short-lived and regionally confined protests against the regional government in Erbil.

The situation in non-Arab neighbouring countries, like Turkey, was very different again. Initially, many Arab Islamists saw Turkey as a model for the successful combination of democracy, economic prosperity and respect for Islamic values. Among the Kurds in Turkey, despite considerable scepticism about the government's intentions, the mood appeared to have been one of cautious optimism and eagerness to exploit the new opportunities rather than widespread disaffection.

Yet, popular pressures for change were largely marginalized if not criminalized by the ruling elites; opposition movements appeared able to mobilize the population only to a limited extent, and for a limited period. A mere four years later, the situation looked grim for the Kurds in both Turkey and Iraq, albeit for very different reasons. Since the spring of 2014, the Kurdistan region in Iraq, which had seemed a beacon of stability and prosperity over the past decade, was crippled by the continuing onslaught of forces of the so-called Islamic State (IS), by an acute and pervasive economic crisis and by continuing squabbles between the different political parties of the region. In the late summer of 2015, ethnic violence between the Kurdistan Workers' Party (PKK) and security forces once again erupted in Turkey, on a scale not seen since the 1990s. These sudden and dramatic developments threatened to undo all the social, political and economic progress that had been made among and by the Kurds, both in Turkey and in Iraq, over the preceding decade. Yet, this political violence occurred in societies that in many respects are very different from those of around the year 2000. Cityscapes have changed dramatically; transnational contacts have intensified; and, perhaps most importantly, an entire newly affluent group of Kurds has emerged.

This chapter attempts to trace some of these recent changes in the political economy of the Kurdish-majority regions of Turkey and Iraq up to the summer of 2015, with a focus on changing opportunities for, on the one hand, representation and participation in civilian politics, and, on the other, mobilization for violent action. I will limit my discussion to Iraq and Turkey, as knowledge about the Kurds in Iran is limited even by regional standards and as the situation in war-torn Syria is so complex and volatile as to make empirical investigation virtually impossible. But even a study of the political economy of the Kurds in Turkey and Iraq faces serious obstacles. For Turkey, detailed data sets are available, but these are rarely if ever differentiated in terms of ethnicity; for Iraq, detailed quantitative data is a scarce commodity, and much of what little information we have is unreliable. Thus, the websites of the various Kurdistan Regional Government (KRG) ministries are notorious for providing few, if any, data, the sources and reliability of which are impossible to determine. For these and other reasons, the following analysis should be seen as merely a preliminary sketch of recent developments. It focuses on two major cities, Diyarbakir in Turkey and Erbil in Iraq, and its analyses and findings are qualitative rather than quantitative.[1]

Ethnicity, Democracy and Violence: Theoretical Perspectives

It is tempting to see political developments in the Kurdish-majority regions of Iraq and Turkey as determined first and foremost, if not exclusively, by ethnicity. Both countries, after all, have seen years of ethnically based guerrilla warfare and a violent counter-insurgency by state-security forces. Yet, there are reasons, both empirical and theoretical, for doubts concerning such reductionist readings. Mobilization along ethnic lines, although massive, was by no means universal among Kurds in either Turkey or Iraq; and some authors have suggested that language-based ethnic identity is in itself not enough to explain the emergence of ethnic conflict. Thus, David Laitin has forcefully argued that language diversity and linguistic grievances are not, in and of themselves, causes of ethnic violence, adducing empirical evidence that ethnic difference is not in itself a cause of conflict; rather, he claims, the open expression of linguistic demands creates possibilities for peaceful political resolution rather than armed conflict.[2] The most obvious other area to look for explanations of violent conflict is, of course, the political economy. Thus, in a recent overview article, James Fearon considered ethnic mobilization and ethnic violence from a political-economy perspective.[3] Earlier, modernist accounts of ethnic and national identity, Fearon argues – such as, most famously, those of Ernest Gellner and Benedict Anderson – tend to explain the politicization of ethnicity in terms of macroeconomic aspects of modernization, like industrialization and 'print capitalism'. Such approaches can hardly account for the emergence of politicized ethnicities in the Ottoman Empire, which knew little capitalism, little industrialization and little printing up until the early twentieth century. According to such theories, he continues, 'local political entrepreneurs find an eager constituency' whenever there are 'ascriptive barriers to upward mobility'.[4] It is not clear if such analyses apply to the Turkish case, where one can speak of industrializing modernization only in the course of the twentieth century; it certainly does not seem to apply to rentier economies like that of Iraq. Fearon himself focuses on the use of tools from microeconomic theory; he takes another suggestion from R.H. Bates, which *prima facie* seems more plausible in the case of the Kurds; according to this view, ethnicity provides a basis for forming coalitions in 'purely distributional conflicts over political goods'.[5] In such a view, ethnic groups are 'minimum winning coalitions' which are 'large enough to secure benefits in the competition for spoils, but also small enough to maximize the per capita value of these benefits'.[6] According to Fearon, such an approach is better placed to explain situational and temporal shifts in ethnic politicization. It remains to be seen, however, whether this focus on distribution does full justice to the particularities of Kurdish ethnicity in both Turkey and Iraq.[7]

Likewise, the oft-invoked opposition between 'strong' and 'weak' states seems unhelpful if not misleading, as the lack of institutionalization of a 'weak' state need not imply a weakness of coercive force. Instead, Peter Evans describes an ideal-typical opposition between 'developmental' states, like Japan and Taiwan, which know a capitalist economy characterized by the strong intervention of a relatively autonomous state, and 'predatory' (or 'weak') states, like Zaire under President Mobutu Sese Seko, which 'prey on their citizenry, terrorizing them, despoiling their common patrimony, and providing little in the way of services in return'.[8] Prima facie, Turkey shares some features with developmental states, while Iraq, including Iraqi Kurdistan, would come closer to the ideal type of the predatory state.[9] It is an open question, however, as to what extent the successive civilian governments in Turkey can be considered autonomous from society; and whatever the levels of predation in Iraqi Kurdistan, services there have never collapsed completely – in contrast with post-Saddam Iraq as a whole.

A more promising factor that can help to explain the dynamics of local social and political life is that of patronage. In the social-scientific literature, patronage tends to be depicted as by definition illegitimate and non-institutional; however, in contemporary Turkey – and especially in Iraq – it has become so firmly entrenched as to virtually form an institution of its own. In Iraqi Kurdistan, novel patterns of patronage under the new Kurdish political elites were already becoming visible in the mid-1990s.[10] Hence, one may ask whether and to what extent the Kurdish regions of both countries have become forms of what Kanchan Chandra has called a 'patronage-democracy' – that is, a democracy 'in which the state monopolizes access to jobs and services, and in which elected officials have discretion in the implementation of laws allocating the jobs and services at the disposal of the state'. According to Chandra, the emergence of such patronage-democracies depends on both the size of the State and the power of elected officials to distribute state-controlled resources to individual voters. A patronage-democracy in this sense also requires the state sector to be larger than the private sector as a source of jobs and services; moreover, it allows for a particular region or even city to qualify as a patronage-democracy even if the country as a whole does not. While admitting that there is insufficient cross-national data to warrant a general concept of patronage-democracy, Chandra suggests that it is particularly likely to develop in postcolonial states where colonial rule has left behind a legacy of state-dominated economies.[11] This suggests one possible line of accounting for the substantial differences between Turkey and Iraq, which share a long Ottoman past but have had rather different experiences with imperialism and colonial rule.

A second prerequisite for a more adequate understanding of recent developments among the Kurds may be the distinction between national and regional dynamics. Although obviously shaped by national politics, local developments – whether on a regional, a provincial or a municipal scale – appear to have been crucial.[12] In Iraqi Kurdistan, the establishment of a substantial region under *de facto* Kurdish rule in 1991, which was also legally recognized in Iraq's 2005 constitution, has marked the development of an entirely new political arena; in Turkey, the election of pro-Kurdish local governments in many – though by no means all – predominantly or primarily Kurdish constituencies in the 1999 municipal elections likewise created unprecedented political, economic and cultural opportunities. Intriguingly, this development almost coincided with, but attracted far less attention than, national political developments such as the capture and imprisonment of PKK leader Abdullah Öcalan in the same year.

The most significant development in early twenty-first-century political economy, it will be argued below, is visible at the regional or local rather than the national level; this is the rise of what may be called 'white Kurds'. In Diyarbakir, the new Kurdish economic elites are sometimes jokingly referred to as *beyaz Kürtler*, or 'white Kurds'; and, as I will argue below, one may similarly speak of a newly affluent class or stratum in Iraqi Kurdistan. I prefer this folk term over more familiar and more analytic ones like 'upper class', 'upper-middle class', 'bourgeoisie,' 'comprador class' or 'elite' for reasons that will become clear below. Some initial clarifications are in order, though. The expression obviously takes its inspiration from the term 'white Turks' (*beyaz Türkler*), which was coined in the 1990s and originally denoted the old urban, republican elites originating from the Balkans and/or living in the coastal provinces and Ankara, who were secular and Western in outlook, as opposed to the 'black Turks', that is, the pious and conservative, lower-class population of the Anatolian provinces. More loosely, it also came to denote a self-conscious elite that looks down on lower strata that it perceives as backward or rural; as such, it may denote newly emerging elites as well as long-established ones. The dichotomy implied in this folk term is an obvious oversimplification – in particular, because it downplays the dynamics of social mobility and the development of conscious elites. Moreover, it may misleadingly suggest an ethnic or geographic differentiation; I have no grounds for thinking that these new elites have a distinct ethnicity, geographical distribution or migration history. Nonetheless, the term may be useful in so far as it calls attention to the novel and locally specific character of these developments. Below, I will explore the political–economic similarities and differences between these groups among Turkish and Iraqi Kurds, in particular with respect to political representation and participation, up to the summer of 2015.

Turkey and Iraq: Diverging and Converging Trajectories

As anybody who has ever crossed the overland border at Ibrahim Khalil can attest, the vast differences between the Kurdish-inhabited regions of Turkey and Iraq are immediately apparent to even the most casual observer. Next to the obvious visual differences in cityscapes, in building styles of houses and in traffic organization, the more abstract economic divergences are almost equally striking. Southeastern Turkey, or Northern Kurdistan, is an integral part of a neo-liberal Turkish economy that is oriented towards the international market and which has witnessed years of sustained growth, especially in industry and construction. By contrast, Southern or Iraqi Kurdistan is a politically autonomous and economically only partly integrated region of Iraq, which displays many of the distinguishing features of a rentier economy;

it has little agricultural or industrial activity, an inflated bureaucracy and a strong reliance on expatriate workers – especially in the construction and services sectors, and in trade.

These discrepancies may be cause for surprise. After all, the Kurds in these regions share a common cultural background and history, their ancestors having been subjects of the Ottoman Empire for centuries. Apparently, then, these differences should be explained in terms of the different structural features of the empire's successor states; these differences became even more pronounced in the years following World War II. Here, I will briefly sketch these diverging (though also, in some respects, converging) patterns as a background for early twenty-first-century developments.[13]

The late nineteenth and early twentieth centuries witnessed the rapid rise of a new, major social actor: army officers – initially at least, of a predominantly Balkan background – with a military-academy education of modern, secular French (and, later, German) inspiration. In the new Republic of Turkey that was established by Mustafa Kemal Atatürk in 1923, it was army officers who constituted the new political elite. The country also witnessed the rapid emergence of new economic elites in the wake of the dispossession, expulsion and, in part, extermination of Greeks and Armenians, who had formed a disproportionately large part of the Ottoman mercantile bourgeoisie.

From the 1920s onwards, an ethnically Turkish middle class emerged.[14] The early 'Kemalist' republic was an authoritarian single-party state in which the ruling elites engaged in a radical project of social engineering, involving a modernization imposed from above and, where deemed necessary, implemented by force. As part of this policy, the Kemalists strove to eliminate all intermediate religious, tribal and other forms of authority that stood between the individual and the State; instead, society was to be supplied with a homogeneous, secular, national, Turkish culture. In the Kurdish regions, the Kemalist elites closed *medreses* (religious schools) and Sufi lodges, both of which had been instrumental in developing literate forms of the Kurdish language; banned the public and private speaking of Kurdish; and sought to destroy tribal structures and practices like blood feuds. These measures hit the Kurds especially hard.

It was not until after World War II that a combination of domestic and foreign pressures forced a greater political pluralism, institutionalized in a multiparty system and regular elections from 1950 onwards. Turkey has remained a civilian democracy ever since: despite being punctuated by military coups in 1960, 1971 and 1980 (not to mention the 'soft coup' ousting the then-prime minister, Necmettin Erbakan, in 1997), and being restricted in practice by the establishment of a military-dominated National Security Council (Milli Güvenlik Kurulu) in 1962, civilian rule and democratic parliamentary politics were never durably abolished.[15] Although deeply involved in political affairs, and temporarily suspending both civilian rule and the constitution when they saw fit, the Turkish military never attempted to directly govern the country themselves. In this respect, Turkey clearly differs from neighbouring countries like Greece, Syria and Iraq. What did emerge with multiparty politics, however, were new opportunities for patronage; below, we will see how these worked in practice.

Turkey's economic policies have undergone dramatic changes over the decades and have known failure as well as success. The national economy pursued in early republican times aimed at import-substituting production; in the 1980s, this largely state-led economy was replaced by economic-liberalization policies, which opened up Turkey for the world market. This liberalization also led to rapid rises in economic inequality, inflation and, above all, a steadily rising public debt, which was increasingly paid for by ever-larger International Monetary Fund (IMF) loans. Socially, the Turgot Özal years (1983–93) paved the way for a new social force that would not become politically visible until the 1990s: a provincial middle class that was considerably more pious and conservative in its outlook than the 'white Turks', that is, the secularized, Westward-looking Kemalist elites of the country's coastal regions.[16] It was primarily this newly affluent, and increasingly vocal, conservative middle class that would ultimately bring the Turkish Islamists to power in 2002.

In this nationalist but politically relatively open climate, Kurds could pursue different strategies; if they were willing to forego any claim to a distinct ethnic identity, they could in principle climb ever higher up the social ladder (although the wealthiest financial elites consisted exclusively of 'white Turks', and still do to this day). For the lower social strata, there were initially few opportunities or channels for specifically ethnic organization and resistance. Rather, (limited) Kurdish ethnic demands were to some extent taken over by the more radical groups of the Turkish Left, as part of a broader class struggle seen as having a higher priority.

The earliest Kurdish parties in Turkey, like the Turkish branch of the Kurdistan Democratic Party (KDP), were headed by sons of leading tribal families. In the late 1970s and early 1980s however, a new and more radical movement emerged: the Kurdistan Workers' Party (Partiya Karkerên Kurdistan, or PKK) headed by Abdullah Öcalan. Basing itself on revolutionary Marxist–Leninist principles, the PKK started a campaign of provoking increased state repression in order to increase or create a national revolutionary consciousness among the predominantly rural and illiterate Kurdish masses. It had a different class base than other Kurdish parties, recruiting primarily among the urban proletariat; this distinct class background has been adduced in explanation of its rather more violent character.[17]

The violent PKK insurgency and the even more violent repression by the Turkish security forces had grave social and economic consequences for the entire region. But increasingly, there were also civilian options for pursuing Kurdish ethnic demands in Turkish national politics. The Halkin Emek Partisi (HEP), established in 1990, and its successors (or reincarnations) emerged as an enduring force, even if they faced formidable difficulties in their attempts to gain a place in mainstream politics.[18] In 1993, the party was banned on the grounds of its alleged links with the PKK, after which it reconvened under a different name (a pattern that would be repeated several times); in 1994, its representatives were stripped of their parliamentary immunity and condemned to long terms in prison; others, like Vedat Aydin in 1991 and Mehmet Sincar in 1993, fell victim to political assassination. Nevertheless, over the years, pro-Kurdish politicians grew increasingly more visible in national politics (more precisely, in gaining access to the Turkish Parliament). The biggest success to date was undoubtedly the June 2015 national elections, in which the People's Democratic Party (HDP), led by Selehattin Demirtas, for the first time ever passed the 10-per cent electoral threshold.[19] Perhaps even more significant than this entrance into national, civilian politics was the consolidation of Kurdish representation at the local level from 1990 onwards – or so I will argue below.

Iraq, of course, has run a rather different trajectory in the twentieth century. Under British mandate rule, the new state of Iraq was turned into a constitutional monarchy; in the national parliament, rural landowning elites were clearly overrepresented.[20] The 1958 coup led by General Abdulkarim Qassim ended the monarchy and moved Iraq closer to the socialist Eastern Bloc. Despite a number of significant – and partly successful – agricultural and other reforms, Qassim's coup initiated a decade of political instability, in part resulting from an unresolved Kurdish question. A new coup in 1968 brought the Arab nationalist Ba'ath party to power; effective leadership in both the party and the regime soon came to be exercised by Saddam Hussain, who consciously modelled his style of rule on Stalin's. Despite its officially pro-Soviet line and its socialist-leaning policies, the Ba'ath regime mercilessly persecuted members of the Iraqi Communist Party (ICP) – as indeed it did with all sources of political opposition including, in particular, Kurdish and Shi'ite parties.

Iraq's economic policies over the years have been erratic, and from the 1970s onwards they became dominated by the oil sector.[21] Saddam's domestic and international ambitions were encouraged by the rapid rise of oil prices in the 1970s. The steadily rising budget increased the regime's autonomy from society. Rather than leading towards socialism, as official rhetoric would have it, Ba'athist rule has in practice produced a form of state capitalism.[22] Socialist land reforms and the collectivization of agriculture in the 1970s were followed by a policy of economic liberalization (*infitah*) in the 1980s. The end of the Iran–Iraq War in 1988 saw a rapid rise in basic food prices, partly as a result of radical market reforms amounting to virtual shock therapy. The instability resulting both from the demobilization of the Iraqi Army and the skyrocketing prices led to considerable violence, ultimately channelled or deflected by Saddam's August 1990 invasion of Kuwait.

Iraq's economic development in the 1990s remained largely hidden behind international sanctions. It was characterized by the further pursuit of a criminalized crony capitalism, by hyperinflation and by Iraq's inability and/or unwillingness to pay the debts that it had incurred during the Iran–Iraq War.[23] It was also during the 1990s that much of the Iraqi welfare state was quickly dismantled and replaced by an increasingly openly predatory state. Although state services, like a food-distribution system and free education and healthcare, largely remained in place, corruption and nepotism steadily increased.

Iraqi society as a whole had become predominantly urban as a result of more or less spontaneous processes by the late 1970s, but the still largely rural Kurdish region was forcibly urbanized for political reasons during the 1970s and 1980s. Government troops systematically evacuated and destroyed villages, deporting their inhabitants to relocation camps (*mujamma'at*). As a result, Iraq's hitherto self-sufficient agricultural economy was destroyed. The rural population was robbed of its means of subsistence and reduced to a position of dependence on government handouts. This forcible social transformation was not necessarily intended to dismantle rural tribal structures, however; during the 1980s war, the regime had strengthened – and, in some cases, actually created – tribal structures by the appointment of 'advisers' (*mustashar*), who headed pro-government Kurdish irregular troops in the countryside. Moreover, Kurdish being, in theory at least, an official language, and Kurdistan being – again, largely theoretically – a constitutionally recognized, autonomous region of the country, there was no taboo on expressions of Kurdishness as there was in Kemalist Turkey.

Thus, unlike in Turkey, members of the Iraqi Kurdish elites had to hide neither their ethnicity nor their tribal affiliation in their attempts to join the national economic – and, to a lesser extent, political – elites. In Iraq, it was political loyalty, primarily expressed through Ba'ath Party membership, rather than cultural or ethnic Kurdish identity that decided one's social standing – if not physical survival. In these circumstances, Kurdish tribal leaders loyal to Baghdad, or at least neutral in the confrontation between the Iraqi regime and the Kurdish insurgency, could become successful entrepreneurs. Among the best-known of such entrepreneurs were the leaders of the Surchi tribe, originally based on the Harir Plain north of Erbil, who during the 1980s became wealthy enough to buy property in London's wealthiest districts. But there were various others who similarly profited from Ba'athist rule.

It is a moot question whether, and to what extent, both the regional parliament in the Kurdish North and local tribal and/or business leaders had any real political leverage, actually succeeded in representing the local population or could provide any kind of patronage. After all, they acted in what was, by any standard, a totalitarian state with an extreme concentration of power in the hands of a narrow elite based on family ties as much as on Arab nationalism. The patronage relations that were allowed or encouraged by the regime tended to be tribal as much as parliamentary in character, and offered mediation rather than representation. The 1991 uprising led to a rapid, and still poorly understood, change of local elites. Below, we will explore some of the new power structures and patronage patterns that emerged in its wake.

In short, the post-World War II trajectories of Turkey and Iraq have been quite distinct – the former developing into a relatively successful, if fragile, market economy integrated into the world market; the latter becoming a rentier economy that remained isolated from the world market for decades, and acquired an increasingly predatory character in the 1990s and beyond. Behind these obvious differences, however, there were also a number of parallel or converging trends. Both countries saw a restricted liberalization and privatization of the economy during the 1980s, high inflation and massive debt in the 1990s and a measure of economic stabilization after tumultuous years during the first decade of the twenty-first century. These distinct and drastically changing economic landscapes yielded rather different political opportunities for the Kurds living in these countries, as will become clear below.

The Kurds in Turkey since 1999: Patronage in a Developmental State?

In 2002, as noted, the Islamist Justice and Development Party (AKP) achieved a landslide victory, primarily on an economic ticket. Its subsequent electoral triumphs were likewise driven primarily by its successes in reforming the national economy. Inflation was much reduced, though not brought entirely under control, by strict monetary policies involving, among others, the introduction of a new currency, the *Yeni Türk Lirasi*, in 2005. The AKP Government also made a point of repaying Turkey's IMF debts, a task that it had completed by 2013, and reduced government debt from 78 per cent to some 40 per cent of GDP.[24] This is not to say, however, that Turkey became a debt-free country; rather, borrowing shifted to the private sector. Thus, according to CIA figures, Turkey's external debt amounted to US$402 billion at the end of 2014.[25] The strength of the Turkish economy is thus a matter for dispute; but the structural changes and the national government's ability to intervene in the economy are not in doubt.

AKP rule marked a new era not only with respect to the economy but also with respect to civilian–military relations. During the initial years of his rule, Erdoğan was engaged in a protracted power struggle with the military elites – a struggle that ended with a decisive victory for civilian politics over the military. The AKP had the reputation of being less corrupt than its secular rivals, the traditional Turkish mainstream parties, and of doing rather more for practically improving the daily lives of its supporters. Over the years, however, it increasingly fell into the familiar pattern of rewarding the political loyalty of its followers, whether in giving handouts or in awarding contracts, for which its predecessors had become notorious. State-sponsored construction projects in Turkey tended to be awarded to AKP voters – in particular, through the government-run Turkish Housing Development Agency (TOKI), the country's biggest property developer, which operates nationwide in providing cheap housing for the poorer strata of society, securing considerable numbers of votes and generating enormous wealth for contractors in the process. In recent years, opposition parties have voiced concern over the agency's success rate.[26] In the Kurdish southeast, TOKI was reported to be involved primarily in private construction works that were of an inferior quality, but which were increasingly out of reach for the local poorer strata for whom they had originally been intended. According to political scientist A. Kadir Yildirim, Erdoğan's recent shift towards authoritarian rule cannot be understood without looking at the 'upgraded clientelism' that supports it; this clientelism, he argues, is unprecedented in its scale and pervasiveness.[27]

On the national level, the 2002 AKP electoral victory constituted a watershed, as it marked the breakthrough of new elites and introduced a rupture with longstanding Kemalist dogmas and taboos (including on the acknowledgment of the cultural and ethnic existence of the Kurds). For the Kurds in Turkey, however, the year 1999 rather than 2002 formed the turning point. On the one hand, the capture and subsequent trial of PKK leader Öcalan in February 1999 spelled an effective end to PKK guerrilla warfare, which already by that time seemed past its prime. Some guerrillas surrendered to the Turkish authorities; many others withdrew across the Iraqi and Iranian borders, establishing new headquarters in the Qandil Mountains in Iraq. Only small numbers of guerrillas remained inside Turkey. But next to these dramatic (trans-)national developments, the Kurdish southeast also witnessed a rather less visible but equally momentous development at the local level. In 1999, for the first time ever, a pro-Kurdish party won municipal elections in several major cities. This development created unprecedented opportunities for the distribution of resources. This opportunity space may have been diminutive in comparison with the richer provinces in western Turkey and with the local private sector, not to mention the central government and its agencies like TOKI, but it was certainly real. Reportedly, pro-AKP cities like Urfa received a rather higher budget from the national government than pro-Kurdish Diyarbakir, but the latter acquired substantial means for distribution nonetheless.[28] The late twentieth and early twenty-first century witnessed the rise of a number of new trade and industry hubs, locally called 'Anatolian Tigers', also in or near the Kurdish southeast, witness the success of cities like Kahramanmaraş and Gaziantep; in general, however, the region continued to lag behind western Turkey economically. Thus, in 2013, per capita income in Diyarbakir Province was 50 per cent of the national average, while the illiteracy rate was twice as high as elsewhere in Turkey; the rates of students graduating from high school, vocational school or university were around half the national average.[29]

This relative poverty increased the opportunities for patronage even for municipalities with a restricted budget. Thus, the pro-Kurdish Diyarbakir municipality appears to have taken over a number of welfare activities formerly (and nationally) associated with the AKP. It also encouraged local villagers to form agricultural collectives, and experimented with redistributing agricultural lands to poorer villagers; in the city, the municipality supplied microcredits to people wanting to start small-scale businesses. Local economists, however, say that demand for such microcredit was small anyway, as aspiring small entrepreneurs either were not poor enough to qualify for such credits or required rather larger investments than could be provided for.[30] Hence, one may doubt whether such programmes marked a substantial economic policy aimed at countering the nationally rising economic inequality rather than populist posturing or small-scale clientelization.

For their part, local PKK activists tried to maintain an influence in political, economic and social affairs, both by setting up formal structures of parallel government in the shape of the so-called Union of Communities in Kurdistan (Koma Civakên Kurdistan, KCK) and by establishing more informal representatives in urban quarters, who could mediate in private matters like marital conflicts and small-scale financial or economic disputes.

Despite the relative economic underdevelopment of the Kurdish southeast, a more conservative middle class emerged here as elsewhere in Anatolia. There are indications that since the effective end of the guerrilla war and the emergence of local pro-Kurdish politics, both traceable to the year 1999, a new Kurdish middle class, or affluent stratum, has emerged and flourished in the southeast; in Diyarbakir, these new elites are estimated at some 10 per cent of the population, and are jokingly referred to as 'white Kurds'. According to local analysts, their wealth was accumulated less through industrial production than through services, notably construction, reportedly supported by funds locally allocated by the pro-Kurdish municipality. The municipality is also said to command a larger budget (and hence, more extensive opportunity for patronage) than the local TOKI branch, which receives its funds directly from the central government.[31]

It was primarily this rising provincial middle class, hitherto un- or under-represented in Turkish politics, that had supported Prime Minister Necmettin Erbakan's Islamist Refah Party in the 1990s, and which brought its successor, the AKP, to power in 2002. Despite the nationwide rise of a pro-AKP business class with roots in Anatolia over the following years, the wealthiest financial elites were and remained 'white Turks' originating from the coastal areas; apparently, Kurds have hardly if at all penetrated these highest financial echelons. Most members of the Kurdish business elite in western Turkey are reported to belong to slightly lower economic strata, being disproportionally represented among hotel and restaurant owners.[32]

Similar patterns of social mobility, it appears, can also be seen in the Kurdish southeast. Although part of Diyarbakir's present-day elite hails from the city's older notable families like the Karakoç family (who formerly were primarily wealthy landowners, but have in recent years become active in construction), most of them are believed to have amassed their wealth over the past two decades. Most of these 'white Kurds' thus form a relatively young elite. The reverse side of this increasing economic inequality is a real loss in purchasing power among the poorer strata, which carries an increasing risk of antagonisms between rich and poor.

Over the past decade, Diyarbakir appears to have seen considerable social mobility among different parts of its population: earlier inhabitants and refugees arriving in the 1990s have tended to move from Suriçi, the old city centre inside the ancient fortification walls, to Bağlar and then on to Yeni Bağlar – and finally, to upmarket new neighbourhoods like 75 Road and Diclekent. In recent years, poorer Kurdish refugees from Syria and from Sinjar in Iraq have tended to rent houses in Suriçi and Bağlar, allowing their earlier inhabitants to move out to more affluent quarters. Richer Syrian refugees are reported to have bought apartments in the latter areas. Increasingly, the relatively affluent Kurds of Iraq have also been buying properties in the Kurdish areas across the Turkish–Iraqi border. Quantitative data is not available, but these and other observations indicate a relationship between the construction boom, increasing inequality and settlement patterns. The Diclekent quarter, newly constructed outside the urban nucleus, forms perhaps the best visualization of Diyarbakir's increasing economic inequality. Initially, there were plans to surround it with a protective wall against intruders; however, local academics reportedly warned against this physical separation, which, they feared, might increase antagonism between rich and poor in the city, and thus undermine Kurdish national solidarity.[33]

The extent to which these economic developments have affected the potential for mobilization remains to be assessed, but there is a widespread perception that the changes of the past 15 years have been not just quantitative but also qualitative.

In March 2012, PKK leader Öcalan publicly announced that his party would enter into peace negotiations with the Turkish Government. Although the ensuing talks showed few if any signs of progress, let alone concrete details of the settlement to be reached, they continued until the spring of 2015. It has been claimed, however, that the very existence of such a peace process, whatever its actual progress or results, has helped the civilian HDP to strengthen its mobilization across class divides. It was the middle class, after all, which stood to lose most by the collapse of the talks and by any resumption of violence, with its concomitant risk of harm to the local economy and of damage to or the loss of private property. As one local observer put it, the success of the HDP in the 2015 elections resulted from its ability to maintain the balance between the conservative middle classes and the poorer (and more easily radicalized) strata. On a similar note, one PKK dissident observed that the class base of the Kurdish movement had changed radically since the turn of the century.[34] Apparently, this 'peace dividend' has even broken existing bonds of patronage: reportedly, even AKP voters formerly working with, or co-opted by, TOKI switched sides to the HDP in the June 2015 elections. It is too early to say whether and how the renewed outbreak of violence in the summer of 2015, and the subsequent destruction of large parts of Suriçi by the Turkish armed forces and government-hired contractors, will affect these settlement patterns and long-term political tendencies.

The Kurds in Iraq since 1991: An Emerging Patronage Democracy?

The turn of the twenty-first century also provided unprecedented opportunities for the Kurds in Iraq, albeit in a setting radically different from the Turkish one. Most importantly, from 1991 onwards, the Iraqi Kurds were able to create a political arena that was largely (though by no means entirely) autonomous. In 1992, the parties united in the Iraqi Kurdistan Front (IKF) organized regional elections, which ended in a 50–50 division of seats between the two biggest parties, the KDP headed by Masoud Barzani and the Patriotic Union of Kurdistan (PUK) led by Jalal Talabani. This 50–50 division soon pervaded, and increasingly paralyzed, all civilian politics in the region. Both parties tried to get out of the stalemate by increasingly bypassing the elected structures; and in May 1994, fights between the two parties broke out, which took an increasing toll on the civilian population and on the urban infrastructure. Although these fights ended with an American-brokered peace agreement in 1998, they left the region effectively split into two single-party statelets marked by pervasive patronage of the locally dominant party. New regional elections would not be held until 2005.

Hence, for Iraq Kurdistan, the 2003 war marks far less radical a rupture than it does for the rest of Iraq: its main political, economic and even ideological features had stabilized well before the war, and met with few radical challenges until long afterwards.[35] Obviously, however, the war and its aftermath did lead to a number of significant political changes – most importantly, a steep rise in revenues (17 per cent of

Baghdad's oil revenues being earmarked for the region) and the official recognition of Kurdish autonomy in the 2005 Iraqi Constitution; nonetheless, these changes consolidated and institutionalized existing arrangements rather than marking a radical departure. Over the following decade, however, the region saw substantial demographic changes. An entire generation of youths came of age without ever having experienced – let alone actively participated in – insurgency and counter-insurgency, guerrilla warfare or its violent repression.

Instead, the younger generation increasingly came to see security, material well-being and employment as entitlements rather than achievements or privileges. The main question here is whether and to what extent this postwar development of a rentier state and consumerist society has affected the prospects for ethnic mobilization, let alone violent collective action, either on behalf of or against the ruling Kurdish authorities.

The sudden rise of revenues dramatically increased the possibilities for building up clientele networks, but apparently it did not lead to any qualitative changes in existing patterns of patronage. All oil revenues appear to have been spent immediately, either on public obligations like salary payments or on personal enrichment; little, if any, thought appears to have been given to building up currency reserves, let alone creating a sovereign wealth fund.[36] An unknown percentage of these funds has flown directly into KDP and PUK party coffers and into the bank accounts of leading politicians; another percentage has gone to various forms of patronage.

The most visible, and undoubtedly the most blatant, of these is the direct allocation of funds to those close to the power elites. Already by 2006, there were an estimated 1,000 millionaires in Sulaimaniya Governorate, and another thousand in Erbil.[37] With possible exceptions like the owners of Korek and Asiacell, the region's two main mobile-phone companies, these millionaires had acquired their fortune through the redistribution of oil income and other revenues rather than by engaging in entrepreneurial activities or providing services. Construction was not in the hands of local entrepreneurs, but primarily of foreign (and especially Turkish) companies. Thus, rather than constituting an affluent business class as a social force in its own right, they remained entirely dependent on – and, hence, loyal to – the parties in power.

A second major channel for building clientele networks was – and is – the distribution of subsidized foodstuffs. A food-distribution system that had been established under the Ba'ath regime remained in place, not only in the Kurdistan Region but in Iraq as a whole. Each family continued to receive a monthly supply of basic foodstuffs (including wheat, sugar, rice, cooking oil and powdered milk) free of charge.[38] In recent years, questions have been raised about the need for and desirability of such a distribution system. Families not wanting or needing their free ration could either get its cash value from the local distributor or acquire better-quality products at a surcharge.

Thus, the distribution system provided ample opportunity for corruption and black-market activities. It also created opportunities for political patronage, as the distribution cards were also used for voter registration. Some local observers alleged that, precisely because of this double use, the KRG authorities have been reluctant to use the distribution cards for the registration of internally displaced persons in local camps: being entitled to food supplies in the north might also be construed as being entitled to vote in the regional elections. Conversely, there are persistent rumours of local ruling parties handing out food-distribution cards to Kurds living in neighbouring areas of Turkey and Iran, in exchange for their coming to Iraqi Kurdistan and voting for them in elections.[39]

Third, even public education – and, in particular, higher education – appears to have become an instrument of patronage rather than a generator of knowledge production or economic innovation. Prior to the 2014 financial crisis, a university degree virtually guaranteed a well-paid job in the state service; reportedly, a staggering 60 per cent of the region's workforce was estimated to be in the service of the KRG in 2011. Given this prospect, it is little wonder that higher education has boomed: in 2013, there were ten public and ten private universities in the region, enrolling some 100,000 students. State education up to and including university level was provided free of charge; however, an increasing number of higher-income families sent their children to the rapidly expanding private schools and universities, which could charge up to US$10,000 annually per student.

There have been serious and well-meant attempts to improve higher education; but these have generally been promulgated in a top-down manner without any serious thought concerning their practical implementation, let alone follow-up. For example, the Ministry of Higher Education has spent some US$500 million on sending students abroad to get PhDs; however, a large proportion of them either stayed abroad or returned without a degree. For those who did return after graduating, the infrastructure to apply or transmit what they had learned abroad was simply lacking; as a result, the returnees were integrated into existing structures, and were unable to put to use anything of what they had learned abroad.[40]

The massive recruitment of university graduates by the KRG not only destroyed any semblance of a labour market, it was equally detrimental to the private sector. The substantial proportion of local youths who received higher education grew up in the belief that they could expect – and, indeed, were entitled to – a secure income through virtually guaranteed government employment; this expectation threatened to thwart all incentive to set up private businesses, let alone to seek employment in the private sector. Thus, local shop owners have complained that Iraqi Kurdish employees expect to be assigned a managerial position immediately, refusing even to pass through an apprenticeship stage in a subordinate position. Likewise, restaurant owners complain that locals have grown to think that menial jobs in the services sector are beneath their dignity.[41]

As a result, a substantial proportion of the personnel in restaurants and shops are Kurds from Turkey, Syria and Iran; a significant percentage of managers in the more upmarket luxury hotels, restaurants and department stores are Lebanese; and a large part of the personnel at hotels and airports hail from the Indian subcontinent. A number of Chinese construction firms had flown in their own workers; but many of these left in 2014 due to the non-payment of salaries and the increased IS threat. The largest number of foreign companies and expatriate workers in construction, however, were Turkish; significantly, these hailed from AKP bastions like the Black Sea coast rather than the Kurdish-majority areas.[42] Until the IS takeover of Mosul, one could also see day labourers from Mosul Province waiting for employers on street corners. These expatriate workers had neither political rights nor political representation.

But it was not only massive government employment that hindered entrepreneurship. Anyone trying to set up a business in the region encountered a kind of patronage in reverse, in that they had to seek a partnership with, or the protection of, someone with party connections. In theory, the KRG welcomed private entrepreneurship and encouraged foreign investment through relatively liberal investment laws;[43] in practice, however, these partnerships amounted to a kind of protection ring that extorted money from entrepreneurs without providing any real services in return, beyond a protection from self-created (and, in part, imaginary) dangers and difficulties. These local partners or protectors could hardly be called a business class; generally, they were less entrepreneurs who invested in risky or innovative business ventures than rentiers who lived off a relatively risk-free income, if not predators who siphoned off others' capital. As a result, the entrepreneurial class – like the employees in the services and construction sectors – included a disproportionately large number of expatriates, mostly from Iran and Turkey; repeatedly, these foreign traders have complained about corruption and about the mistrust of foreigners in the region.[44]

There was thus increasing popular disaffection with the region's staggering corruption and pervasive patronage; but this hardly translated into any large-scale demonstrations or enduring political mobilization, let alone widespread violent protest. Opposition parties – like the Yekgirtuy Islamî (Islamic League) early in the twenty-first century and Gorran, a splinter faction from the PUK, towards the end of its opening decade – appear not to have succeeded in seriously challenging or changing this arrangement of affairs. Led by a veteran peshmerga, Noshirwan Mustafa, Gorran pushed for greater transparency in discussions of the KRG budget, with some initial successes; in the longer run, however, it appeared to pursue a greater share in, rather than any substantial change to, the existing redistribution system. Parliamentary debate was dominated by largely symbolic questions at the expense of rather more pressing topics like the endemic corruption and the acute currency crisis. It came to a virtual standstill anyway after the ousting of all Gorran members from both cabinet and government in the autumn of 2015 following violent anti-KDP demonstrations in Sulaimaniya that were openly supported by Gorran. Even after the ousting of IS from Mosul in the spring of 2017, the Kurdistan Region remained deadlocked in a self-inflicted political and financial crisis.

Contrasting Patterns of Ethnic Violence

During the first decade of the twenty-first century, the prospect of renewed ethnic violence in both the southeast of Turkey and the north of Iraq appeared to be steadily receding. Yet, in 2015, both regions were once again arenas of major armed confrontation. However, one question that has become particularly pressing in the wake of the August 2014 IS offensive and the July 2015 escalation in Turkey is whether and to what extent the local population can be mobilized for a prolonged armed struggle, as it could in the 1970s and 1980s.

As noted above, the rise of the 'white Kurds' in the Turkish southeast did not necessarily lead to the disappearance or upward social mobility of the poorer social strata. Nonetheless, in the Kurdish-majority provinces of Turkey, the emergence of a newly affluent class and the dividend of civilian politics do appear to have changed attitudes. Despite a persistent distrust of the central government, a large part of the local population appeared to have progressively lost its taste for radical discourse of any kind – whether Turkish, Kurdish-nationalist or Islamist. The dramatic events of the summer of 2015 proved, however, that another quite substantial population segment could still be mobilized for violent collective action. Hence, the HDP, the Barış ve Demokrasi Partisi (BDP) and other incarnations of what remained largely the same party in substance and personnel had to perform a continuous balancing act between mainstream (and civilian) politics and (pro-)PKK radicalism. These two strands were represented primarily by, respectively, the more conservative and increasingly affluent strata that would otherwise vote AKP as they had done before, and the impoverished youths in the cities, who were the main victims of the increasing economic inequality and who showed a permanent potential for radical political action. It is unclear to what extent the HDP has succeeded in durably garnering the support of this urban proletariat; reportedly, in several violent episodes – like the October 2014 urban riots in the wake of the AKP Government's perceived support of ISIS during the siege of Kobani (northern Syria), and the June 2015 bombing of an HDP election rally in Diyarbakir – HDP officials made strenuous efforts to avert further escalation. In the summer of 2015, however, it was primarily these youths who resorted to violent urban protests against Turkish security forces, erecting barricades in the streets of

Diyarbakir and a number of other cities and declaring autonomy. The violence appeared to be concentrated in the poorer quarters of cities like Diyarbakir, Cizre, Silopi and Nusaybin.[45] It may have been no coincidence that these were predominantly Kurdish cities near the Syrian border: ethnically mixed cities like Mardin were reportedly relatively quieter, as were most Kurdish towns further north.

The concentration of the insurgency in these towns has been explained by the presence of veterans from the siege of Kobani in 2014: veterans who could put their experience in urban guerrilla warfare to good use in Turkey.[46] Other observers have emphasized the spontaneous, grassroots action by local youths; but the similar tactics of declaring autonomy suggest a rather stronger inspiration, if not organization, by PKK forces and ideas.[47] At present, it is difficult to determine the degree of spontaneity and organization of these protests; however, what matters more in the present context is the participation of large groups of urban youths who can apparently be mobilized for collective violence.

The character of the violence has also changed dramatically. To the extent that these clashes can be seen as a PKK strategy, they appear to reflect a shift away from the primarily rural guerrilla tactics of the 1980s and 1990s to a new form of urban guerrilla warfare. This may reflect the fact that the PKK no longer has the personnel or the means to conduct a large-scale rural insurgency; significantly, the 2015 clashes involved relatively few rural incidents; those that did take place occurred primarily in areas near the Iraqi and Iranian borders, like Hakkari and Dogubeyazit. The shift may also reflect a shift towards urban guerrilla warfare as a more effective, and more easily publicized, form of insurgency – possibly shaped by the unprecedented, and unprecedentedly sympathetic, media coverage of the Kobani siege in the autumn of 2014. Whatever the organization behind it, the events of the summer of 2015 proved that among part of the local population, there remained an enduring mobilization potential for urban violence. Generally, however, the uprisings failed, in so far as they did not secure mass support or mobilization: most residents of the quarters where autonomy had been announced tried to leave before a curfew was imposed and the Turkish Army moved in.[48]

Ethnic mobilization and ethnic violence in Iraqi Kurdistan display a rather different pattern. Thus far at least, competition between the main political parties in Iraqi Kurdistan has led to hardly any further ethnic fragmentation. There are some indications of an increasingly vocal, cultural self-assertion in the Badinan region in the northernmost part of the Kurdistan Region, but this has hardly if at all translated into a distinct political mobilization. Other ethnic groups like the Assyrian Christians, the Yezidis, the Turkomans and others appear to be numerically too small and politically and economically too weak to mount a serious challenge. Of these groups, only the Christians and the Turkomans were represented as such in the regional parliament. In the wake of the summer 2014 IS onslaught, which specifically targeted the region's minorities, calls increased for the separate representation of groups like Yezidis, Kakais, Arabs and others; one proposal suggested two separate councils for, respectively, ethnic and religious minorities.[49]

It remains to be seen whether the creation of such councils will lead to a greater representation rather than to a more diffuse patronage. In fact, coinciding with these efforts, there are indications that the KRG's conceptions of 'Kurdishness', and hence of full citizenship, were becoming increasingly restrictive. On several occasions, minorities like the Yezidis, the Christians, the Shabak and the Turkmens in the Nineveh Plain and Sinjar protested against being treated as second-class citizens, and against the alleged appropriation of ruling positions and other goods by individuals close to the KRG or the KDP. Some locals interpreted the collapse of the KRG front against IS, which left the Yezidis unprotected, as a reflection of the regional government's indifferent attitude towards minorities.[50] Moreover, especially since 2014, the KRG's rhetoric and practices appear to have become increasingly anti-Arab. On one level, the confrontation between KRG troops and IS forces reproduces the confrontation between Kurds and Arabs of the 1980s; however, in the present circumstances, anti-Arab sentiment among the population is notably stronger than it was under Ba'ath rule, and in fact seems to be encouraged by the regional government. In both official rhetoric and popular parlance, one increasingly often hears expressions like *arabî pîsekan* ('dirty Arabs'); and locals born outside the Kurdish region, or of mixed marriages, have complained of being humiliated or discriminated against by officials for being insufficiently 'Kurdish'.

The KRG's failure to pay peshmerga salaries on a regular basis has apparently not led to any mass desertion; but the enduring loyalty of the regional forces, let alone the civilian population, could not even be taken for granted in the face of the IS threat. Among the public, irritation about the government's corruption and mishandling of the current economic and political crisis grew steadily. Although it was – and is – doubtful that such disaffection will develop into violent, organized opposition (radical armed groups being largely absent in the regional political landscape), the KRG is clearly alarmed. Undoubtedly triggered by the August 2015 demonstrations in Baghdad, which had forced Prime Minister Haidar Abadi's cabinet to announce major reforms, the KRG took precautions against any public display of discontent, putting riot police and water cannons on alert in the major cities.[51] Given the depth of the ongoing financial crisis – which, in the summer of 2017, was no nearer resolution than in the autumn of 2015 – one should perhaps not ask whether more serious and massive protests could break out, but rather why they had not already occurred much earlier.[52]

The current shortage painfully exposes a number of structural weaknesses in the regional government. With measures partly inherited from the Ba'athist welfare state and partly introduced by the ruling Kurdish parties, the KRG has long been able to effectively buy the loyalty of the bulk of the population. Its continuing ability to do so, however, depended not merely on the continuation but on a steady increase in revenues, if only to accommodate the ever-larger numbers of university graduates in the government-paid workforce. Baghdad's discontinuation of oil payments in January 2014 immediately left the KRG – which had not built up any substantial currency reserves – unable to continue salary payments on a regular basis, dramatically exposing its structural dependency on external revenues and on the goodwill of the central government. In the same year, the sudden – and equally dramatic – fall in oil prices on the international market demonstrated the economic vulnerability of both the Erbil and the Baghdad governments.

In an optimistic scenario, the crisis that erupted in 2014 might ultimately force the KRG to recognize that its economic policies have been unsustainable, and to revise them accordingly; however, even three years later, no substantial reforms plans had been formulated – let alone implemented.[53] Various politicians and policy advisers have floated plans for greater transparency, for attracting foreign investment and/or for introducing taxation, but none of these appear to have materialized. The expectation in KRG circles seemed to be that either payment from Baghdad would quickly resume or that local oil production could be rapidly expanded to meet the region's cash demand. However, several foreign oil companies left the region because of the KRG's inability to pay them; furthermore, given the dramatically fallen oil prices, the Baghdad government appeared to be virtually as short of cash as the KRG was.

For the most part, the KRG appears to have taken only short-term emergency measures. The most important tactic, the resort to selling its own oil, well predated the crisis, and was in fact a cause as much as a consequence of friction with Baghdad. In 2015, the KRG tried to offset the fall in revenues by trying to raise oil sales of its own, but its capacity to increase oil production and export was restricted by several factors. Oil extraction was and remained largely in the hands of foreign companies in the service of the KRG; however, as the latter had not been paying their salaries, these companies limited or even suspended their activities, which made it difficult to maintain – let alone raise – production levels.

Oil export was also hampered by the technological difficulties of transporting regional crude through the existing national pipeline. Finally, oil sales were hampered by potential juridical ramifications: few countries appeared to be willing to buy crude directly from the KRG and thus to risk legal action by the Iraqi central government.[54] Given the legal limbo in which this trade took place, one may surmise that oil is being sold at prices well below those of the world market.

Conclusions

The past two decades have witnessed the creation of political spaces in both Turkey and Iraq in which Kurdish actors could compete on an unprecedented scale. The new opportunities for the allocation and redistribution of resources, moreover, facilitated the rise of similar, newly affluent groups or classes. Following local usage, these have been dubbed 'white Kurds' in this chapter rather than a bourgeoisie, a comprador class or a political elite, given the major political–economic differences between the two regions. The structural contrasts between the two strongly suggest that neither class position nor ethnicity is the sole or main explanatory factor here. In Iraqi Kurdistan, these new strata can hardly be called a bourgeoisie in virtue of their business activity or their position in the production process, given the virtual non-existence of a regional productive economy. Moreover, the top-down character of local politics also makes it difficult to call these groups elites in a strictly economic sense. In Turkey, by contrast, the newly affluent strata appear to have had more of a productive role in the economy, and more leverage in local, and partly in national, politics – witness how some of them switched sides between parties like the AKP and the pro-Kurdish HDP, especially during the 2015 elections. Unlike in Iraq, however, the changes resulting from increased civilian participation and from new opportunities for allocation did not lead to the co-optation or 'disappearance' of significant numbers of the urban poor and, in particular, of radicalized urban youths with a permanent potential for violent protest. In Iraqi Kurdistan, the lower social strata appear to have been more effectively co-opted or appeased.

These differences can in part be explained as resulting from distinct state traditions. Indeed, despite long-standing and increasingly intensive cross-border traffic, and despite considerable political and cultural interaction between the different Kurdish-inhabited regions, the nation states established in the 1920s are still the main arenas for economic competition and political contestation. Moreover, concepts like those of the rentier state, the developmental state or of patronage-democracy turn out to have only a limited applicability to the Kurdish case, or cases.

First of all, they should not blind us to the vast differences between the two regions. Despite some superficial similarities and increasing convergence, there are marked structural economic differences between the two regions, and consequently between their patterns of political representation and participation – let alone mobilization for violent collective action. At present, Iraqi Kurdistan has little if any local proletariat or working class. What labour there is, is generally found in the services sector rather than in agriculture or industry and tends to be done by expatriate workers. Officially, the region has regional elections every four years; yet, it seems the local population is co-opted rather than represented by the leading political parties. This massive co-optation seriously limits possibilities for the effective contestation of the status quo; the bulk of the population appears to have lost all appetite for violent political action. Instead, the KRG conducted the fight against IS primarily through a professional army: present-day peshmergas constitute a paid militia rather than an ideology-driven guerrilla movement. Again, this is an important difference with Turkey, where the Kurdish region has an enduring reservoir of disaffected and easily radicalized youths; as the events of the summer of 2015 show, these groups maintained a potential for violent mass protest, if not organized urban insurgency.

One may doubt whether the Kurdish-majority region in Turkey qualifies as a patronage-democracy in Chandra's sense. Turkey as such does not have a colonial past, and although it had a strongly state-led economy geared towards import-substituting industrial production in the 1950s and 1960s, the privatizations realized since the 1980s may make it difficult to speak of a state-led economy as Chandra requires.

Second, party patronage, although by no means absent, is nowhere near as dominant a factor in Turkish social life as it is in Iraq. Hence, in some of these respects, Iraqi Kurdistan would seem to qualify rather better as a patronage-democracy; however, its democratic character has been disputed and, in some respects, has come to resemble a predatory rather than a developmental state. On the whole, developments in the regional political economies since the 1990s have been instrumental in creating newly affluent and vocal strata of the local population. They have also vastly increased the possibilities for the political representation – and, to a lesser extent, participation – of the Kurds in both Turkey and Iraq. But in both countries, the more peaceful, pluralist and inclusive forms of politics, and the greater economic affluence, have proved fragile gains indeed.

Notes

1. I am indebted to a large number of people. First of all, my thanks to Faleh Abdul Jabar and Abir Khaddaj of the Iraq Institute for Strategic Studies in Beirut for making possible the field research on which this work is based. Next, for their logistic support and their hospitality, I am indebted to a large number of local friends who may prefer to stay anonymous. Likewise, given the uncertainties, my various interviewees on both sides of the border may wish not to have their names revealed. Finally, I am grateful to Jelle Verheij, Yektan Türkyilmaz, Gülfer Coskun, Murat Bayram, Mehmet Kaya, Bilal Wahab, Raber Jawhar, Djene and Sara Bajalan, Bora Shamlo, Hussein Kordnejad and Roger Guiu, for sharing their thoughts with me. I would like to state even more emphatically than is customary that none of them necessarily agrees with, or can be held accountable for, any of the statements of fact and interpretation below.

2. David D. Laitin, 'Language conflict and violence: the straw that strengthens the camel's back', *Archives européennes de sociologie* XLI (2000), pp. 97–137.
3. James D. Fearon, 'Ethnic mobilization and ethnic violence', in Donald E. Wittman and Barry R. Weingast (eds), *The Oxford Handbook of Political Economy* (Oxford: Oxford University Press, 2009), pp. 852–68.
4. Ibid., p. 859.
5. Ibid., p. 860.
6. Ibid.
7. For more detailed criticism of both Fearon and Laitin, see, e.g., L.-E. Cederman a.o., *Inequality, Grievances, and Civil War* (Cambridge: Cambridge University Press, 2013).
8. Peter Evans, *Embedded Autonomy: States and Industrial Transformation* (Princeton, NJ: Princeton University Press, 1995), p. 45.
9. Ibid., especially chapter 3; see also Boaz Moselle and Benjamin Polak, 'A model of a predatory state', *Journal of Law, Economics, and Organization* 17 (2001), pp. 1–33.
10. In an earlier article, 'Urbanization, privatization, and patronage: The political economy of Iraqi Kurdistan', in F. Jabar and H. Dawod (eds), *The Kurds: Nationalism and Politics* (London: Saqi Books, 2006), pp. 151–79, I discussed developments in the political economy of the region up to the late 1990s. Unfortunately, Veli Yadirgi's *The Political Economy of the Kurds in Turkey* (Cambridge: Cambridge University Press, 2017) appeared only after my article was finished.
11. Kanchan Chandra, *Why Ethnic Parties Succeed: Patronage and Head Count in India* (Cambridge: Cambridge University Press, 2004), pp. 6–8.
12. For reasons of space, I will largely ignore the considerable variation within each region; for example, in Duhok, tribal relations have long been, and remain, at least as important a factor in determining upward social mobility and elite membership as party membership, and rather more so than in Sulaimaniya.
13. For a comparison of the post-World War II economies of Turkey and Iraq, see also Roger Owen and Sevket Pamuk, *A History of Middle Eastern Economies in the Twentieth Century* (London: I.B.Tauris, 1998), pp. 104–26 and 162–74.
14. See Çaglar Keyder, *State and Class in Turkey: A Study in Capitalist Development* (London: Verso Books, 1987).
15. It remains to be seen whether Erdoğan's push for a presidential system, still very much ongoing in 2018, will durably affect this constellation.
16. See Sami Zubaida, 'Turkish Islam and national identity', *Middle East Report*, no. 199 (Summer 1996).
17. For an early analysis of the PKK and its distinct class base, see Martin van Bruinessen, 'Between guerrilla war and political murder: The Workers' Party of Kurdistan', *Middle East Report*, no. 153 (1988), pp. 40–6. See also Paul White, *Primitive Rebels or Revolutionary Modernizers?* (London: Zed Books, 1999).

18. Its successors were, respectively, Demokrasi Partisi (DEP, 1993–4), Halkin Demokrasi Partisi (HADEP, 1994–2003), Demokratik Halkin Partisi (DEHAP, 1997–2006), Demokratik Toplum Partisi (2005–9), Baris ve Demokrasi Partisi (2009–14), and Halklarin Demorkatik Partisi (2013–present).
19. These gains were partly undone by the violence that broke out in the summer of 2015, the November 2015 elections and the nationwide purges in the wake of the July 2016 coup attempt; but these developments are beyond the scope of this book.
20. The classic account of Iraq's social structure before and after the 1958 coup is, of course, Hanna Batatu's *The Old Social Classes and the Revolutionary Movement of Iraq* (Princeton, NJ: Princeton University Press, 1978).
21. For more detailed discussion of the Iraqi economy under the Ba'ath, see Abbas Alnasrawi, *The economy of Iraq: oil, wars, destruction of development and prospects, 1950–2010* (Westport, CT: Greenwood Press, 1994); Marion Farouk-Sluglett and Peter Sluglett, *Iraq since 1958: From Revolution to Dictatorship* (London: I.B.Tauris, 1990), chapter 7; and the papers collected in Kamil A. Mahdi (ed.), *Iraq's Economic Predicament* (Reading: Ithaca Press, 2002).
22. See Sluglett and Sluglett, *Iraq since 1958*, chapter 7.
23. Thus, during the early 1990s, the Iraqi dinar (ID) plunged from the official rate of 3.10 to the US dollar to ID3,000 to the dollar; public debt rose at the same time to some US$100 billion.
24. Bloomberg Business, 14 May 2013. Available at www.bloomberg.com/news/articles/2013-05-13/erdogan-s-imf-triumph-masks-surge-in-private-debt-turkey-credit (accessed February 2018).
25. www.cia.gov/library/publications/the-world-factbook/rankorder/2079rank.html (accessed February 2018).
26. 'State's property developer a failure, opposition CHP says', *Hürriyet Daily News*, 28 April 2015. Available at www.hurriyetdailynews.com/states-property-developer-a-failure-main-opposition-chp-says.aspx?pageID=238&nID=81680&NewsCatID=338 (accessed February 2018).
27. See A. Kadir Yildirim, 'Clientelism 2.0 vs. Democracy in Erdogan's "New Turkey"', *Washington Post*, 13 March 2015. Available at www.washingtonpost.com/blogs/monkey-cage/wp/2015/03/13/clientelism-2-0-vs-democracy-in-erdogans-new-turkey (accessed February 2018).
28. Interviews, local observers, Istanbul, Diyarbakir, August 2015.
29. Erhan Demirhan (ed.), 'Istatistiklerle Sanliurfa-Diyarbakir', report, Karacadağ Kalkinma Ajansi [Karacadağ Developement Agency]. 2013, pp. 34, 23–4.
30. Interview, Diyarbakir, August 2015.
31. I should emphasize that these are mere estimates based on qualitative assessments rather than quantitative statistical data; interviews with local observers, Diyarbakir, August 2015.
32. I have no quantitative data to back up this claim, but it was independently confirmed by several observers; interviews, Greater Istanbul area, August 2015.

33. Interviews, local analysts, Diyarbakir, August 2015.
34. Interviews, Istanbul, Diyarbakir, August 2015.
35. For a more detailed argument concerning these continuities, see Michiel Leezenberg, 'Iraqi Kurdistan since 2003', *Arab Studies Journal*, 23 (2015), pp. 154–83.
36. Bilal Wahab (personal communication). According to official KRG figures, some US$100 billion has been spent locally since 2004; however, the actual allocation of this amount, let alone its relation to the revenues from Baghdad and from levies at the borders with Turkey and Iran, is less than clear.
37. Denise Natali, *The Kurdish quasi-state: development and dependency in post–Gulf War Iraq* (Syracuse, NY: Syracuse University Press, 2010), p. 100. These particular estimates have been contested by locals, but there is no denying the emergence of a substantial class of newly affluent party clients.
38. One local source estimated the monthly rations per person at 2.5 kg of rice, 1 kg of sugar and 1 litre of cooking oil; through separate channels, each family would also receive some 40 to 50 kg of flour and two barrels of heating oil per year.
39. Interviews, Erbil, Sulaimaniya, August 2015.
40. Interview, local higher-education specialist, Sulaimaniya, August 2015.
41. Interviews, local business owners, May 2014, August 2015.
42. Interviews, Turkish entrepreneurs, Diyarbakir, March 2013; Erbil, May 2014.
43. Frank Gunter, in *The Political Economy of Iraq* (Cheltenham: Edward Elgar Publishing, 2013), chapter 10, argues that Iraq, partly because of its bureaucratic tradition, has generally been hostile to private entrepreneurship and tended to encourage speculative rather than innovative entrepreneurs.
44. Interviews, local and foreign tradesmen, Erbil, Sulaimaniya, August 2015.
45. Interviews, personal observations, Diyarbakir, Mardin, Silopi, August 2015.
46. Jiyar Gol, BBC World News, 8 September 2015.
47. For an analysis of the ideology informing the 2015 uprisings, see my 'The Ambiguities of Democratic Autonomy: The Kurdish movement in Turkey and Rojava', *Southeastern European and Black Sea Studies* 16 (2016), pp. 671–90.
48. See Mahmut Bozarslan, 'Why the PKK shifted to urban warfare', *al-Monitor*, 29 March 2016. Available at www.al-monitor.com/pulse/originals/2016/03/turkey-why-pkk-carry-clashes-cities.html (accessed February 2018).
49. Sharon Behn, 'Minorities in Iraq's Kurdistan Push for Greater Political Voice', VOA News, n.d. Available at www.voanews.com/content/minorities-in-iraq-kurdistan-push-for-greater-political-voice/2910051.html (accessed February 2018).
50. Interviews, Yezidi representatives, Brussels, July 2015.
51. Personal observations, Duhok, Erbil, August 2015.
52. In part, the announcement by regional President Barzani of a referendum on independence for the Kurdistan Region, which was to be held in September 2017, may be interpreted as an attempt to gain, or regain, legitimacy among the population.

53. Some successful attempts at countering double salaries and ghost employees have been reported, but no structural reforms have been carried out.
54. Israel appears to be foremost among these states, reportedly acquiring some three quarters of its current petrol needs from Iraqi Kurdistan. 'Israel turns to Kurds for three quarters of its oil supplies', *Financial Times*, 23 August 2015. Available at www.ft.com/content/150f00cc-472c-11e5-af2f-4d6e0e5eda22 (accessed February 2018).

CHAPTER 5

FORMS AND PROSPECTS OF KURDISH ARMED STRUGGLE

David Romano

In the modern era, the forms that Kurdish uprisings take must be understood in order to examine the likelihood of further armed conflict breaking out in states with a significant Kurdish minority – namely, Turkey, Iraq, Iran and Syria. States dealing with Kurdish insurgencies in the twentieth and twenty-first centuries have thus far sought to avoid labelling the violence as 'Kurdish uprisings'. Instead, they preferred labels such as 'terrorist', 'tribal or religious reactionary', 'imperialist pawn' or 'political opportunists'. This is a clear policy of the Turkish and Iranian state media today when discussing PKK (Kurdistan Workers' Party) or PJAK (Free Life Party of Kurdistan) attacks, which are almost never described as 'Kurdish uprisings' involving 'Kurdish nationalist movements' but rather as 'terrorist' or 'secessionist' acts.[1] Describing such violence as 'Kurdish' would imply that the states in question have been less than successful in integrating or accommodating their Kurdish populations. Terminology such as 'nationalist revolts' necessarily conjures up notions of a nation struggling for self-determination – a concept that much of the international community views positively.[2]

This chapter focuses on the use of armed struggle by Kurdish nationalist movements as a means of addressing grievances. It further analyzes the types of armed struggle that Kurdish leaders have used against their respective central governments. The central question is:

FORMS AND PROSPECTS OF KURDISH ARMED STRUGGLE 119

what explains the use of militant tactics, and what forms of violence have Kurdish movements adopted? The chapter concludes with a reflection on the future of armed struggle in the various Kurdistans. Armed struggle can erupt from myriad and non-mutually exclusive causes. Social-science literature on the issue has produced a number of different explanations for the phenomenon, each relying on various assumptions and three different, broad levels of analysis: the individual, group and structural levels.[3]

Frustration–aggression theories maintain that blocked desires or the depriving of basic needs leads to frustration, followed by aggression and violence towards the perceived source of the block. Johan Galtung, John Burton and Edward Azar provide well-known approaches regarding how the denial of basic needs – such as security, housing, food or identity – leads to violent conflict.[4] Moreover, *relative deprivation*, meaning the difference between one's current status and that of others (or, more generally, the status that one thinks they should have), produces violent conflict.[5] In either case, the Kurdish regions of Turkey, Iraq, Iran and Syria have historically been the most impoverished peripheral regions of each state.[6]

Group-identity theories focus on individuals' desires for satisfactory group identity, and as such stipulate that the new twentieth-century states dominated by a *Staastvolk*[7] of Turkish, Arab or Persian ethnicity favoured their own groups and discriminated against the Kurds. The discrimination was not only material, in terms of access to economic or political resources, but also symbolic, in the form of the denial of Kurdish identity, culture, history and symbols. The result of such discrimination (or perceived discrimination) causes a dynamic similar to the above-described relative deprivation and frustration–aggression theories, but with the causal factors operating at the group rather than the individual level. The work of Donald Horowitz, Lars-Erik Cederman, Kristian Gleditsch, Halvard Buhaug, Simon Hug, Andreas Schädel and Julian Wucherpfenng explains violent conflict as often breaking out from such factors.[8]

In communitarian theories, low levels of interaction result in few shared norms and the absence of a community or a 'social glue'. Fewer constraints on non-cooperative actors desiring gain allows for more aggressive behaviour and ultimately violent conflict. However, Kurds, Turks, Arabs, Persians and others lived in close proximity and intermingled for hundreds of years and continuously interacted; most shared the religion of Islam as their social glue.

Another explanation is aggressive-group theory, which views the culture and/or the political–economic organization of a group as either inherently peaceful (such as the 'democratic peace' theories in international-relations approaches)[9] or particularly aggressive and prone to violence. For instance, stereotypes of the Kurds as mountain bandits, fierce warriors, unredeemable miscreants and a people quick to anger and take up arms are popular in the region, and often used by state elites to describe, delegitimize and dismiss Kurds, who are therefore cast as unwilling to listen to reason.[10]

Vested-interest theories postulate that certain individuals or subgroups benefit from violent conflict. State elites in Turkey, Iraq, Iran and Syria frequently assert that any armed opposition to their rule stems from vested interests, as rebels seek personal power and influence.

Finally, rational-actor explanations view violent conflict as one among many options for pursuing one's interests. As such, violence generally occurs if the structural context is such that actors feel they have more to gain from resorting to violence than from restraining themselves. For instance, if the alternatives to armed opposition are viewed to be continued repression, humiliation, poverty, human-rights abuses and even death, then taking a chance with armed insurrection may indeed seem preferable.[11] More critically, the risks of taking up arms against a weakening central government may appear much smaller.[12] This helps to explain numerous Kurdish uprisings against weak unitary states, including the Turkish Republic in its early years; the Republic of Kurdistan in Mahabad in 1946, when Tehran appeared impotent; the Iranian Kurdish revolt following the 1979 revolution and collapse of the Shah's rule; the Iraqi Kurdish uprising following the 1990–1 Gulf War and the weakening of Saddam Hussein's power; and the current Kurdish bid for autonomy in Syria following Bashar al-Assad's loss of power in the peripheries.

Linked to this, spiral-anarchy theories claim that distrust between states or actors under conditions of anarchy unintentionally lead to armed conflict. Paul Roe posits that uncertainties and insecurities arising from the collapse of a 'just' central state authority, or a government able to deliver law and order with some semblance of fairness, force people to turn to their communities for protection.[13]

FORMS AND PROSPECTS OF KURDISH ARMED STRUGGLE 121

In present-day Iraq, for example, the failure of Shi'i leaders in Baghdad to share power with Sunni Arabs and Kurds has led the country to a state of political turmoil.[14]

The aforementioned theoretical approaches to understanding outbreaks of violent conflict are not mutually exclusive. In my application of social-movement theories to Kurdish cases in 2006, I showed how such a combination and synthesis of various approaches can explain the outbreak of various modern Kurdish revolts.[15] While it is not the intention of this chapter to provide a lengthy and definitive explanation of a particular Kurdish uprising or the general phenomenon of Kurdish armed struggle, the aforementioned theories provide a theoretical background for the logic of armed resistance. The number of armed revolts emanating from the Kurdish regions of Turkey, Iraq, Iran and Syria represent Kurdish resistance to the Turkish, Arab and Persian nationalist programmes. That the revolts also included other causes and motives need not contradict this narrative. Indeed, all major collective political undertakings occur for a variety of different reasons and reflect the myriad goals of the multiplicity of people behind them.

Social-movement logic argues that alienated, deprived, frustrated, repressed and angry individuals will erupt in random acts of violence or the occasional riot. If a number of such people band together and create an organization or movement, however, they can develop an ideology and the means to communicate it to others.[16] Ideologies that politicize ethnicity explain the source of people's dissatisfaction in ethnic terms and point the finger of blame at ethnic outsiders (as well as ethnic traitors and collaborators). The movement tries to 'awaken' people to their (now politicized) ethnicity, and offers them a vehicle with which to take corrective action. In the right structural context, such movements can mount serious challenges to already weakened state authorities – especially if they enjoy outside support. In other contexts, very well-organized movements with committed leaders and activists can nonetheless survive and eventually impact on the structures in which they operate. They can sustain an armed revolt even in the face of a strong state, eventually weakening it enough to secure some of their objectives. In the course of the resulting conflict, different ethnic (or religious) communities come to increasingly distrust each other, sundering bonds of community and leading to an ethnic polarization that in turn helps to further fuel the conflict.

On the other hand, states that manage to address the underlying grievances of disaffected populations can counter the narrative of opposition groups and more easily achieve long-term peace and stability. Exclusively military state 'solutions' to such revolts must deploy extreme levels of force for any chance at long-term pacification. Insurgent groups generally have great difficulty convincing people to risk their lives fighting political systems that are mutable by other means and open to meaningful, peaceful and legal participation.

Examples of Kurdish Armed Struggles

A list of major Kurdish uprisings of the twentieth and twenty-first centuries includes, at the very least, the following:

- the 1920 Barzinji revolt in Iraq;
- the 1925 Shaykh Said uprising in Turkey;
- the 1927–30 Mount Ararat uprising in Turkey;
- the 1937–8 Dersim revolt in Turkey;
- the 1946 creation of the Republic of Mahabad in Iran;
- the 1961–6, 1968–70 and 1972–5 rebellions in Iraq;
- the 1979 rebellion in Iran;
- the 1984–present day PKK conflict in Turkey;
- the 1991 uprising at the end of the Gulf War in Iraq;
- the 2005–11 PJAK insurgency in Iran; and
- most recently, the post-2011 Democratic Union Party (PYD) movement in Syria.[17]

A slightly closer look at three Kurdish armed uprisings demonstrates the various forms that Kurdish armed revolts can take. The first case is the 1925 Shaykh Said revolt, which was a fairly pre-modern Kurdish uprising in Turkey that represented the resistance of feudal, religious and tribal elites to the increasing control of central governments. The second case is post-1979 Iran, where fighting between the newly formed Islamic Republic and the Kurdistan Democratic Party of Iran (KDPI) featured a more modern and clearly Kurdish nationalist uprising that nonetheless continued to rely on tribal fighters and elites. The third case is the post-1984 PKK insurgency in Turkey, where the movement was a non-tribal, leftist, Kurd-focused insurgency that spawned sister movements in Syrian Kurdistan (the PYD – Democratic Union Party) and Iranian Kurdistan (the PJAK – Free Life Party of Kurdistan).

The form that Kurdish armed struggles take, however, may play an important role in determining how long they endure and the extent of the challenge that they pose to states in the region. For example, if all three of these uprisings occurred in part due to Kurdish national aspirations – primarily, but not exclusively, linked to the aforementioned *frustration–aggression* and *group-identity* sorts of explanations for conflict – one can expect further violence as long as key elements of these aspirations remain unfulfilled for the Kurdish populations in question.[18] Also, different kinds of Kurdish armed struggle may be easier for affected central states to compromise with than others.

The Shaykh Said Revolt of 1925

The Shaykh Said revolt broke out only two years after the founding of the Republic of Turkey. The new state was still weak at the time, and Kurdish tribes that had supported the Turkish War of Independence now found themselves increasingly shut out of power in Ankara. The uprising was planned and organized by Azadi (the Society for Kurdish Independence), a Kurdish nationalist party founded in 1923 by Kurdish former military officers in the Ottoman Army and intellectuals. They chose Shaykh Said to lead the revolt because he was an important Sunni religious figure of the large Naqshbandi Sufi movement, which had many followers in eastern Anatolia. As Robert Olson explains, the Azadi leadership 'had decided at its first congress, held probably [...] sometime in the late summer or fall of 1924, that it would be doubly advantageous to give the coming revolt [...] a religious appearance'.[19] Olson adds that while the Shaykh Said rebellion was a nationalist rebellion, its mobilization, propaganda and symbols were those of a religious rebellion. For the average Kurd who participated in the rebellion, the religious and nationalist motivations were doubtless mixed. Most of the Kurds thought that the shaykhs who led the rebellion were religious and, more importantly, Kurds.[20]

The revolt therefore sought to mobilize both Kurdish nationalists and religious conservatives upset by the new Republic of Turkey's abolition of the Sultanate in 1923 and the Caliphate in 1924. Many people were both Kurdish nationalist and religiously conservative, as these are not mutually exclusive categories.

It is important to note that the Shaykh Barzinji revolt in Iraq (1920–32) bears many similarities with that of Shaykh Said, including the mobilization of both Kurdish-nationalist and conservative-religious sentiment against the British, who were in the process of creating Iraq and imposing their rule on Kurdistan via the new Arab government in Baghdad. Like Shaykh Said, Shaykh Barzinji was a Naqshbandi religious and tribal Kurdish leader, and the two revolts would both fall into the same archetype of 'pre-modern'.

The largely religious, conservative and tribal base of the Shaykh Said revolt — and, similarly, of the Shaykh Barzinji revolt — did not preclude the incorporation of modern nationalism. Bruinessen describes the issues that Azadi organizers used to attract Kurdish nationalists and give the revolt its Kurdish nationalist character:

> In the name of populism, the Kurdish language was forbidden in public places (1924); in the name of the abolition of feudalism, Kurdish aghas, but also intellectuals, were sent into exile to western Turkey. A new law (No.1505) made it possible to expropriate the land of Kurdish big landlords and give it to Turkish-speakers who were to be settled in Kurdistan. Azadi's propagandists took up the grievances resulting from this, and found many willing ears.[21]

In 1924, after Ankara dismissed their demands for Kurdish autonomy within Turkey,[22] many local Kurdish leaders opted to pursue secession from the new republic. In the republic's place, Shaykh Said wanted to erect a sort of Islamist Kurdish state. A letter that he sent to religious leaders and Kurdish tribes shows how he viewed Islam as the basis for fraternity between Turks and Kurds: 'previously, we had a common Caliphate, and this gave our religious people a deep feeling of being a part of the same community as the Turks. Since the abolition of the Caliphate, the only thing left to us is the sense of Turkish repression'.[23] Shaykh Said and his compatriots, as well as Shaykh Barzinji to the south, had not seen the need to resort to armed opposition until the contours of the emerging new state order became clear; authoritarian and centralizing governments with strong nationalisms based on ethnicities other than theirs were leaving little or no room for Kurdish elites in the new order.

Nonetheless, the revolt also failed to attract support from Alevi Kurds because of Shaykh Said's status as a prominent Sunni Muslim leader and a history of Sunni predations on Alevis in the region. Many tribal rivals who joined the revolt likewise chose not to act even though they would stage their own revolts against the Turkish state in subsequent years. Tribes concerned about relative power would not want to see their rival tribes successfully lead a revolt, even if they largely agreed with the reasons for and the objectives of such a revolt.[24]

The Said rebellion nonetheless posed a serious threat to the new central government, which had to mobilize large numbers of troops to suppress parts of eastern Anatolia that had risen en masse. However, if a return to Islam-based politics constituted one of the key demands of Shaykh Said and his cohorts, then the new government in Ankara could hardly compromise given its central vision of a secular, European-style revolution in Anatolia. Turkey's founder and leader at the time, Mustafa Kemal Atatürk, used the opportunity to declare martial law and to clamp down on other, non-Kurdish opponents and critics in Ankara.[25] In this sense, the revolt could be described as having seriously retarded the introduction to Turkey of democracy and multiparty elections – which had to wait until 1950, and even then took a very illiberal form.

The uprising was eventually suppressed, and Turkish officials hanged Shaykh Said and other rebel leaders in the eastern city of Van on 29 June 1925. The victorious Turkish state then wrote the history of the conflict as a campaign to suppress religious reactionaries, feudal elites resisting modernization and self-serving bandits.[26] The followers of the rebel leaders were cast as ignorant, poor people who did not know any better. The new Republic went on to deny Kurdish identity, minority rights and any public manifestations of Kurdishness. It quashed several more uprisings until 1938, after which it enjoyed more stability until the PKK, in 1984, began its insurgency, which is still ongoing at the time of writing.

Early Kurdish Resistance to the Islamic Republic in Iran

Just as the Shaykh Said revolt in Turkey took advantage of a moment of state weakness to press a Kurdish nationalist agenda, the Kurds in

Iran chose a similar moment of state collapse in 1979.[27] Like much of the Iranian population, the Kurds enthusiastically welcomed the overthrow of the Shah's dictatorship. The Iranian state under the Shah had pursued a Persian nationalist ideology that repressed any manifestations of Kurdish particularism, and the Kurds looked forward to a new regime under which they could realize their rights and basic needs. According to Nader Entessar, however, '[i]nitial Kurdish euphoria over the demise of the Pahlavi monarchy gave way to the bitter realization that Kurdish autonomy demands would go unheeded by the new Islamic Republic. It became evident that Ayatollah Khomeini's objective of establishing a strong centralized Islamic Republic would clash with the goals of the autonomy-seeking Kurds'.[28]

As various political groups jockeyed for power in the post-Shah political vacuum of Tehran, the Kurds pushed for autonomy and recognition of their linguistic and national rights. They insisted that their goal was not secession but rather autonomy within a democratic and federal Iran.[29] Ayatollah Khomeini and other elites in Tehran remained sceptical, fearing that their real agenda was secession and Kurdish statehood. Within just a few weeks of Khomeini's return to Iran, clashes erupted in Iranian Kurdistan between Kurdish fighters and the new regime's forces. While KDPI leaders continued to try to negotiate with Tehran, pitched battles between the tribal-aligned peshmerga and the new Islamic Republic's Pasdaran (the Iranian Revolutionary Guards Corps) saw major Kurdish cities change hands several times. Efforts by President Bani Sadr and Prime Minister Mahdi Bazargan to forge an acceptable compromise with the Kurds were repeatedly vetoed by the increasingly ascendant hard-line clerical authorities, who soon ousted Sadr and Bazargan.[30] Since the Kurds had already agreed to recognize and support an Islamic republic in Iran, their demands for some measure of democracy and decentralization could have been met by authorities in Tehran.[31]

Instead a distrustful Khomeini and his inner circle chose the path of repression. Khomeini feared that giving in to the Kurds would lead to more demands by them and other minorities in Iran. He also feared foreign powers using the Kurds and others as proxies against his new regime. Additionally, despite major purges of officers loyal to the Shah, Tehran's military was not as weak as Kurdish rebels might have hoped. Kurdish disunity similarly helped to set the scene for the eventual collapse of the insurgency. While the KDPI was mostly secular, leftist and boasted leading Kurdish intellectuals and urbanized professionals in the core of its ranks, the party relied upon mostly Kurdish tribal fighters for its armed forces. According to David McDowall,

> If indiscipline was one problem, acknowledgement of KDPI leadership was another. The KDPI could count on unanimous if undisciplined support in its traditional heartlands around Mahabad and Urumiya, but less so further north or south. In the north it faced competition from the Iraqi KDP, led by the Barzani brothers, which now sought to rally Kurmanji-speaking tribes in support of the republic and against Kurdish autonomy.[32] To the south the KDPI was challenged by Komala (The Organization of Revolutionary Toilers of Iranian Kurdistan) which took issue on ideological grounds and [...] resented the KDPI's presumption as representative of the Kurdish people.[33]

At the cost of tens of thousands of lives, the new Iranian regime thus re-established firm control over Iranian Kurdistan in 1980, only to briefly lose it again when Kurdish forces took advantage of the Iraqi invasion to once more pursue their goals militarily. By 1983, Tehran again pacified Kurdistan, and original Kurdish demands for more decentralization and autonomy were never granted.

At the time of writing, low-intensity warfare is still being waged on-and-off by both KDPI forces[34] and other Iranian Kurdish opposition parties. These groups appear outmatched by Iranian state forces, but this does not prevent instability and armed struggle on the part of the Kurds. Although the international media lacks access to report on the resistance movements, we know that riots have periodically broken out in Iranian Kurdistan over sparks such as executions of political prisoners, human-rights abuses and the recent suicide of a young Kurdish hotel maid, who allegedly tried to escape rape at the hands of a regime security official.[35] In Iranian Kurdistan, personal, tribal and ideological conflicts hamper the utilization and directing of discontent in order to mount a more effective challenge to Tehran similar to what the PKK has done in Turkey.

The PKK Insurgency in Turkey

Unlike the previous two examples of armed struggle – or, in fact, the majority of Kurdish rebellions listed at the outset of this chapter – the PKK insurgency in Turkey did not flare up at a time of central-state weakness. The PKK began organizing in the 1970s, when the Turkish political scene was paralyzed by fighting between leftists and rightists but the central state remained intact. The PKK emerged out of Turkey's political Left, founded by a group of students at the University of Ankara. Beginning with very little in the way of resources or networks, the founders of the movement – led by former political-science student Abdullah Öcalan – left Ankara for rural Kurdistan and went on to build a mass movement that has challenged the Turkish state for more than three decades.[36]

Organizing itself clandestinely in both the rural areas and the cities of Turkey's impoverished Kurdish regions, the PKK built a network of guerrilla fighters along Maoist lines rather than turning to pre-existing Kurdish tribal forces. This differentiated the organization from those behind most other large Kurdish armed struggles. The group avoided many of the divisions that came with the fusion of tribal loyalties with modern nationalist politics. Although some Kurdish clans and tribes in Turkey, such as the Bucaks around Severek, sided with the government and others largely supported the PKK, the movement was not dependent on tribes and recruited a mass base from both the rural peasantry and the impoverished urban classes. Non-tribe-based guerrillas proved more difficult for government authorities to identify and isolate, as they were not associated with particular regions or communities and did not need to defend or return to these areas after fighting.

While initial strategies focused on eliminating leftist and Kurdish rival groups in eastern Turkey and attacking unpopular, feudal Kurdish landlords, the PKK began attacks on the Turkish security forces in 1984 and initially sought to establish an independent Kurdish state.[37] Turkey's denial of Kurdish identity, repressive assimilation policies, the impoverishment of the Kurdish regions of the country, the 1980 military coup and three years of authoritarian military rule provided ample justification for taking up arms against the Turkish state. Although heavily repressive military rule provided little in the way of improved opportunities for rebellion, the PKK nonetheless managed to

FORMS AND PROSPECTS OF KURDISH ARMED STRUGGLE 129

launch its insurgency at this time – all of which circumstances support group-identity explanations for conflict over rational-choice ones.

The willingness to engage in armed struggle played a central part in the PKK's strategy from the outset. A sympathizer describes a crucial difference between the PKK and its local competitors, such as Ala Rizgari:

> In the early 1980s, the uneducated, poor peasants or townspeople would go to cadres of other 'revolutionary' organizations and complain about a local official or gendarmes commander who abused them or enforced laws onto them too assiduously. The cadres would say, 'Yes, let's discuss these. The officials are part of the government and class system that oppresses us, and we must unify against them.' When they approached the representatives about such a matter, however, the response was most often: 'You have a problem with this official? O.K. He will be gone by next week.'[38]

This kind of action-oriented response quickly earned the PKK a great deal of credibility with the local populace. The Turkish state had learned how to co-opt or repress and deport tribal leaders as necessary, but it did not have an effective response to a more amorphous, Maoist-style guerrilla movement. As the PKK's armed campaign expanded, Ankara in 1987 imposed a state of emergency on most of the country's predominantly Kurdish provinces. Emergency rule only ended in the two most affected Kurdish provinces (Hakkari and Sirnak) in 2002. The state also recruited Kurdish tribes and villages into a 'village guard' system to counter the PKK, to which the PKK responded by targeting the village guards and, for a time, their families as well (most of the civilian casualties at the hands of the PKK occurred in this way).

The PKK declared a number of unilateral ceasefires beginning in 1993, but these were never reciprocated by the Turkish state lest Ankara implicitly recognize the movement. The insurgency and counter-insurgency reached its height in the 1990s, by which time PKK guerrillas appeared to be on the verge of establishing 'liberated zones' on a significant scale. The PKK fielded some 15,000 fighters at any one time, and boasted several hundred thousand to several million supporters. Increased deliveries of US military hardware, a shift to special-forces-based commando tactics, and a counter-insurgency campaign that included the forced evacuation of some 3,500 Kurdish villages turned the tide against the PKK by the late 1990s.[39] Between August 1984 and March 2009, the estimates of casualties from the conflict went as high as 41,828.[40]

Intermittent ceasefires occurred until 2013, when substantive peace talks between the imprisoned Öcalan (captured in Kenya in 1999) and elements of the Turkish state led to a PKK ceasefire and promise to withdraw armed militants from Turkey. In July 2015, however, armed conflict between Ankara and the PKK resumed. This time, the PKK also seemed to rely on effective new tactics from nearby conflict zones in Iraq and elsewhere – roadside, improvised explosive devices followed by small-arms fire – as well as a new strategy that included mass urban insurrection in Kurdish cities. In 2015, the majority Kurdish city of Cizre in southeastern Turkey fell under weeks of curfew and siege by Turkish security forces as armed, PKK-affiliated youth apparently dug trenches in the streets and fought house-to-house.[41] This mass urban-based warfare strategy, according to Marcus, was one that the PKK had decided against in the early 1990s due to Öcalan's fear of losing control of the movement.[42] With Öcalan currently still imprisoned near Istanbul, such considerations no longer seem to apply and the strategy may have been adopted. As such, the type of violence is dynamic and changing in order to reflect realities on the ground.

Around the late 1990s, the PKK also briefly flirted with a strategy of suicide bombings.[43] The PKK was the only non-Islamist Kurdish organization to do so,[44] sending some 15 suicide bombers (most of whom were female militants) against Turkish police and military targets. Although the PKK still glorifies the suicide bombers that it sent,[45] it refrained from further suicide attacks at least until August 2015.[46] The choice to refrain from such a strategy had to do with the popular view that 'suicide bombing is a jihadi tactic', the 'Tamil Tigers' (LTTE) in Sri Lanka notwithstanding, and the secular PKK had no wish to be associated with its jihadist enemies in the region.

Future Prospects for Kurdish Armed Struggles

Whether involving 'primitive rebels', a label that many used to describe Shaykh Said, Shaykh Barzinji and others; 'revolutionary modernizers', such as the PKK; or something in between, such as the Iranian Kurdish rebels after the fall of the Shah, Kurdish armed struggles all invoked and further developed political demands based on a Kurdish national identity.[47] A politicized Kurdish identity thus crystallized and developed considerably in the course of the myriad uprisings of the twentieth and twenty-first centuries in Turkey, Iran, Iraq and Syria,[48] and the intra-Kurdish divisions and even fighting that characterized earlier revolts has become less likely as Kurds' loyalty to a larger sense of nation increasingly takes hold. This Kurdish nationalist 'genie' cannot be put back into some bottle, either. However, with the right policies it may be accommodated within existing states, or it may be used by currently ruling-state elites to resist calls for democratization.[49] In sum, given a chance at meaningful political participation, Kurds in Iraq, Turkey and Iran have already demonstrated a preference for the non-violent pursuit of their goals.[50]

As the renewed conflict between the PKK and the Turkish state demonstrates, however, future Kurdish armed struggles may unfold in new ways. Turkish Kurdistan has urbanized and modernized a good deal in the last several decades. Part of the urbanization was also a result of previous guerrilla wars and the state's counter-insurgency programmes, which emptied rural areas of their populations. Urban unrest appears to be a new strategy available to Kurdish rebels; citywide disturbances in the large metropolises may bedevil Turkey in particular for as long as it refuses to come to terms with its Kurdish rebels. The resulting instability may cost dearly in the economic, political and social spheres.

The progress that Iraqi Kurds have made towards self-sufficiency and independence offers improved possibilities for Kurdish insurgents in neighbouring states. Although the Iraqi Kurds have been very careful to present themselves as moderates who will not interfere in the politics of neighbouring Kurdish populations and their governments, the high mountains of Iraqi Kurdistan seem likely to offer safe haven to political parties and militant groups from other parts of Kurdistan for the near future. For example, the PKK continues to base its operations in part in the Qandil Mountains. Given the maturing of Kurdish nationalism, Iraqi Kurdish political parties will remain loath to take up arms against Kurdish groups from other parts of Kurdistan – the cost to their legitimacy with their constituents in southern Kurdistan would be too high should they return to the old 'divide-and-rule' behaviour that saw regional states use Kurds against Kurds. Ankara, Tehran, Baghdad and Damascus may thus find that there really is no long-term military solution to Kurdish unrest. The need for elites in these capitals to politically accommodate the Kurds has also never been more pressing, given the instability sweeping through the region and the Kurdish tendency to take advantage of moments of central-state weakness.

The trend of armed conflict, in view of the consolidation of Kurdish parties' control over majority-Kurdish territories in Iraq and Syria, seems to involve a shift towards more regular warfare. The military forces of the Kurdistan Regional Government in Iraq and the PYD in Syria have been holding territory and cities and fighting much more conventional wars than hitherto against challengers. The main challenger has been the so-called Islamic State, which has been trying to hold and expand its own territory.

The conflict, therefore, looks increasingly like inter-state warfare – albeit conducted by relatively weak states. Irregular warfare will nonetheless continue to play a prominent role in all parts of Kurdistan as well. This seems particularly true if, following its collapse, the 'Islamic State' focuses again on terrorism and guerrilla-style attacks. Should Iran turn to Shi'ite militias to harass a new Kurdish state in the former Iraq, or the autonomous Kurdish regions in Syria, then Kurds in both locales will ironically take on the role of states facing guerrilla fighters.

If, as Charles Tilly has observed, 'war made the state and the state made war',[51] then this too will have significance for the development of Kurdish nationalism. The regional context wherein state authorities are either in collapse or appear to strongly favour some ethnic and religious communities over others seems likely to encourage continued Kurdish armed struggle in one form or another.

Notes

1. To take just one example out of thousands in Turkey, see Nurbanu Kizil, 'Turkey to continue to fight ISIS and PKK terrorists at full speed, says President Erdoğan', *Daily Sabah*, 12 August 2015 – the article manages to quote President Erdoğan at length and discuss the conflict between the state and the PKK without once mentioning the words 'Kurdish' or 'Kurds'. Available at www.dailysabah.com/politics/2015/08/12/turkey-to-continue-to-fight-isis-and-pkk-terrorists-at-full-speed-says-president-erdogan (accessed February 2018). Although Iranian state media is generally less averse than its Turkish

counterpart to using the term 'Kurdish', for an example of this phenomenon see '2 PJAK Terrorists Killed, 5 Arrested in Border Clashes in Western Iran', Fars News Agency, 8 September 2015. Available at english.farsnews.com/newstext. aspx?nn=13940617000346 (accessed February 2018).
2. For a discussion of different kinds of sources on this topic, see Robert Olson, 'The Kurdish Rebellions of Sheikh Said (1925), Mt. Ararat (1930), and Dersim (1937–8): Their Impact on the Development of the Turkish Air Force and on Kurdish and Turkish Nationalism', *Die Welt des Islams*, vol. 40, issue 1 (March 2000), pp. 67–94.
3. Thomas Homer Dixon, 'Appendix to a Typology of Common Theories of Conflict', *Environmental Change and Violent Conflict* (1990), pp. 25–31.
4. For example, Johan Galtung, *Peace By Peaceful Means: Peace, Conflict, Development and Civilization* (Thousand Oaks, CA: Sage Publications, 1996); John Burton, 'Conflict Resolution: The Human Dimension', *International Journal of Peace Studies*, 3:1 (1998); and Edward E. Azar, 'Protracted Social Conflict: Theory and Practice in the Middle East', *Journal of Palestine Studies* 8:1 (1978), pp. 41–60.
5. For example, see Ted Robert Gurr, *Why Men Rebel* (New York: Routledge, 1970).
6. For more on this in the Turkish context, see Ahmet Icduygu, David Romano and Ibrahim Sirkeci, 'The environment of insecurity and the Kurdish question in Turkey', *Journal of Ethnic and Racial Studies*, 22:6 (1999), pp. 991–1010.
7. A German term literally meaning 'people of a state', *Staatsvolk* in this context refers to a national/ethnic group that defines the State's identity in its image.
8. Donald Horowitz, *Ethnic Groups in Conflict* (Oakland, CA: University of California Press, 1985); Lars-Erik Cederman, Kristian Skrede Gleditsch and Halvard Buhaug, *Inequality, Grievances and Civil War* (Cambridge: Cambridge University Press, 2013); and Lars-Erik Cederman, Simon Hug, Andreas Schädel and Julian Wucherpfenniig, 'Territorial Autonomy in the Shadow of Conflict: Too Little, Too Late?' *American Political Science Review*, 109:3 (2015), pp. 354–70.
9. Steve Chan, 'In Search of Democratic Peace: Problems and Promise', *Mershon International Studies Review*, 41 (1997), p. 1.
10. When the author gave a lecture at the University of Sulaimaniya (Iraqi Kurdistan) in 2003 on 'theoretical explanations for violent conflict', the largely Kurdish audience's reaction to this approach was extremely indignant. Audience member after audience member pointed out that 'it was Arabs, Turks and Persians who attacked and conquered Kurds, not vice-versa'.
11. For more on the rational-actor theories' application to the Kurdish cases, see David Romano, *The Kurdish Nationalist Movement* (Cambridge: Cambridge University Press, 2006), chapters 3, 5 and 8.
12. Recent political-science work in this tradition can be found in James Fearon and David Laitin, 'Ethnicity, Insurgency, and Civil War', *American Political Science Review*, 97(1) (2003), pp. 75–90; and David Laitin, *Nations, States and Violence* (New York: Oxford University Press, 2007). Fearon and Laitin, for instance,

argue that the apparent resurgence of ethnic conflicts following the end of the Cold War resulted from a steady accumulation of conflicts that could not be resolved under strong, authoritarian states. Once these states collapsed, scores could be settled by violent means. Such 'opportunity and rational calculus' explanations stand in contrast to the aforementioned group-identity explanations in that they assume that there will always exist motivations for insurgency, but look for the key explanatory variable in opportunity and the rational calculus of insurgents.

13. Paul Roe, 'The Intrastate Security Dilemma: Ethnic Conflict as a "Tragedy"?' *Journal of Peace Research*, 36:2 (March 1999), pp. 183–202.
14. For more on this subject, see David Romano, 'Iraq's Descent Into Civil War: A Constitutional Explanation', *Middle East Journal*, 68(4) (2014), pp. 547–66.
15. Romano, *Kurdish Nationalist Movement*.
16. The founders and key organizers of a movement may act altruistically, out of a sense of identity and ideology, but they may also be frustrated individuals whose entry into the halls of wealth and power was blocked by the already-existing elite of a state.
17. All casualty figures are approximate:

    - 1920 Barzinji, 6,000 casualties, see Johan Franzén, 'Iraq, Revolt of 1920', in *The International Encyclopedia of Revolution and Protest* (London: Blackwell Publishing, 2009);
    - 1925 Sheik Said, 40,000–250,000 casualties, see Kristiina Koivunen, 'The Invisible War in North Kurdistan', 2002, available at ethesis.helsinki.fi/julkaisut/val/sospo/vk/koivunen/theinvis.pdf (accessed February 2018);
    - Dersim, at least 10,000 casualties;
    - Mahabad, 1,000 casualties;
    - 1961–6 Barzani rebellion (Iraq), 10,000 casualties;
    - 1968–70 Barzani rebellion (Iraq), 60,000 casualties;
    - 1972–5 Barzani rebellion (Iraq), 10,000 casualties, see Dynamic Analysis of Dispute Management Project, University of Central Arkansas, Conway, AR;
    - 1979 Iran, 1,000–2,000 casualties, see Mehrdad Izady, *The Kurds: A Concise History And Fact Book* (Washington, DC: Taylor and Francis Inc., 1992);
    - PKK–Turkey, 40,000 casualties, see 'Who are Kurdistan Worker's Party (PKK) rebels?', BBC, 4 November 2016], available at www.bbc.com/news/world-europe-20971100 (accessed February 2018);
    - 1991 Iraq, 1,247 casualties; and
    - PJAK–Iran, 434 casualties, excluding 2010, see Uppsala Conflict Data Program, Uppsala University, Sweden.

18. Fulfilling Kurdish national aspirations does not necessarily mean establishing an independent Kurdish state, of course. Just as the Spanish and Canadian governments have hitherto fulfilled enough of their Basque and Quebecois

populations' aspirations through recognition and the provision of extensive levels of autonomy and democratic rights, so too might most Kurds' demands be sufficiently met. Failing autonomy within genuinely democratic states, however, the chances of more armed dissent and the secession of predominantly Kurdish regions increases. For more on this topic, see David Romano and Mehmet Gurses (eds), *Conflict, Democratization and the Kurds in the Middle East: Turkey, Iran, Iraq, and Syria* (New York: Palgrave Macmillan, 2014).

19. Robert Olson, *The Emergence of Kurdish Nationalism and the Sheikh Said Rebellion, 1880–1925* (Austin, TX: University of Texas Press, 1989), p. 92.
20. Ibid.
21. Martin van Bruinessen, *Agha, Shaikh and State: The Social and Political Structures of Kurdistan* (London: Zed Books, 1992), p. 281. Bruinessen describes the motives of the rebellion as 'neither a purely religious nor a purely nationalist one [...] The primary aim of both Shaykh Said and the Azadi [nationalist] leaders was the establishment of an independent Kurdistan. The motivation of the rank and file was equally mixed, but for them the religious factor may have predominated' (pp. 298–9).
22. Ugur Ümit Üngör, *The Making of Modern Turkey: Nation and State in Eastern Anatolia, 1913–1950* (Oxford: Oxford University Press, 2011), p. 123.
23. Cited in Hamit Bozarslan, 'Kurdish Nationalism in Turkey: From Tacit Contract to Rebellion (1919–1925)', in Abbas Vali (ed.), *Essays on the Origins of Kurdish Nationalism* (Costa Mesa, CA: Mazda, 2003), p. 180. Bozarslan also provides a much more in-depth discussion of the causes of the Shaykh Said revolt and the state of Kurdish nationalism at the time (well developed among only a small group of Kurdish elites, but intuitively understood by the Kurdish masses) than is possible here.
24. For more on this subject, see Romano, *Kurdish Nationalist Movement*, chapter 2 as well as Hussein Tahiri, *The Structure of Kurdish Society and the Struggle for a Kurdish State*, Kurdish Studies Series No. 8 (Costa Mesa, CA: Mazda, 2007). The same logic applied to Shaykh Barzinji to the south, and even many elements of more modern Iraqi Kurdish uprisings – Kurdish tribes equally opposed to Baghdad would not lift a finger to help their tribal rivals wrest power from the State.
25. Feroz Ahmad, *Turkey: The Quest for Identity* (Oxford: One World, 2003).
26. The museum attached to Atatürk's mausoleum (Anitkabir) includes exhibits on the revolt, which is described as 'a disturbance in the east'. The exhibits do not once use the words 'Kurds' or 'Kurdish', and instead describe 'religious extremists' and 'feudal landlords' resisting the State's authority. For a discussion of Turkish scholarship on the issue that follows this official state line, see Olson, 'The Kurdish Rebellions', pp. 68–72.
27. This was actually the second time that the Kurds in Iran tried to take advantage of such a moment of weakness: the first was in 1946, when the Iranian state at the time was severely weakened and occupied by British, US and Soviet forces as

a result of World War II. With the initial support of the Soviet Union, the Kurds established the short-lived Republic of Kurdistan in Mahabad.
28. Nader Entessar, *Kurdish Politics in the Middle East* (Lanham, MD: Lexington Books, 2010), p. 34.
29. David McDowall, *A Modern History of the Kurds* (London: I.B.Tauris, 2004), p. 262.
30. Ibid., p. 264.
31. Entessar describes a 1979 meeting between Shaykh Ezzedine Husseini, a leading Sunni Kurdish religious figure in Iran, and Ayatollah Khomeini: 'he [Husseini] asked Khomeini to support autonomy for Kurdistan and to draft an Islamic constitution, as opposed to a Shi'a or Sunni one. According to Husseini, Khomeini said that everyone in Iran was oppressed, but that things were going to be better for everyone. Upon leaving, Khomeini told Husseini, "What I am asking from you is the security of Kurdistan." Husseini responded, "What I ask from you is autonomy for Kurdistan." The two religious leaders never met again.' Entessar, *Kurdish Politics*, pp. 38–9. Accommodating the full extent of Kurdish territorial demands for an autonomous region would not have been so easy, however, given that these extended well into Azeri-populated areas. Such things are, of course, precisely what negotiations are supposed to address.
32. They did so presumably in order to secure Teheran's assistance for their struggle against Baghdad.
33. McDowall, *A Modern History*, p. 265.
34. While PJAK's offensives against Iranian regime forces since 2004 are reasonably well known, KDPI forces have now apparently returned to armed operations as well – see, for instance, 'A bold move: KDPI Peshmerga enter Iranian Kurdish city, group says', *Rudaw*. Available at rudaw.net/english/middleeast/iran/17092015 (accessed February 2018). The KDPI has suffered three different splinter groups, however, which in addition to PJAK and two Komala-armed Iranian Kurdish parties, attests to enduring divisions among Iranian Kurds.
35. Shima Sharabi, 'Iran Riots Over Maid's 'Honor Killing'', *Daily Beast*, 8 May 2015. Available at www.thedailybeast.com/articles/2015/05/08/iran-riots-over-maid-s-honor-killing.html (accessed February 2018).
36. For a resource-mobilization social-movement-theory account of how the PKK's founders accomplished this, see Romano, *Kurdish Nationalist Movement*, chapter 3.
37. This goal changed around 1993, by which time the PKK had moderated its objective to some form of local self-government, minority rights and increasing democracy within Turkey. After around 2001, the organization further shifted its ideology from its original Marxist–Leninism to a more anarchist, community-based sort of direct democracy, known as 'democratic autonomy'. Cengiz Gunes, *The Kurdish National Movement in Turkey: From Protest to Resistance* (New York: Routledge, 2012).

FORMS AND PROSPECTS OF KURDISH ARMED STRUGGLE 137

38. Cited in Romano, *Kurdish Nationalist Movement*, p. 76 (author's interview with a PKK sympathizer from Mardin).
39. For more details and figures on the matter, see Gunes Murat Tezcur, 'The Ebb and Flow of Armed Conflict in Turkey: An Elusive Peace', in Romano and Gurses, *Conflict, Democratization and the Kurds*, pp. 171–88. The drastic reduction in Syrian aid to the PKK that accompanied Syrian–Turkish détente in the late 1990s also had a very negative impact on the PKK.
40. Ibid., p. 173.
41. 'Turkey Kurds: Many dead in Cizre violence as MPs' march blocked', BBC, 10 September 2015. Available at www.bbc.com/news/world-europe-34206924 (accessed February 2018).
42. Aliza Marcus, *Blood and Belief: The PKK and the Kurdish Fight for Independence* (New York: New York University Press, 2007), p. 208.
43. Dogu Ergil, 'Suicide Terrorism in Turkey', *Civil Wars*, 3:1 (2000), pp. 37–54.
44. Islamist groups such as Ansar al-Islam in Iraq, which was mostly Kurdish in its membership but not organized as a Kurdish nationalist group, conducted a number of suicide bombings in the late 1990s and early 2000s. For more on this, see David Romano, 'An Outline of Kurdish Islamist Groups in Iraq', Jamestown Occasional Papers Series, 17 September 2007.
45. Zeynep Kinaci, whose *nom de guerre* was 'Zilan', was the PKK's first suicide bomber in June 1997, when she killed eight Turkish soldiers along with herself. She is widely revered in the movement, with songs and commemorations in her honour still occurring.
46. On 2 August 2015, an individual whom Turkish authorities claim was a PKK militant drove a bomb-laden tractor into a military outpost in Dogubeyazit, eastern Turkey, killing two soldiers and wounding 31. 'Turkish troops killed in Kurdish militant "suicide attack"', *Guardian*, 2 August 2015. Available at www.theguardian.com/world/2015/aug/02/turkish-troops-killed-suicide-attack-blamed-on-pkk (accessed February 2018).
47. While 'primitive rebels' refers to Eric Hobsbawm's theories, 'primitive rebels or revolutionary modernizers' in the Kurdish context is a dichotomy explored by Paul White, *Primitive Rebels or Revolutionary Modernizers: The Kurdish Nationalist Movement in Turkey* (London: Zed Books, 2000).
48. For more on this, see Romano, *Kurdish Nationalist Movement*, chapters 4 and 8.
49. The chances of the Kurdish issue promoting either democratization or authoritarianism is the principal theme explored in Romano and Gurses, *Conflict, Democratization and the Kurds*.
50. In the examples cited above, the Shaykh Said revolt was preceded by attempted participation in the new Grand National Assembly in Ankara, and the Iranian Kurdish rebellion was preceded by attempted negotiations over the constitution and form of the new regime in post-Shah Iran. In the case of the PKK, the issue appears a little more opaque – the group claims that the 2013 ceasefire was broken by the Turkish state when it resumed building dams and police stations in Kurdish areas during this period, when Ankara refused to pass a law

guaranteeing withdrawing PKK fighters safe passage, and finally by alleged Turkish connivance with an Islamic State suicide bomber who struck a Kurdish youth group in Suruc in July 2015. Ankara meanwhile claims that the PKK never withdrew all its fighters from Turkey and never stopped its provocations and attacks, culminating in the post-Suruc killing of two Turkish police officers that the PKK initially claimed responsibility for (but later withdrew) in revenge for their alleged assistance to the suicide bomber. (Whether the PKK was tricked into killing the police officers or freely chose to do so, providing Ankara with a ready justification to resume the war, this most probably constitutes gross ineptitude on the PKK's part.) In the meantime, the PKK-sympathetic and peaceful, legal HDP (People's Democratic Party) enjoyed unprecedented success in the 7 June 2015 elections, in which they garnered 13 per cent of the nationwide vote, including from many non-Kurdish voters. For more on the recent PKK–HDP–Ankara intrigues, see Lucy Kafanov, 'End of Turkey-PKK ceasefire puts HDP in a tough spot', *Al Jazeera*, 10 August 2015. Available at www.aljazeera.com/news/2015/08/turkey-pkk-ceasefire-puts-hdp-tough-spot-150806110231827.html (accessed February 2018). Finally, although they would probably be glad of the opportunity, Kurds in Syria have never really been given a chance to pursue their goals from within the political system.
51. Charles Tilly, *Coercion, Capital and European States, AD 990–1992* (Malden, MA: Wiley-Blackwell, 1992).

PART II

OLD SOCIETY: PERENNIAL CONTINUITY

CHAPTER 6

TRIBES AND ETHNIC IDENTITY

Martin van Bruinessen

Forty years ago, during Mulla Mustafa Barzani's last and largest-scale uprising, anthropological field research took me, among other places, to the 'liberated areas' of Iraqi Kurdistan. One of the questions that occupied me then was whether and how the 'primordial' loyalties of family and tribe were giving way to the wider solidarities of class or nation. I was aware that several major tribes that had long been hostile to Barzani were fighting on the government side, but was expecting that the armed confrontations might strengthen a sense of common Kurdish identity among Barzani's allies and those who happened to live in the areas controlled by him and the Kurdistan Democratic Party (KDP). At the time of my stay, in the winter of 1974–5, there were allegedly around 50,000 peshmerga (guerrilla fighters) defending the liberated areas, many of whom appeared to be tribesmen under the command of their own chieftain or another prominent member of the tribe. The Barzanis – recognizable by their red, tightly wound turbans – were reputedly the most effective fighters among the peshmerga.

The Barzanis were not a typical tribe, however, nor was Mulla Mustafa Barzani a tribal chieftain. He hailed from a family of religious leaders associated with the Naqshbandi Sufi order, in whose village of Barzan a devoted following of diverse origins had settled, who venerated the shaykhs as holy men with superhuman qualities. In the course of decades of confrontation between the shaykhs and large neighbouring tribes, several of the smaller tribes of the region allied themselves with the shaykhs and were gradually incorporated as Barzanis. Mulla Mustafa was a younger brother of the incumbent shaykh, and had since the 1920s led the Barzanis in numerous battles – against the British and Iraqi military, against hostile Kurdish tribes and later also against rivals within the KDP. In 1946, he had, with a fighting force of some 1,000 Barzanis, joined the short-lived Kurdish Republic of Mahabad in Iran, becoming one of its three generals, and following its collapse had taken refuge in the Soviet Union with his men, only returning to Iraq after the 1958 Revolution.

These adventures had made Mulla Mustafa into a symbol of the Kurds' struggle for self-determination – and the urban, educated men who led the Kurdish nationalist party (the KDP) made him its president, hoping thereby to extend the party's influence from cities and towns to the tribal environment. After the onset of fighting between the Kurds and the new revolutionary regime in 1961, Mulla Mustafa gradually marginalized the party's urban, educated leaders and took direct control of the party apparatus as well. He actually fought his main rivals in the party, the Ibrahim Ahmad–Jalal Talabani faction, in 1966; by the time of the 1974–5 war, these rivals had reconciled with him but had lost all positions of influence in the party (they would, however, later establish a rival party, the Patriotic Union of Kurdistan – PUK).

The 'liberated areas' were in theory administered by the KDP party apparatus, which still included educated, urban Kurds; they were in practice ruled by the peshmerga commanders. In the hills overlooking the town of Ranya, where I spent some time, the commander was one of the men who had accompanied Mulla Mustafa to Mahabad and the Soviet Union. He was, it was said, a poor peasant's son, had studied agriculture during his Soviet years, and believed in empowering peasants against landlords (who, in this region, were tribal chieftains).

The major tribal chieftain and landlord had, in fact, fled this 'liberated area' for the safety of government-held land, but many of the commoners of the tribe stayed behind to cultivate the land. Young party workers spoke proudly of the liberation of the peasants from feudal oppression by the *agha*, the tribal chieftain. I found, however, that the traditional 'feudal' obligations (corvée labour and a share of the harvest) had not disappeared but that the peasants now had to deliver them to the party, as taxation in kind. The KDP, or the peshmerga commander, had taken the place of the tribe *agha* and integrated the tribesmen into a larger entity, without however changing much in the way that the tribe functioned at the local level. The village community and the tribe were still the social entities with which the villagers identified themselves in the first place. They saw themselves as Kurdish because they belonged to a Kurdish tribe. Tribal identity was not giving way to ethnic or ethnonational identity but was considered as a condition for it. In the KDP's discourse, everyone in the region was a Kurd, including the Christians, Yezidis and non-tribal Muslim villagers; but for my interviewees, belonging to a tribe and respecting tribal custom was an essential part of Kurdishness.

In Turkish Kurdistan, I found that it was especially the tribes that identified strongly with the Kurdish movement in Iraq and looked to Mulla Mustafa Barzani as not just another tribal leader but a unifying national figure. I met tribesmen who had spent time in Iraqi Kurdistan and joined the peshmerga in some battles. Others had supported the Iraqi Kurdish movement by smuggling food and arms. 'My religion is Kurdistan, and Barzani is my prophet', one of these men told me; he was committed to his own tribe but placed the ideal of Kurdistan above it. In 1965, a sister party of the KDP had been established clandestinely in Turkey; its founders were educated men of tribal background. Most of the Kurdish nationalist groups that became active in Turkey from the mid-1970s onwards were, however, urban-based and explicitly critical of tribalism and of the Iraqi KDP's policies – even though many of their prominent members also were of tribal background.

The final collapse of Mulla Mustafa Barzani's movement in March 1975 and his subsequent exile in the United States seemed to mark a turning point in the history of Kurdish nationalism. The armed insurrection and the counter-insurgency response had mobilized tribes on both sides, providing favoured chieftains with arms and money and strengthening tribal moral values. Following Barzani's defeat, the Iraqi regime initially embarked upon a policy of winning hearts and minds by financial handouts, accelerating urbanization and undermining the foundations of the tribal economy. Turkey's Kurds seemed to be taking the lead in the nationalist struggle along with, a few years later, those in Iran awakened by the 1978–9 revolution there. In both cases, the movement was led by urban-based parties that claimed to be opposed to tribalism. By the time I submitted my dissertation, in 1978, I believed that the tribal society that I had studied was gradually vanishing, or at least becoming irrelevant to Kurdish nationalist politics.[1]

The developments of the following decades forced me to nuance my views. Settlement of the last nomads and massive urbanization loosened many Kurdish families' ties to the land, and thereby their dependence on their tribes; mass education broadened people's horizons and opened up more individualized perspectives on life. These developments have undeniably contributed to an ongoing process of de-tribalization. On the other hand, however, tribes and tribalism have in some places made a remarkable comeback, as a direct result of state intervention or of social insecurity. The resumption of guerrilla warfare in Iraq in the late 1970s, the Iran–Iraq War of 1980–8 and the Kurdistan Workers' Party (PKK)-led guerrilla campaign in Turkey of the 1980s and 1990s led to the mobilization of tribal militias against the Kurdish movement on an unprecedented scale. In Iraq as well as Turkey, existing tribes were mobilized, paid and armed, and also some new tribe-like entities were created by the State. In response, the neighbours of these militias had either to leave their region or to strengthen their own tribal organization and defensive potential. This re-tribalization was probably a temporary and reversible process, lasting only as long as the military confrontations took place and there was special government funding for the tribes (as is suggested by the case of Iraq, where the militia tribes have gradually lost power and influence since the mid-1990s).

There was yet another way in which the tribes made a comeback, or have become more visible. The massive influx of tribespeople, fleeing from war or forcibly expelled from villages, into the towns and cities has made a noticeable impact on social life and public morality. Tribes have provided their members in the urban environment with a social 'safety net', but have also brought conservative social norms and a violent code of honour.

Women's-rights activists have complained of a strengthening of patriarchal structures constraining women's lives in Iraqi Kurdish towns.[2] This, too, may be a passing phenomenon, due to the geographical movement of people holding 'tribal' values rather than a general resurgence of those values, but it shows that tribes, tribalism and the associated practices and values may persevere even when the economic and political conditions to which they were adaptations have changed.

Tribes have shown a remarkable ability to adapt to changing circumstances and environments, and to assume new functions. In the final part of this chapter, I shall return to the various modalities of adaptation accounting for their survival and lasting importance. I begin with an overview of attempts, from standpoints close to the State, to understand and 'domesticate' the tribes. I then pass on to anthropological analyses and theoretical explanations of tribal dynamics and state–tribe interaction, and the analysis of two other social formations that have contributed to shaping, and have been shaped by, Kurdish tribal society; Sufi orders and the nationalist association or party, both of which appeal to loyalties broader than those of the tribe.

Ziya Gökalp, Sultan Abdulhamid and the Kurdish Tribes

Not long after the establishment of the Republic of Turkey, the ideologist of Turkish nationalism and pioneer of sociology in the country Ziya Gökalp, who was himself at least partly of Kurdish descent and had grown up in Diyarbakir, wrote an important study of the Kurdish tribes of his region, to which he added proposals on how best to 'civilize' them and integrate them into the new nation state. The study was commissioned by a confidant of Atatürk much concerned with nation-building, Minister of Health Rıza Nur, and long remained unpublished but had a significant impact on later official thinking and policies.[3] Tribal organization, in Gökalp's analysis, was an adaptation to environmental factors. In the desert and in the high mountains, only pastoral nomadism is possible, and Gökalp appears to consider tribalism as the natural form of organization of nomads. Agricultural populations of the plains and the edge of the desert face the permanent threat of incursions by armed nomads, and they have adopted tribal organization and tribal custom (such as the blood feud) in a defensive response to the danger posed by their nomadic neighbours.

From this follow Gökalp's counsels on how to modernize and civilize the Kurds; the nomadic mountain people should be brought down from the mountains, for instance by offering them land in the plains. This would remove the threat from the other villages in the plains, which would then no longer need tribal organization and would gradually de-tribalize and become fully settled communities obedient to the government and its laws.

Gökalp notices significant differences between Arab, Turkish and Kurdish tribes. Arab tribes, he claims, are genealogically homogeneous; chieftains and followers are each other's relatives. Kurdish and Turkish tribes are more similar to each other in that they are often led by families that have a different ethnic origin than the commoners. Most Turks, he notes, were de-tribalized much earlier than the Kurds; he considers Turkish culture as more advanced than Kurdish culture, at least in part because of its stronger association with urban life and settled agriculture. He notices examples of Kurdish tribes that once were tribal Turks and of Kurds adopting Turkish identity in an urban environment, and he perceives a close correlation between de-tribalization, sedentarization and assimilation into Turkish culture. Ethnic identity, for Gökalp, is not primordial but a consequence of social dynamics, and historically the balance between Turkicization and Kurdicization had often shifted depending on ecological conditions. Modernization and nation-building demanded, in his view, deliberate assimilation policies based on settlement and de-tribalization.

Echoes of Gökalp's counsels can be found in numerous later policy proposals, from the 1927 Settlement Law to President Turgut Özal's 'last will' on the Kurdish question of 1993. The Settlement Law envisaged the complete evacuation of the more inaccessible, mountainous parts of Kurdistan and the deportation of their inhabitants to the regions where Turkish culture was dominant, as well as the settlement of Turkish pioneers among the population of those parts of Kurdistan believed to be capable of being civilized.[4] Özal was concerned with the increasing strength of the separatist PKK, which he believed to depend on support from nomads and mountain villagers. His proposal for a solution involved the wholesale deportation of this mountain population to western Turkey along with economic investment in the parts of the region that were effectively controlled by the State.[5]

Gökalp associated tribalism and the tribes with ecologically marginal regions (mountains and deserts), with pastoral nomadism and with social and cultural backwardness, and he firmly believed that it was possible as well as desirable to de-tribalize these entities and assimilate them into (in his view) superior Turkish culture. Changing their ecological environment, through settlement in a different part of the country and/or urbanization, was in his view the crucial factor in this civilizing process. Gökalp's analysis no doubt owed much to his familiarity with the new French sociology, but his dim view of the backwardness and the threat to progress represented by tribalism was inspired by his disgust with the policies of the last great Ottoman Sultan, Abdulhamid II (ruling 1876–1909), who had armed and empowered the larger Kurdish tribes in order to strengthen his grip on the eastern provinces of the empire. As a young man, Ziya Gökalp belonged to the reform-minded opponents of Abdulhamid's authoritarian rule, and had led protest actions by Diyarbakir's citizenry against the incursions of a tribal chieftain favoured by the Sultan – Ibrahim Pasha, of the Milli tribe.

Sultan Abdulhamid famously established the tribal light cavalry regiments known as Hamidiye, primarily to defend the Ottoman frontier against the Russian threat – in the Russian–Ottoman War of 1877, Russian troops had penetrated deeply into Ottoman Kurdistan, and vulnerability of the frontier had remained a major concern ever since – and secondarily against the threat of Armenian separatism. Beginning in 1890, ultimately some 64 Hamidiye regiments were established, each consisting of men from a single tribe under the command of their own chieftain.

The Ottoman civilian administration had no jurisdiction over these regiments, which answered only to the military general charged with establishing and overseeing the Hamidiye and who, in turn, reported directly to the sultan. Armed, salaried and privileged with virtual impunity, the Hamidiye commanders and their tribesmen considerably strengthened their position vis-à-vis the other segments of the population, including not only the Armenian and Muslim peasantry and townspeople but also the non-Hamidiye Kurdish tribes as well as rivals for leadership within the tribes that provided the regiments.[6]

Reform-minded members of the administration and urban notables resented the impunity enjoyed by the Hamidiye and the empowerment of the tribes over the educated elite. For the Sultan, however, these regiments, which were personally loyal to him, constituted a more reliable chain of command than the civil administration. To the reform-minded elite of the region, the Hamidiye represented a return to lawlessness, barbarism and insecurity. Seen from the centre, however, the establishment of these regiments was a means to tie the Kurds more firmly to the empire. It was, moreover, part of a broader range of tribal policies aiming to integrate and 'civilize' the Kurds without de-tribalizing them and sacrificing their military potential.

It had long been an established practice, both in Iran and the Ottoman Empire, for the ruler to keep tribes in check by offering positions of honour at court to members of the most powerful and influential tribal or religious families, so that they could serve as go-betweens as well as guarantors of the tribes' loyalty. Rebellious leaders were forced into exile, but their sons in many cases were recruited into the higher levels of the state bureaucracy, as had happened to the Kurdish lord of Cizre, Bedir Khan Beg, and the religious leader Shaykh Ubaydullah of Hakkari, both of whom led large-scale uprisings that were considered proto-nationalist by later generations.[7] Under Abdulhamid, these policies were modernized by the establishment of a special school, the *aşiret mektebi*, for the children of the tribal elite in Istanbul, opening up bureaucratic careers to at least some of them.[8] Leading families of Kurdish, but also of Arab, tribes were thereby more systematically integrated into the central Ottoman state while maintaining their authority over their followers in the periphery.

The Kurdish policies of Turkey and Iraq — and, to a lesser extent, of Iran — have oscillated between 'Gökalpian' efforts at de-tribalization and cultural assimilation, and the 'Hamidian' empowerment of certain tribes against security threats, which in the twentieth century mainly meant the Kurdish nationalist movement. In Iraq, this process culminated in the physical destruction of virtually all Kurdish villages in the 1980s, except those of tribes that had joined the pro-state militias. In Turkey, the de-tribalization drive reached its first culmination with the brutal pacification campaign against Dersim in 1937–8 and the ensuing massive deportations and forced assimilation. The policy was resumed with renewed vigour in the 1990s with the forced evacuation of numerous mountain villages and the recruitment of tribal militias (*korucu*, i.e., 'village guards') to conduct counter-insurgency operations against the PKK.[9]

There is hardly any nomadism left in Kurdistan today. All large nomadic tribes have been forced to sedentarize, and only here and there do small groups of tribesmen take their — now much-reduced — herds to the old mountain pastures in summer, while spending the winter in town or a nearby village.

Many tribespeople have, in fact, moved to the large cities and do not flaunt their tribal affiliation. Surprisingly, however, even in the urban

What is a Tribe?

In the anthropological literature, tribes have often been discussed as kinship-based social formations preceding the State and/or continuing to exist in peripheral regions where the State's authority is not effectively exercised. Evolutionary anthropology has postulated a development from small bands of hunters and gatherers through egalitarian, segmentary tribes to more hierarchically organized chiefdoms and finally the full-fledged state.[10] British anthropology especially has often described and analyzed tribes as if they existed in a vacuum, independent of the pervasive influence of states. There may in the twentieth century still have been human communities, here and there, that lived in isolation and were hardly affected by the existence of states. This was, however, not the case for Kurdish and other Middle Eastern tribes, which had long lived in intensive interaction with highly developed states in the region.

Many structural features of the Kurdish tribe, such as its internal hierarchy, can best be explained as a result of this interaction with the State. To the fourteenth-century North African author Ibn Khaldun, we owe a brilliant sociological analysis of tribe–state interaction as an explanation of history and dynastic change in the Maghreb.[11] The State is represented in Ibn Khaldun's model by a city, where the ruler lives, surrounded by agricultural lands that feed the city. Beyond these well-protected domains belonging to the State (*makhzan*) lies the wild periphery of mountain and desert (*siba*), where unruly Bedouin tribes roam. These tribesmen periodically raid the state lands and may even conquer the city and overthrow the ruling dynasty, taking its place. They are militarily superior to the townsmen due to two main factors: their harsh living conditions have made them sturdy and have forced them to develop a strong social cohesion and group feeling (*asabiyya*), essential to survival.

The concept of *asabiyya* is central to Ibn Khaldun's analysis. The Bedouin tribes have strong *asabiyya*; settled groups also have it, but in weaker form. Once the conquering tribesmen, who owed their victory to their strong *asabiyya*, settle down to urban life and get used to luxury, their physical prowess as well as their *asabiyya* weakens, making them vulnerable to the next wave of conquerors. The main source of a group's *asabiyya* is, according to Ibn Khaldun, the blood relationship but he recognizes that it may also be generated in patronage relations. A group needs to permanently cultivate its awareness of kinship (as the Bedouin tribes do); if not, it will gradually lose its *asabiyya*.

Ibn Khaldun thus appears to define the tribes by their relationship with the State – although he also believes that the Bedouin tribe precedes the emergence of the State – and attributes their distinctive characteristics of sturdiness and *asabiyya* to the harsh ecological conditions of their existence. He does not consider tribes and urban populations as different by nature; tribesmen may turn into civilized urbanites, but in the process lose much of their *asabiyya*. (There seem to be some unacknowledged echoes of Ibn Khaldun in Ziya Gökalp's comments on how Kurdish tribes may be civilized and assimilated; he may have read Ibn Khaldun as well as Émile Durkheim.)

Ibn Khaldun appears to equate tribalism with pastoral nomadism and the rough life encountered in resource-poor environments. Gökalp, however, makes the interesting observation that settled communities living on the edge of the desert or mountains also adopt tribal organization in order to defend themselves more effectively against raids by the desert or mountain tribes. Collective self-defence, no doubt, is a major function of tribal organization, and it may well exist in the absence of nomadism. Many of the major Kurdish tribes have a memory of once having been nomadic or at least semi-nomadic, but nomadism has virtually disappeared while the tribes are still there.

Kurdish tribes: the segmentary and hierarchical principles

There is a considerable range of variation in the degree of complexity of the social organization of Kurdish tribes but they all share two basic structural principles, which are also found in other tribes in the Middle East.[12] The first of these is the *segmentary lineage*, defined by patrilineal descent and endogamy. The tribe consists of a number of sections that are, at least structurally, equal to one another. Each of these sections consists again of several sub-sections, which in turn are divided into yet smaller sections, and there is a strong preference for endogamy down to the lowest level of the extended family. A man is expected to marry his father's brother's daughter or, if that is not possible, another close relative. (Or rather, a father is expected to give his daughter in marriage to a brother's son or another close relative within the same descent group.) This marriage pattern keeps the daughters' reproductive potential within the extended family or shallow descent group, and thereby strongly reinforces its cohesion at the expense of its integration into the tribe as a whole or its larger segments (which might be better served by different marriage patterns).[13] And, we should add, it significantly reduces women's individual freedom and ability to negotiate.

Lineages would keep breaking up into smaller segments if this pattern were not balanced by common interests keeping the segments together, the most important of which is common rights to pasture and agricultural land. Tribes claim traditional rights to land, which have to be unceasingly asserted and defended against rival claimants. Conflicts are the 'glue' of tribal organization, and the segmentary structure of the tribe is best seen at times of conflict. Tribes unite in conflicts with rival tribes but they are also often riven by internal conflicts, in which alliances and opposition closely follow the segmentary structure of the tribe. In the case of a blood feud, it is not only the families of the original perpetrator and victim that are involved but the conflict mobilizes the largest possible segments to which these families belong; each member of the perpetrator's larger lineage is a legitimate target for revenge, followed by counter-revenge against the entire lineage of the original victim.[14]

Segmentary-lineage theory was dominant in British anthropology in the mid-twentieth century and inspired the first anthropological studies of Kurdish society,[15] but from the 1970s onwards it came increasingly under critique.[16] My own field research and oral-history interviews in the mid-1970s convinced me that segmentary lineage was not just a model invented by anthropologists but that it also corresponded to the way that many Kurds believed their social organization worked. However, segmentary lineages coexist with another structural principle that complements, and may override, the egalitarian principle of segmentary alliance and opposition − namely, *hierarchy and authoritarian leadership*.

In theory, the most senior male in a household, extended family or lineage is also the most respected person and the natural leader; there may be relations of seniority among the lineages of a tribe as well, and the senior elder of the most senior lineage might act as the chieftain of the entire tribe.

However, this is rarely the case – and even then, only in relatively small tribes. In the larger tribes, it is more common to have a chiefly family or lineage that is not closely related to any of the commoner lineages that together constitute the tribe.[17] Some chiefly families deliberately emphasize the fact that they are not genealogically related to their tribes – some even claiming descent from the Prophet or early Muslim dynasties, others maintaining memories of different regional or ethnic origins. As outsiders, they are not party to any conflict between the segments of the tribe and are in a position to mediate, negotiate and impose solutions – especially when aided by an armed retinue personally loyal to the chieftain. In fact, a chieftain's position is dependent on his ability to manage conflict within the tribe as well as with the outside world. Similarly, as we shall see below, the influential position of religious leaders, especially of Sufi shaykhs, in Kurdish society is to a large extent based on their ability to manage conflicts *between* tribes.

For similar reasons, the marriage pattern of the chiefs of larger tribes often deviates from the endogamous norm. Many members of chiefly families do in fact marry cousins (i.e., closely related women of the same social stratum), but strategic marriage alliances result in a conspicuous degree of exogamy. Chiefs may marry women from other Kurdish tribes; it is not uncommon for chiefs of rival tribes to seal the end of a conflict by an exchange of daughters as spouses for themselves or their sons. They may also take wives from other ethnic groups in the region, or intermarry with urban notables or families of bureaucrats. Polygamy allows them to balance such exogamous alliances with cementing ties within the family.[18]

Important though conflict management within the tribe may be, the authority of a chieftain over his tribe depends even more on his ability to represent the interests of the tribe towards the outside world – which has, in the first place, traditionally meant the State. Both Iran and the Ottoman state dealt with tribal populations as collectivities, developing various forms of indirect rule in which the tribal chieftains constituted the crucial interface. In Safavid Iran (sixteenth–eighteenth centuries), the State in fact consolidated or even created large tribal confederacies (*il*, pl. *ilat*), appointing a chieftain (*ilkhani*) over them and incorporating these confederacies into a decentralized military-command structure.

The Ottoman system of indirect rule allowed for large, autonomous Kurdish principalities in the sixteenth century; as the central administration penetrated more deeply into Kurdistan in the nineteenth century, large tribal confederacies replaced the region's principalities as the units of indirect rule; and with further expansion of the state bureaucracy, ever-smaller regions were left under indirect rule and the relevant tribal units became smaller and less complex.[19]

The cohesion and group feeling (*asabiyya*) of the tribe is no doubt in part due to the awareness of blood kinship among its major sections, but is also fostered by the patronage that the chieftain can dispense due to his privileged relationship with the State. A good chieftain is generous, and a model of manly virtues of whom the entire tribe can be proud. He takes care of the interests and problems of individual commoners as well as the collective. Belonging to a strong tribe provides security in an otherwise insecure environment. And yet, in spite of strong *asabiyya*, tribes are fissiparous and prone to internal conflict. The segmentary structure of their lineage is not the only reason tribes are often riven by conflict.

Another major factor is that there may be competing contenders for the position of paramount chieftain, each of whom may mobilize external resources in the pursuit of his interests. Their rivalry may result in breaking up the entire tribe into two feuding factions, in which each contender was supported by entire sections of the tribe, or each of the sections was in turn divided into factions supporting one or the other.[20]

The geographical position of Kurdistan on the periphery of several states often gave ambitious chieftains the opportunity to strengthen their position by playing one state off against another; some of the more successful chieftains switched allegiances more than once in the course of their careers. It also happened regularly that two contenders for leadership within a tribe allied themselves with different states. These were, until the late nineteenth century, the Ottoman Empire and Iran; later, Russia occasionally had its Kurdish tribal allies and, since World War I, so did Britain. In the postwar years and under Iraq's mandate, British political officers propped up the power of 'loyal' tribal chieftains and found that there were also 'traitors' in the same tribes, who were in collusion with Turkey.[21] Later still, when Kurdish nationalist movements emerged in Iran, Iraq and Turkey, we often find members of the leading family of a tribe active in a Kurdish party, and others working with the central government.[22]

Transcending Tribal Boundaries: Religious and Ethnic Loyalties

The years 1880 and 1925 mark the beginning and end of a period that saw a number of major Kurdish uprisings led by religious leaders, in which Kurdish ethnic identity was a major factor and in which many different tribes took part, temporarily overcoming traditional hostilities. Shaykh Ubaydullah of Nehri in Hakkari (1880) and Shaykh Said of Palu (1925) were leaders of different branches of the Naqshbandi Sufi order, Shaykh Mahmood of Sulaymaniya (1919, and again 1923) was the head of a major branch of the Qadiri order. All three belonged to families that had long been established in their region, claimed descent from the Prophet Muhammad and were highly (though by no means universally) respected. The shaykhs of Barzan, who also were Naqshbandis but not *sayyids* (descendants of the Prophet) and who were looked down upon as heterodox upstarts by the more established families, also established their reputation and gained a wide following in anti-Ottoman and later anti-British uprisings during this period.[23]

These and other great religious families were not affiliated with any tribe but had religious followers in many different tribes, and among the commoners as well as the leading stratum. Their religious charisma and the widespread belief in their ability to perform miracles enabled such shaykhs to play a mediating role in conflicts between tribes and make peace between rival chieftains, and thereby acquire considerable worldly power and wealth. The Sufi orders (*tariqa*) superimposed a centralized network structure on the fissiparous, segmentary structure of the tribes, thus making coordinated action possible. The network consisted of the shaykh and his deputies (*khalifa*), whom he had appointed to represent him in different districts. These deputies would lead the Sufi rituals, initiate new followers, bolster the shaykh's charisma by their devotional stories and act as his representatives and propagandists. Around each of these *khalifa* were groups of men who regularly took part in the spiritual exercises of the order, and perhaps one or more second-level deputies as well as a more diffuse and much larger group of followers who looked upon the shaykh and his *khalifa* as spiritual advisers, protectors and healers.[24]

The said shaykhs, or rather the Sufi networks established by their families, strengthened regional identities that transcended the individual tribe. As the highest authorities recognized by the tribes of Hakkari, Shaykh Ubaydullah and his descendants could arbitrate in conflicts and maintain a degree of cohesion among these tribes. Ubaydullah's son, Muhammad Siddiq, was in the early twentieth century reported to actually rule over four settled tribes of the region and have influence in a much larger region.[25] In the case of the Barzinji family, to which Shaykh Mahmood belonged, the network included tribes as well as non-tribal peasants in the Sulaimaniya region of southern Kurdistan, but it was also strongly opposed by other tribes that felt threatened by the shaykhs' ambitions.[26] Shaykh Said's family had established a dense network of *khalifa* and village mullahs in the Zaza-speaking districts between Erzurum and Diyarbakir. (Zaza is considered a distinct language by most linguists, and a Kurdish dialect by Kurdish nationalists.) Prior to the uprising, the shaykh had toured those districts, resolving conflicts between tribes and persuading chieftains to sign up to the rebellion. The uprising spread well beyond the Zaza districts, and Shaykh Said, who was publicly hanged after the suppression of the rebellion, became a national hero to Kurds even beyond Turkey. Almost a century later, the shaykh's family still is at the centre of a dense network of *khalifa* and village mullahs spread throughout the Sunni, Zaza-speaking districts, which in a sense serves to integrate the Sunni Zaza tribes with one another.[27]

From Sufi Orders to Political Parties

The role of coordinating corporate action by various tribes has shifted from Sufi orders to formal associations and parties, but Sufi orders remain influential in Kurdish society, in urban centres as well as in rural districts. In Turkey, the Naqshbandi order has profoundly shaped religious sensibilities and had an impact on Islamist politics.[28] It has a number of distinct Kurdish branches that are now also active in major cities in western Turkey, presumably especially among Kurdish migrants.[29]

All Sufi orders were formally banned in Turkey in 1925, and most Kurdish Naqshbandi shaykhs – including those not involved in the Shaykh Said uprising – were sent into exile. Teacher–disciple networks persisted, however, especially among the Kurds, and after the return to multiparty politics in 1950 *tariqa* shaykhs have acted as vote-getters for political parties, which in turn enabled them to dispense patronage and strengthen their positions.[30] In this respect, they differed little from the tribe *aghas*, many of whom also consolidated their positions by taking part in political-party-based patronage politics.

In Iraq, several branches of Sufi orders transformed themselves into politico–military entities that positioned themselves in the tribal environment as a sort of warrior tribe, fighting other tribes and at the same time attempting to incorporate them. The most remarkable example, no doubt, is that of the Barzanis. Although originally it was the Naqshbandi network and veneration of the charismatic shaykhs that gave this heterogeneous coalition its cohesion, under Mulla Mustafa Barzani the shaykh and his pious followers faded into the background and the Barzanis became a sort of Praetorian Guard, a confederation of tribal and non-tribal groups unconditionally loyal to him and later to his sons Idris and Masud. With the help of this formidable fighting force, the Barzani family brought most of Badinan, the Kurmanci-speaking northern part of Iraqi Kurdistan, under its control (with the exception, until 1991, of the large tribes that remained allied with and were armed by the central government). In the course of the armed confrontation with Baghdad, Barzani also wrested control of the KDP from the hands of its originally urban and Sulaimaniya-based leadership and gained the allegiance of some southern tribes. Iranian, Israeli and finally covert US support helped him to further consolidate his position as the *Serok* (headman, president) of the Kurdish movement, ruling a complex chiefdom of tribes and non-tribal groups through a tightly controlled party apparatus and intelligence service, with the Barzani 'Praetorian Guard' as the main enforcers.

Mulla Mustafa Barzani's main rival, Jalal Talabani, who in the mid-1960s not only fought the government but also clashed with Barzani's peshmerga, and who in 1976 established the PUK as a 'progressive' alternative to the KDP, also belonged to a well-known family of Sufi shaykhs – this time, of the Qadiri order.

The rival parties, the KDP and the PUK, have occasionally been described as fronts for the Naqshbandi and Qadiri Sufi orders, respectively – an unwarranted exaggeration that appears to reflect secularist Kurds' perceptions of the lasting influence of these Sufi orders.[31]

Most of the Barzanis were not practising Naqshbandis, and there were to my knowledge no Qadiri Sufis among Talabani's collaborators and political followers. The Talabanis are a large notable family with influence and land in Kirkuk and in Koy Sanjaq, and the Talabani shaykhs of Kirkuk have a large religious following but Jalal Talabani and his associates were always secular, urban intellectuals. Neither is there a Talabani Praetorian Guard to balance the Barzanis' one as a tribal fighting force. The core of the PUK has been urban and non-tribal; the party has recruited tribal allies, but few of these were firmly committed and many changed sides repeatedly in the course of the conflicts with Baghdad.[32]

There were, however, Qadiris who did become a politico–military force without giving up being Sufis. These are in the Kasnazani branch of the Barzinji family, the most conspicuous Qadiris nowadays, who have numerous followers in Iraq as well as Iran and Turkey. In the 1960s, the incumbent shaykh, Abdulkarim, and his followers in the Kirkuk region constituted a pro-government militia force that actively fought the peshmerga. His son, Shaykh Muhammad, was likewise both a Sufi teacher and a militia commander. Unlike the Barzanis, the Kasnazanis were both a quasi-tribal fighting force and actively participated in Qadiri Sufi rituals. In the 1990s, the shaykh lived in Baghdad, where he had disciples in all branches of the state apparatus and was involved in various business deals with Saddam Hussein's sons. After a falling out with Saddam, he fled Baghdad and was offered asylum in Sulaimaniya by Jalal Talabani. Throughout the years of fighting on opposite sides, the shaykh and the nationalist politician had always kept lines of communication open. In Sulaimaniya, he remained politically active and a force to be reckoned with due to his ability to mobilize followers. In the years following the US invasion of Iraq, one of his sons established a political party, attempting to translate his father's Sufi network into votes in the country's first elections – with limited success.[33]

Iraqi Kurdistan

Kurdish pro-government militias, the Kurdish movement and Kurdish ethnic identity

Shaykh Muhammad's Kasnazaniyya was not the only Kurdish militia to maintain ambivalent relations with the Kurdish nationalist movement that they were supposed to be fighting. During the Iran–Iraq War, unprecedented numbers of tribesmen were recruited – voluntarily or under duress – into pro-government militias (nicknamed *jash*, 'donkey foals' by the Kurds). Each militia battalion was commanded by a *mustashar* ('adviser') – in many, but not all, cases a tribal chieftain who besides his own salary received a sum for each of his men.

Kurdish young men could evade being drafted into the army by enrolling in the *jash*, which obviously caused the militias' numbers to swell. Their enthusiasm for engaging the peshmerga varied; some *mustashar* were firmly committed to defeating the KDP and PUK forces, but on the whole active participation in military campaigns appears to have been limited; many avoided open clashes with the peshmerga when they could, and mainly restricted themselves to guarding their own tribal territories against peshmerga incursions and a possible Iranian offensive.

These militia tribes' villages enjoyed immunity when the other Kurdish villages were evacuated and destroyed, culminating in the 1988 genocidal *Anfal* operations. In these operations, *jash* were deployed on a large scale to round up villagers; there are numerous reports about cruel behaviour and massive plunder of villages by *jash* but also many accounts of individual *jash* saving the lives of villagers marked for deportation and annihilation.[34]

Less than three years later, in the aftermath of the Kuwait war, many *jash* took active part in the massive Kurdish uprising of March–April 1991. By some accounts it was in fact *jash* who initiated the rebellion, capturing towns and the centres of Ba'ath party control; the nationalist parties were at first allegedly reluctant and only later brought the uprising under their control. (Other accounts, less convincingly, claim that the parties organized the uprising from the very beginning.) Many of the *jash*, like the nationalists they had fought, appeared to be eager for Kurdish autonomy.

In the safe haven created by international intervention later that year, former *jash* tribes such as the Surchi, Herki and Zibari – long-time enemies of the Barzanis – remained a significant force; they were armed and prosperous, though no longer in league with Saddam's regime. The KDP and PUK had to reach an accommodation with them (in which the PUK was the more flexible party), and were forced to accept that they were politically active. The early and mid-1990s were a period of increasing tension between the KDP and the PUK, each of which was now in control of a major part of Iraqi Kurdistan and building up an administration. Both co-opted remnants of the previously existing civil service and the urban middle classes, and relied on the tribes for territorial control. The sociologist Andreas Wimmer, who visited the region a few times in the early 1990s, described both parties as 'a mixture of tribal confederation and patronage-based party apparatus'. The KDP had long incorporated tribes in its command structure, which is why it was the stronger of the two parties and could offer protection to urban populations and the numerous internally displaced in camps. The PUK had depended less on tribal support but now allied itself with several large former *jash* tribes to consolidate its territorial control and form a defensive anti-KDP coalition. As Wimmer observed, perhaps somewhat overstating his case, the PUK 'in a sense took over the role of Baghdad in relying on the tribal enemies of the Barzani coalition'.[35] Although there was no significant armed confrontation with the central government, this was a period in which tribes were very prominent and the position of tribal chieftains bolstered.

A few dozens of these chieftains, led by Umar Khidr Surchi, formed an alliance that they called the Mosul Vilayet Council, which announced its intention to renegotiate the inclusion of the province of Mosul in Iraq by the League of Nations, demanding self-determination on behalf of the Kurds and other ethnic and religious communities of the region. They invited the KDP and PUK to join their efforts to get the United Nations involved in a revision of the status of the region – apparently with little success.[36] Some of the same men established the Kurdistan Conservative Party (KCP) as a vehicle to defend the interest of tribal chieftains.

The Surchis' habitat is in the KDP-controlled northern part of Iraqi Kurdistan, but the Surchi and the KCP cultivated relations with the PUK and remained hostile to the KDP. They were punished for this when in 1996, at the height of the fratricidal KDP–PUK war, KDP peshmerga overran the central Surchi village, killing the head of the leading family. The KCP moved its base to the PUK region, where it briefly had one minister in the regional government at Sulaimaniya. A reconciliation with the KDP finally took place in 2005, when the two major parties reached agreement over a jointly ruled Kurdistan regional government.[37] Not much later, however, in preparation for the 2008 provincial council elections, the Herki, Surchi and Zibari tribes were reported to be seeking cooperation with Arab Sunni tribes against the Kurdish nationalist parties.[38]

As the parties consolidated their rule, they lessened their dependence on the tribes — especially, one may presume, on those of doubtful loyalty. The KDP and PUK held a monopoly of financial resources in their respective regions, and could weaken the positions of chieftains by withholding or re-channelling patronage. The reconciliation between the two parties gave the chieftains in between less leverage.

The reorganization of the peshmerga army along non-tribal lines is also likely to have weakened the position of tribal chieftains — but very little concrete information on the peshmerga army is publicly available. Officially the PUK and KDP peshmerga have been integrated in a single force with mixed regiments, but there are doubts as to how seriously the integration was carried out. Party loyalties remain strong, and the all-pervasive patronage has allowed commanders at all levels to continue recruiting trusted men, which often means men of their own extended family or tribe.[39]

Turkish Kurdistan: Various Modes of Integration in the State

The dominant political movement of Turkey's Kurds, the PKK, identified tribal chieftains in its earliest broadsheets as collaborators with the colonial state and carried out its first major attack against a chieftain closely linked to the then-ruling party, Mehmet Celal of the large Bucak tribe. Unlike the Iraqi Kurdish parties, the PKK has never attempted to accommodate the tribes. There are tribespeople in its ranks — men as well as women — but they joined as individuals and not on the basis of their tribal affiliation. Wherever it could exercise influence, the PKK has attempted the break the power of tribal chieftains and other powerful families.

Many tribal chieftains were in fact closely allied with the State. During the period of high Kemalism, in the 1930s and 1940s, the State had attempted to de-tribalize Kurdish society by sending numerous chieftains and their families into exile, thus separating them from the tribe, and by deploying the usual institutions of national integration, the school and the army. The return to multiparty democracy, from 1950 onwards, had the effect of revitalizing many of the tribes and strengthening the positions of tribal chieftains. Competitive elections, in which each province elected a number of deputies, propelled tribal *aghas* (as well as Sufi shaykhs) who could command a significant proportion of the vote in their provinces into the role of political brokers allied with one of the parties. New structures of patronage emerged, in which Kurdish members of parliament – who were in some cases *aghas* themselves, or more often educated men representing an *agha* – served their constituencies by giving them access to various resources, from infrastructural investments and marketing of goods to legal representation, employment and education. Similarly, the army units that policed the countryside found it easiest to deal with the population of their district through village and tribe *aghas*, and the same was true of other centrally appointed officials. Not all tribes were thus revitalized, but in each province several chieftains could position themselves at the interface of state and society and consolidate their tribes.

These *aghas* and shaykhs were typically allied with conservative parties of the political centre – this was one of the reasons why military and civilian bureaucrats were suspicious of the first of these parties, the Democratic Party, which was brought down in the 1960 military coup – but the other parties also found tribal allies in the Kurdish provinces, including even the ultranationalist MHP (Nationalist Action Party). As politicians, they represented some of the interests of their constituencies, which were by and large Kurdish, but most of them cautiously stayed aloof from the emerging Kurdish nationalist movement.

A different type of Kurdish representation in parliament began with the establishment, in 1990, of the first of a series of short-lived 'pro-Kurdish' parties that were in fact rooted in the Kurdish movement and took up such issues as recognition and cultural and political rights. With a few exceptions, tribal chieftains have not been much in evidence in the pro-Kurdish parties; both for the chieftains and their dependents, alliance with one of the establishment parties was more useful for purposes of patronage. Until the spectacular rise of the pro-Kurdish

HDP (People's Democratic Party) in 2015, most Kurdish members of parliament owed their seats to patronage politics rather than their views on the Kurdish question.

Turkey's military and intelligence services kept a close watch on the tribes, and distinguished sharply between those that were (more or less) reliable and those that had once taken part in uprisings or given other signals of dissent.[40] Since Ottoman times, 'loyal' tribes have been called upon to put down rebellions. When the PKK, which started a genuine guerrilla war in 1984, became a serious security threat that could not be effectively contained by the police, Turkey recruited 'reliable' tribes as a counter-insurgency militia: the *korucu*, or 'village guards.' Initially drawn from only a few tribes, the numbers of village guards gradually increased, reaching almost 50,000 salaried militiamen and an additional 25,000 volunteers.

Some units consisted of existing tribes or sections of tribes, others of apparently randomly recruited men under a local strongman. The *korucu* were integrated into a military-command structure but have had licence to exert violence on their own behalf. Money, arms and virtual impunity before the law gave the favoured chieftains unprecedented power and led to the intensification of inter-tribal conflicts. Local as well as outside observers spoke of the 're-tribalization' of society. It would be misleading, however, to think of this in terms of a return to the past: the *korucu* system introduced new forms of patronage relations, based on a mix of kinship, class and political interests.[41]

Final Observations

The massive destruction of much of the rural economy in the counter-insurgency operation of the 1980s (in Iraq) and 1990s (in Turkey) has undermined the economic foundations of tribal organization in large parts of Kurdistan. Pastoral nomadism has virtually disappeared (but there has been a significant revival of transhumant pastoralism in eastern Turkey as a complement to agrarian or urban economic activities) and a high proportion of the rural population has been displaced. On the other hand, the Iraqi and Turkish states' establishment of tribal and quasi-tribal militias bolstered tribal organization with new resources (and changed the balance of power between tribal groups).

Tribal organization remains complementary to the administrative structure of the State. Tribes exist where the State cannot exert its authority effectively or where it deliberately delegates tasks to them. In this respect, tribal organization is comparable to civil society (although it lacks the voluntary character and benevolent qualities commonly associated with civil society).[42] Tribal militias such as the *jash* and *korucu* – or, in an earlier period, the Hamidiye – are extreme examples in that they were deliberately created out of previously existing tribes (but never fully coinciding with those tribes). There are numerous less-extreme examples, in which tribes are left to perform tasks that are too costly for the State to implement. I briefly mention two such examples, in a rural and an urban setting.

Land conflicts are perpetual. Land registration by the State started in the mid-nineteenth century and has not yet been fully completed. There are often competing claims to the same piece of land, and control of land is frequently seized from the person with the strongest legal claim by a rival who can mobilize sufficient local backing. It is possible to go to court and register one's claim against an illegal occupant (and, in fact, people do go to court and do win verdicts). The court verdict determines legal ownership, but the State in many cases does not have the resources to enforce such decisions. So even where state law is recognized and appealed to, a claimant may need to invoke the support of his tribe, or even of his tribe's allies, to press his claim against the usurper (who also has tribal support) and actually obtain his right – or not.[43]

The numerous cases of seizure of entire villages by *korucu* in Turkey, which could not be undone by court decisions in favour of the original owners – or could be, but only with great difficulty – underline the importance of tribal support (and, incidentally, also bring out the role of the PKK as a new arbiter alongside the shaykhs).

A considerable proportion of the Kurdish population of tribal background has migrated to such metropolises as Baghdad, Tehran, Istanbul and Cologne. No doubt many of them have individualized and loosened ties with their tribal origins. Yet for recent migrants, and probably especially for those of low education and low economic position, networks based on region of origin or tribal affiliation remain essential resources that allow them to survive in the new environment.

'Hometown' associations, in which people from the same town or district in Turkey organize themselves for sociability and mutual aid, are a well-known phenomenon about which there is a growing body of academic studies.[44] At least some tribes also perform that role very effectively, as is documented for the case of the Koçkiri in Istanbul by Günter Seufert.[45] Early migrants of this tribe, arriving in the 1960s, found themselves a particular niche in the labour market, which they had to defend against other Kurdish tribesmen. Newly arriving Koçkiri found lodging, jobs and protection in their tribal network, and the need for these services kept that network intact and solidarity high. Anecdotal information suggests that there are many such economically specialized tribal networks in the major cities.

In all these examples, the tribes that we encounter are hardly the tribes of segmentary theory but rather patronage networks in which kinship and (the belief in) common descent is only one factor. The alliances and oppositions in conflicts involving militias, voting in elections, land conflicts or scarce resources in the urban environment do not neatly follow the segmentation of descent groups but do involve vertical relations of patronage in which physical prowess, loyalty, abilities and political convictions are also important factors. The tribes involved have names and in many cases a documented history going back centuries. Corporate action by the entire tribe has been extremely rare in modern history (and may very well always have been rare). When we see a tribe in action, it is often one or more members of the leading family with a following consisting of relatives and assorted clients and dependents. It is in this form that tribes are likely to remain part of the political landscape of Kurdish society.

Notes

1. M.M. van Bruinessen, 'Agha, shaikh and state: on the social and political organization of Kurdistan', PhD thesis, Utrecht University, 1978. An abridged and updated version was published by Zed Books in 1992. Further observations and reflections on state–tribe relations, partly based on the developments of the following decades, can be found in Martin van Bruinessen, 'Kurds, states and tribes', in Faleh A. Jabar and Hosham Dawod (eds), *Tribes and power: nationalism and ethnicity in the Middle East* (London: Saqi, 2003), pp. 165–83.
2. Nazand Begikhani, Aisha K. Gill and Gill Hague, *Honour-Based violence: experiences and counter-strategies in Iraqi Kurdistan and the UK Kurdish diaspora* (Farnham, Surrey: Ashgate, 2015); Andrea Fischer-Tapir, *Brave men, pretty women? Gender and symbolic violence in Iraqi Kurdish urban society* (Berlin: Europäisches Zentrum für Kurdische Studien, 2009).

3. It was eventually published as Ziya Gökalp, *Kürt aşiretlei hakkında sosyolojik tetkikler* [Sociological studies on the Kurdish tribes], ed. Şevket Beysanoğlu (Istanbul: Sosyal Yayınlar, 1992).
4. The Settlement Law is discussed extensively in İsmail Beşikçi, *Kürtlerin 'Mecburi İskan'ı* [The Kurds' 'Forced Settlement'] (Ankara: Komal, 1977).
5. Özal's 'testament', a letter written not long before his death to then-Prime Minister Süleyman Demirel, in which he advised how the Kurdish question could be solved ('Özal'ın Demirel'e Kürt Vasiyeti'), was leaked to the press not long after his death, appearing in the newspaper *Hürriyet* on 12 November 1993. It was summarized in English by Hugh Pope: 'Voice from grave airs a Kurdish solution: Ozal letter published advocating forced migration to defeat PKK', *Independent*, 13 November 1993.
6. Janet Klein, *The margins of Empire: Kurdish militias in the Ottoman tribal zone* (Stanford, CA: Stanford University Press, 2011); Stephen Duguid, 'The politics of unity: Hamidian policy in Eastern Anatolia', *Middle Eastern Studies*, 9(2) (1973), pp. 139–55; Martin van Bruinessen, *Agha, Shaikh and State: the Social and Political Structures of Kurdistan* (London: Zed Books, 1992), pp. 185–9.
7. Wadie Jwaideh, *The Kurdish National Movement: its Origins and Development* (Syracuse, NY: Syracuse University Press, 2006), pp. 62–74, 88–101; Ahmet Kardam, *Cizre-Botan beyi Bedirhan: sürgün yılları* [The years in exile of Bedir Khan, the lord of Jazira-Botan] (Ankara: Dipnot, 2013).
8. Eugene L. Rogan, 'Asiret mektebi: Abdülhamit II's school for tribes (1892–1907)', *International Journal of Middle East Studies* 28 (1996), pp. 83–107; Alişan Akpınar, *Osmanlı devletinde aşiret mektebi* [The school for tribes in the Ottoman state] (Istanbul: Göçebe Yayınları, 1997).
9. Martin van Bruinessen, 'Genocide in Kurdistan? The suppression of the Dersim rebellion in Turkey (1937–38) and the chemical war against the Iraqi Kurds (1988)', in George J. Andreopoulos (ed.), *Conceptual and historical dimensions of genocide* (Philadelphia, PA: University of Pennsylvania Press, 1994), pp. 141–70; Netherlands Kurdistan Society, *Forced evictions and destruction of villages in Dersim (Tunceli) and the western part of Bingöl, Turkish Kurdistan, September-November 1994* (Amsterdam: SNK, 1995); Joost Jongerden, *The settlement issue in Turkey and the Kurds: an analysis of spatial policies, modernity and war* (Leiden: Brill, 2007).
10. Marshall Sahlins, *Tribesmen* (Englewood Cliffs, NJ: Prentice Hall, 1960).
11. Ibn Khaldun, *The Muqaddimah. An introduction to history*, vol. 1, translated from the Arabic by Franz Rosenthal (New York: Bollingen Foundation Inc., 1958). The British anthropologist and philosopher Ernest Gellner adopted Ibn Khaldun's theory of dynastic change in his influential study *Muslim society* (Cambridge: Cambridge University Press, 1981). More recently, the political scientist Hamit Bozarslan has drawn attention to the usefulness of Ibn Khaldun's conceptual model for understanding state–society relations in the modern Middle East: Hamit Bozarslan, *Le luxe et la violence: domination et contestation chez Ibn Khaldûn* (Paris: CNRS Editions, 2014).

12. For a general discussion of Middle Eastern tribes, see Dale F. Eickelman, *The Middle East, an anthropological approach* (Englewood Cliffs, NJ: Prentice Hall Inc., 1989), chapter 6; Richard Tapper (ed.), *The conflict of tribe and state in Iran and Afghanistan* (London: Croom Helm, 1983); Philip S. Khoury and Joseph Kostiner (eds), *Tribes and state formation in the Middle East* (London and New York: I.B.Tauris, 1991).
13. Marshall Sahlins, 'The segmentary lineage: an organization of predatory expansion', *American Anthropologist* 63(2) (1961), pp. 322–43; Fredrik Barth, 'Father's brother's daughter marriage in Kurdistan', *Southwestern Journal of Anthropology* 10(2) (1954), pp. 164–71; Bruinessen, *Agha, shaikh and state*, pp. 50–9.
14. Examples of feuds in Kurdistan, and analysis are given in Bruinessen, *Agha, shaikh and state*, pp. 64–74. For a more general statement and comparative analysis, see Jacob Black-Michaud, *Cohesive force: feud in the Mediterranean and the Middle East* (New York: St Martin's, 1975).
15. E.R. Leach, *Social and economic organisation of the Rowanduz Kurds* (London: Percy Lund Humphries & Co., 1940); Fredrik Barth, *Principles of Social Organization in Southern Kurdistan* (Oslo: Universitets Etnografiske Museum, 1953). For the broader context, see Martin van Bruinessen, 'Kurdish studies in Western and Central Europe', *Wiener Jahrbuch für Kurdische Studien* 2 (2015), pp. 18–96.
16. For overviews of the criticism, see the contributions by Richard Tapper and Steve Caton in Khoury and Kostiner, *Tribes and state formation*; Eickelman, *The Middle East*, pp. 131–8.
17. Examples are given in Barth, *Principles of Social Organization*; Bruinessen, *Agha, Shaikh and State*, pp. 78–94. As noted above, Ziya Gökalp also commented on this phenomenon of 'alien' leadership in Kurdish tribes, which he believed distinguished them from Arab tribes.
18. Celadet Bedirkhan, one of the pioneers of Kurdish nationalism, was a scion of one of the great aristocratic families of Kurdistan in which exogamy was the rule; his own mother was Circassian and the entire family was an ethnic mix. Daughters also married out (and were thereby lost to the family, although some of their descendants later rediscovered their Kurdish backgrounds). Bedirkhan, being a nationalist, took the deliberate decision to marry his paternal cousin, conforming with the Kurdish marriage preference. See Ahmet Serdar Aktürk, 'Female cousins and wounded masculinity: Kurdish nationalist discourse in the Post-Ottoman Middle East', *Middle Eastern Studies*, 52(1) (2016), pp. 46–59.
19. This process is traced in some detail in Bruinessen, *Agha, Shaikh and*, chapter 3.
20. For a description of one complicated case, the Hevêrkan tribe in the Tor Abdin and the Syrian Jazira in the late nineteenth and early twentieth centuries, see Bruinessen, *Agha, Shaikh and State*, pp. 94–105.
21. Portraits of such 'loyal' and 'unreliable' chieftains may be found in W.R. Hay, *Two years in Kurdistan. Experiences of a political officer 1918–1920* (London: Sidgwick & Jackson Ltd, 1921); C.J. Edmonds, *Kurds, Turks and Arabs. Politics,*

Travel and Research in North-Eastern Iraq, 1919–1925 (London: Oxford University Press, 1957).
22. Examples are given in Martin van Bruinessen, 'Kurds, states and tribes', in Jabar and Dawod, *Tribes and power*, pp. 165–83.
23. Among the Kurds, the term 'shaykh' does not refer to tribal leaders but to religious authorities, and more especially to the leaders of Sufi orders. The uprisings mentioned in this paragraph are studied in some detail in Jwaideh, *The Kurdish National Movement*, and David McDowall, *A Modern History of the Kurds* London: I.B.Tauris, 1996); the role of the Sufi orders in the emergence of Kurdish nationalism is a major theme of Bruinessen, *Agha, Shaikh and State*.
24. Bruinessen, *Agha, Shaikh and State*, chapter 4.
25. Basile P. Nikitine and Ely B. Soane, 'The tale of Suto and Tato', *Bulletin of the School of Oriental Studies* 3(1) (1923), pp. 69–106; Martin van Bruinessen, 'The Sâdatê Nehrî or Gîlânîzâde of Central Kurdistan', *Journal of the History of Sufism* 1–2 (2000), pp. 79–91, reprinted in Bruinessen, *Mullas, Sufis and heretics: the role of religion in Kurdish society. Collected articles* (Istanbul: Isis Press, 2000).
26. In the 1950s, Fredrik Barth's informants of the Jaf tribe were very suspicious of the Barzinji shaykhs and especially their non-tribal followers, whom they believed to be using the mobilizing potential of the Qadiri Sufi order as an instrument of class struggle against the landowners. Barth, *Principles of Social Organization*.
27. Mehmed S. Kaya, *The Zaza Kurds of Turkey: a Middle Eastern minority in a globalised society* (London: I.B.Tauris, 2011), pp. 54–74, 195–9.
28. Serif Mardin, 'The Naksibendi order in Turkish history', in Richard Tapper (ed.), *Islam in modern Turkey. Religion, politics and literature in a secular state* (London: I.B.Tauris, 1991), pp. 121–42; Hakan Yavuz, 'The matrix of modern Turkish Islamic movements: the Naqshbandi order', in Elisabeth Özdalga (ed.), *Naqshbandis in western and central Asia* (Istanbul: Swedish Research Institute in Istanbul, 1999), pp. 129–46.
29. Thierry Zarcone, 'Les branches à Istanbul des ordres soufis kurdes', *Annales de l'autre islam* 5 (1998), pp. 109–23. One of these branches, named after the shaykhs' village of Menzil (near Adıyaman), has adopted a Turkish nationalist discourse and has been a strong supporter of the Justice and Development Party (AKP), for which it was rewarded with a number of deputies in parliament and ministerial posts in government. It is also strongly represented among the Turkish diaspora in western Europe.
30. On these developments, see the interesting study by Müfid Yüksel, *Kürdistan'da değişim süreci* [The process of change in Kurdistan] (Ankara: Sor, 1993), which focuses especially on the shaykhs of Norşin. See also the biography of Shaykh Said's grandson Abdülmelik Fırat, who lived part of his life in exile but also became an influential and widely respected member of parliament – Ferzende Kaya, *Mezopotamya sürgünü. Abdülmelik Fırat'ın yaşam öyküsü* [Exile from Mesopotamia: Abdulmelik Fırat's life story] (Istanbul: Anka, 2003).

31. In several conversations that I had with Iraqi Kurds in the 2000s, this association of the two parties with Sufi orders was made explicitly. The political scientist David Romano appears to reflect these perceptions when he writes that 'Talabani's PUK rallied a disproportionate number of Sorani-speaking Kurds, tribes in opposition to Barzani, members of the Qadri [sic] Sufi religious brotherhood, and people from the southeastern part of Iraqi Kurdistan [...] Barzani's KDP [...] was disproportionately composed of Kurmanji-speaking Kurds, Barzani tribes and their allies, Naqshibendi [sic] Sufis, and people from the northwestern part of Iraqi Kurdistan.' Romano, *Kurdish Nationalist Movement*, p. 197.
32. Noshirwan Mustafa, one of the PUK's commanders (who was later to found the Gorran party), spoke at large about the unpredictable nature of tribal alliances in south Kurdistan. PUK-allied tribes might suddenly join the irregular militias established by the government, and militias might suddenly join the PUK, bringing along their government-supplied weapons and ammunition. The militias commonly avoided full-scale confrontations with the PUK Peshmerga, and often gave warnings of military operations (interview, Nawzeng, Iraq–Iran border, April 1979).
33. While in Sulaimaniya, Shaykh Muhammad and his sons Nehru and Gandhi remained well-connected in Baghdad and became important CIA assets, enabling the CIA mission in Sulaimaniya to meet people of all branches of the state apparatus prior to the US invasion. See Bob Woordward, *Plan of attack* (New York: Simon and Schuster, 2004) (where the shaykh and his sons appear pseudonymously as 'the Pope' and 'the Rockstars'). Annabelle Böttcher made valuable observations, partly based on her own fieldwork in Iraq, in an unpublished paper, 'Sufi resistance in Iraq', presented at the Deutsche Orientalistentag (DOT) in Freiburg in September 2007. The Kasnazaniyya is the subject of a forthcoming PhD dissertation by Awaz Kadir at the École Pratique des Hautes Études in Paris, provisionally titled 'La Kesnazaniyya en Irak: le passage d'une confrérie soufie au parti politique (1980–2014)'.
34. Human Rights Watch/Middle East, *Iraq's crime of genocide: the Anfal campaign against the Kurds* (New Haven, CT: Yale University Press, 1995), pp. 28–30 (on recruitment into the militia battalions), 109–12 (on the *jash*'s ambivalent role in the *Anfal*).
35. Andreas Wimmer, 'Stammespolitik und die kurdische Nationalbewegung im Irak', in Carsten Borck et al. (eds), *Ethnizität, Nationalismus, Religion und Politik in Kurdistan* (Münster: LIT, 1997), pp. 11–43 (especially the section on state-building by clientelism, pp. 32–8). See also Andreas Wimmer, 'Stämme für den Staat: tribale Politik und die kurdische Nationalbewegung im Irak', *Kölner Zeitschrift für Soziologie und Sozialpsychologie* 47 (1995), pp. 95–113.
36. The Mosul Vilayet Council hired the services of a Swiss lawyer to press their claims (which ultimately came to nothing). Their petitions and other

documents, which are of some historical interest, can be retrieved from the website www.solami.com/a33c.htm (accessed February 2018).
37. Michiel Leezenberg, 'Urbanization, privatization, and patronage: the political economy of Iraqi Kurdistan', in Faleh A. Jabar and Hosham Dawod (eds), *The Kurds: nationalism and politics* (London: Saqi, 2006), pp. 151–79, esp. 163–74; Martin van Bruinessen, 'Iraq: Kurdish challenges', in Walter Posch (ed.), *Looking into Iraq* (Paris: European Union Institute for Security Studies, 2005), p. 65.
38. Denise Natali, *The Kurdish quasi-state: development and dependency in post–Gulf War Iraq* (Syracuse, NY: Syracuse University Press, 2010), p. 124.
39. Some US documents released by WikiLeaks provide a glimpse of the reorganization process. See, for instance, 'Peshmerga force unification, Iraqi Kurdistan', dated 6 July 2007, available at www.wikileaks.org/plusd/cables/07BAGHDAD2242_a.html (accessed February 2018).
40. See the anonymous Aşiretler raporu [Report on tribes], Istanbul: Kaynak, 1998, a leaked intelligence report that contains for each of the Kurdish-majority provinces detailed information on the tribes and their loyalty to the state.
41. Bruinessen, 'Kurds, states and tribes'; Hamit Bozarslan, 'Kurdistan: Kriegswirtschaft - Wirtschaft im Krieg', in: Carsten Borck et al. (eds), *Ethnizität, Nationalismus, Religion und Politik in Kurdistan* (Münster: LIT, 1997), pp. 79–112; Gilles Dorronsoro, 'Les politiques ottomane et républicaine au Kurdistan à partir de la comparaison des milices Hamidiye et korucu', *European Journal of Turkish Studies* 5 (2006), available at ejts.revues.org/778 (accessed February 2018); Semsa Özar, Nesrin Uçarlar and Osman Aytar, *From past to present, a paramilitary organization in Turkey: village guard system* (Diyarbakir: Diyarbakir Institute for Political and Social Research, 2013); Mehmet Seymen Önder, *Devlet ve PKK ikileminde korucular* [The village guards, caught between the state and the PKK] (Istanbul: İletişim, 2015).
42. Richard Antoun and others have argued that in non-Western societies, forms of civil society exist that may not be recognized as such because they differ from the formal, associational type to which much of the relevant literature usually restricts itself. Antoun focused on the tribal councils (*diwaniyya*) of Arab society as performing many of the functions attributed to civil society elsewhere. Richard T. Antoun, 'Civil society, tribal process, and change in Jordan: an anthropological view', *International Journal of Middle East Studies* 32 (2000), pp. 441–63. For a more general statement, see Chris Hann and Elizabeth Dunn (eds), *Civil society: challenging western models* (London: Routledge, 1996).
43. Kaya, *The Zaza Kurds of Turkey*, pp. 34–41 provides interesting examples from Solhan district, where several tribes are represented in each village and where local tribal factions may call upon their tribesmen from outside the village, and where ultimately shaykhs and other respected great men are capable of acting as the arbiters in land conflicts.

44. For instance, the special issue of the *European Journal of Turkish Studies* on hometown organizations, *EJTS* 2 (2005), available at ejts.revues.org/359 (accessed February 2018); Anna Grabolle-Çeliker, *Kurdish life in contemporary Turkey: migration, gender and ethnic identity* (London: I.B.Tauris, 2013).
45. Günter Seufert, 'Between religion and ethnicity: a Kurdish-Alevi tribe in globalizing Istanbul', in Petra Weyland and Ayse Öncü (eds), *Space, culture and power: new identities in globalizing cities* (London: Zed Books, 1997), pp. 157–76.

CHAPTER 7

TRIBES AND POLITICS

Hamit Bozarslan

On 9 May 2015, some 300 members of the Alpahan tribe of Batman – who, until then, had supported the ruling AKP (Party of Justice and Development) – changed their political affiliation and adhered collectively to the HDP (Democratic Party of Peoples), which openly defends the Kurdish cause.[1] The day after, the Alikans and the Ramans (comprising 20,000 electors) followed the Alpahans' example.[2] During this pre-electoral period, leaders or members of some other tribes in Siirt, Urfa and Adiyaman also declared that they would henceforth be supporting the HDP.[3] However, it would be difficult to give an accurate picture of the political engagements of the roughly 750 tribes that comprised the Kurdish tribal landscape in Turkey during this electoral period.[4] On the basis of the available data, however, one can easily affirm that tribes continue to play an important role in the Kurdish political space in Turkey. But are they still the major players that they were only a few decades ago?

In this chapter – which focuses mainly on Turkey but also takes into account 'Kurdish situations' in Iraq, Syria and Iran – I will first suggest that the tribal factor has been one of the major determinants of Kurdish politics throughout the twentieth century. It is thus no wonder that French and British mandate officers as well as Turkish, Iranian, Syrian and Iraqi authorities and scholars have paid specific attention to tribes and tribalism in Kurdistan.[5] However, the recent state of violence in the Middle East[6] invites a revisiting of this question in relation to the reinforcement or weakening of extra-tribal dynamics. In fact, recent experiences amply show that the tribal world follows sundry trajectories in different countries. In Egypt and Tunisia, which have been extensively centralized since the beginning of the nineteenth century, tribal dissidence remains active only at the margins of society. As Mohammed Hachemaoui argues, in Algeria, the tribes, which have been rehabilitated by post-civil war power holders, play a decisive political role at the local level.[7] In some other countries, such as Libya and Yemen, which face a massive phenomenon of violence, tribes have become major agents of territorial, social and political fragmentation. In contrast, in Iraq and Syria, the Sunni tribes enjoyed an expanded field of autonomous action only in the first stage of the disintegration of the State – respectively, between 2004 and 2007; and 2011–12. During the second phase of the conflict, they had to accept a subordinated position vis-à-vis sectarian actors, who had, and still have, a higher capacity for using violence, controlling time and space, and imposing their own military order. In contrast, broadly speaking, the tribal actors in Kurdistan have lost the central position that they had enjoyed during most parts of the twentieth century, albeit for entirely different reasons than those observed in the Arab regions of Iraq and Syria. The existence of a strong political authority, such as the KRG (Kurdish Regional Government), in Iraq and the capacity of the PYD (Party of Democratic Unity), a hegemonic actor, in monopolizing instruments of coercion, have considerably narrowed tribal autonomy.

The Imperial Past and the Tribal Factor

In spite of some excellent historical studies, our knowledge on the Kurdish tribes under the first Muslim empires and, later, under the Ottoman and Persian empires[8] remains quite elementary. As Boris James shows convincingly in his study on the Kurds during the medieval era, the area that would one day be known as Kurdistan hosted many tribes that were aware of their 'Kurdishness'.[9] But the impression that one gets from the available literature is that, in spite of their durability in space and across time, these tribes were subordinated either to imperial authorities or to the emerging, local, supra-tribal Kurdish powers known as 'emirates'.[10]

This trend seems to be even more obvious after the Ottoman–Persian wars of the early sixteenth century, which marked on one hand the division of the Kurdish geographical space between these empires and on the other hand the consolidation of the emirates, which were also referred to as *hukumet*s, or 'governments'.[11] This situation did not constitute an exception to a well-established rule that one could observe in many parts of the Muslim world: contrary to widespread opinion, the 'rural sphere' in this region has always been dominated by its urban centres. Power can be exerted by former tribal elements possessing a strong *asabiyya* (group feeling) but, as Ibn Khaldun (1332–1406) understood, these tribes were doomed to fully urbanize themselves – the tribes that he knew had done so within a generation of his first observing them.

Like their Muslim predecessors, however, both the Persian and Ottoman empires – and the Kurdish emirates that were subordinated to them – shared a common will to preserve, or even reinforce, existing tribal structures in the Kurdish space. Although tribes were in no way fixed entities and evolved in size, localization and strength, they enabled power holders to subordinate their society; the presence of the Kurdish *aghas* (lords) allowed them to establish a category of 'most-favoured lords', who helped them to maintain order and security at the local level and in some cases collect taxes as well. The existing literature seems to suggest that Ottoman power tried its best, from the reign of Sultan Mehmed II (1432–81) onwards, to destroy any kind of tribal solidarity among the Turks in Asia Minor and the Balkans, and recruited high-ranking civil and military bureaucrats from among the populations of converted Christians. Yet, it preserved tribal structures in Kurdistan and the Arab provinces. Weaker than its Ottoman neighbour, Persia was obliged to preserve the tribes not only in its peripheries but also at the heart of its empire.

The tribal actors won considerable autonomy after the policy of centralization that these two empires developed from the beginning of the nineteenth century onwards. The framework of this chapter will not allow us to analyze all the outcomes of this policy; suffice it to say that it was successful in destroying the Kurdish emirates and in implementing the State's administration in the main Kurdish cities, often at the cost of much violence and brutality. However, it was unsuccessful in realizing its goal of transforming these empires into a fabric of citizenry (*fabrique des citoyens*). In fact, the State remained external to Kurdish society, and its military and fiscal presence has been regarded by Kurds as a predatory form of intervention in the local Kurdish environment. The destruction of the Kurdish emirates created a real power vacuum, which gave rise to massive security concerns and thus led to a wide-scale re-tribalization of Kurdistan.

Notwithstanding their discourses on 'common ancestors' and their genealogies attached to the Prophet, here, as elsewhere,[12] tribes re-emerged or consolidated themselves as narrowly defined solidarity structures. In the Ottoman Empire, mainly, the first and 'spontaneous' reaction from the central authorities to this tribal 'renaissance' was an 'ethnographic' and coercive one: the Westernized Ottoman bureaucrats who orchestrated the reforms known as Tanzimat ('Reorganizations') had rather poor knowledge of their society. Thus, they tried in vain to understand the tribal social fabric, which had an obvious trans-border dimension,[13] and to reduce tribal 'unrest' through state coercion – but without any tangible results.

It was only under Abdulhamid II (r. 1876–1909), who developed a project of 'restoration' under which he imagined and described the old Ottoman *nizam* (order) and successfully re-centralized power in his own hands, that Ottoman rule understood that it could have another approach to the Kurdish tribal domain. The formation in 1891 of the Hamidiye Light Cavalries, which regrouped some 65 tribes (and their sub-branches, or clans) with some 37,500 men, allowed the Ottoman sultan to have a loyal Kurdish tribal force under his command. This force, which could be considered the sultan's 'Cossack army', not only divided the Kurdish tribes but also prevented potential tribal violence from succeeding anti-state narratives, and was also used against Armenian revolutionary activities. The formation of these units additionally allowed the State to present a generally efficient barrier against the Russian Empire, whose presence in the Kurdish space was perceived as a threat to Istanbul.[14] The cavalries also attested to the profound sophistication of Abdulhamid's political engineering and corresponded to the establishment of an Ottoman type of *makhzan*,[15] sharing many features with those observed in past (and present) North African societies. The enrolled tribes were all located in the northern tiers of Kurdistan, which partly overlapped with historical Armenia.

In the southern parts of Kurdistan, where centrifugal dynamics were quite strong, the sultan could limit his *rapprochement* with the Kurds to classical paternalistic policies. As the case of Ibrahim Pasha of Milli shows,[16] some of these tribes have indeed been loyal to the sultan and have acted as his security agents, but did not take part in the persecution of the Armenians or other Christian communities; others, however, did participate in the wide-scale massacres of Armenians between 1894 and 1896, as well as to the genocide of 1915–16.

The genocide of the Armenians, as well as of the Aramaic-speaking communities (Syriacs and Chaldeans), which took place only six years after the fall of Abdulhamid, largely contributed to the religious and ethnic homogenization of northern Kurdistan.[17]

From the 1920s to 1946

As Hakan Özoğlu suggests,[18] the complex relationship between some Kurdish tribes and the Hamidien regime resulted in two contradictory outcomes. On the one hand, it undeniably reinforced the State and – in spite of a series of Kurdish uprisings, which took place between 1909 and 1914 – constituted one of the preparatory conditions of the so-called war of independence led by general Mustafa Kemal Atatürk in the wake of the military debacle suffered by the Ottoman Empire in World War 1.

On the other hand, it also contributed to the formation of a political 'microclimate' in Kurdistan and, more broadly speaking, reinforced the Kurds' awareness of being 'Kurds' in spite, or perhaps because of, being privileged allies of the State.

After the dismemberment of the Ottoman Empire, the Kurdish tribal world was divided between four countries – Iran, Iraq, Syria and Turkey – and was at one and the same time fragmented and radicalized. Since then, it has simultaneously expressed many forms of collaboration with or resistance to these new authorities. In Turkey, some tribes collaborated with Kemalist power even during the repressive military campaigns against the Kurdish movement; in spite of this fact, some tribes, such as the Heverkans, could not avoid being the new victims of the State.[19] Other tribes, whose chieftains were appointed deputies in the Great National Assembly, were more fortunate.[20] Many other tribes, on the other hand, opted for armed dissidence vis-à-vis Ankara and, on the other, constituted the main militant forces of the 1925 and 1927–30 rebellions. In Iraq, too, some Kurdish tribes accepted collaboration with the (in this case, mandate) authorities during the same period, while others allied themselves with the resisting Barzandji and, subsequently, Barzani forces. This was also the case in Iran where Reza Pahlavi's policy of destruction of the tribal world appeared to be widely inefficient; indeed, many Kurdish tribes joined, for various periods, the Simko rebellion (1918–22), which comprised forces belonging to the Shikak tribal confederation.[21]

During the early period of the French mandate, Kurdish tribes in Syria did not evolve in a violent environment and had rather good relations with the mandate authorities. However, some of these tribes, which had been divided by the inter-state frontiers established in 1921, participated in the Kurdish rebellions in Turkey. The strong opposition to these heavily militarized borders would become one of the key factors of the long-lasting armed struggle in Turkey, Iraq and Iran, in each of which the struggle continued until 1946.[22]

It is true that during these two-and-a-half decades many tribes adopted ambivalent positions, acted under heavy constraints and opted either for co-optation with the states or for resistance against them. Here, as elsewhere, the rebellious tribes could not legitimize their actions by any discourse other than particularistic–tribal concerns. As Eli Amarilogo suggests, tribes needed a broader ideology and a more inclusive framework.[23] Islam could meet this ideological 'call' only during the Shaykh Said rebellion of 1925 in Turkish Kurdistan. But even in this unique case, the religious *da'wa* (call) was combined with Kurdish nationalism. This was due to the nature of the leadership. Shaykh Said, the head of the movement, was a well-known figure of the Naqshbandi Sufi order, but most of the movement's leaders – including the atheist Fehmiye Bilal, Said's secretary, and Hesen Heşyar Serdi – belonged to the Westernized Kurdish elite.[24]

All the other Kurdish revolts that took place both in Turkey and elsewhere had a strong Kurdish tonality.[25] The reason for the inefficiency of Islam as an ideology of resistance could be found in the fact that the official Islam of the State was largely absent in Kurdistan or had very weak local implementation – and also that although the Sufi orders, mainly the Naqshbandiyya and Qadiriyya, were strong they nevertheless were fragmented and did not have the 'cultural' and 'ideological' capital necessary to lead an armed rebellion. 'Kurdism', for its part, was the doctrine of the intelligentsia, a rather thin social stratum, whom much of the ruling elite as well as the tribal chiefs disdained as *mutegallibe* (oppressors/usurpers). Nonetheless, the intelligentsia not only had the capacity to formulate a structured political discourse but also had a supra-social standing that could place it in the privileged position of an arbiter. Although it was alien to segments of the tribal world by virtue of its Westernized profile, it was able to offer them a set of meanings. On the other hand, the intelligentsia was heavily dependent on the prevailing rural dynamics: the submission of the cities, where the State was strongest, had left it with no force other than the tribal one with which to mobilize.

Tribes and Kurdish Contest from 1946 to 1991

The second period under consideration here began in 1946 with the fall of the autonomous Kurdish Republic of Mahabad, and ended with the Gulf War of 1991. This long period has experienced a diffuse but non-armed Kurdish opposition in Iran; the rise and fall of the Barzani rebellion in Iraq (1961–75); and violent, defiant guerrilla warfare in entire regions of Kurdistan after 1979. The formation of a Kurdish autonomous administration in Iraq after the Gulf War of 1991 constituted the last important event of this almost half-century-long period.

Throughout these decades, tribes have been involved in Kurdish politics and in the shaping of Kurdish–State relations in a variety of ways; they constituted the main fighting force of the Mahabad Republic (1946) and of the Barzani rebellion (1960s), which saw a formal tribal commission led by Mustafa Barzani himself.

Barzani also enjoyed special relations with some Kurdish tribes in Turkey, where many tribes entered the political space after the adoption of the multiparty system in 1950. Nurettin Yilmaz, who had an openly outspoken Kurdish identity, and Ahmet Türk, who would become one of the leaders of the Kurdish legal movement in the 1990s, were among the tribal figures who had agreed to cooperate with the right-wing AP (Party of Justice) of Süleyman Demirel, before switching to the 'centre-left' CHP (Republican Party of People) of Bülent Ecevit.[26] Many other tribes, among them the Bucaks, have also played an important political role and experienced internal schisms: while PDK-Turkey (the wing of the Kurdistan Democratic Party in Turkey) founder Faik Bucak and, subsequently, his children have been involved in 'Kurdish' politics, others – organized mainly around Celal Bucak, the tribe's official head – adopted a strongly pro-state position and acted as the State's paramilitary force. After the constitution of the so-called Village Protectors' Battalions in 1987 in the wake of Ankara's counter-insurgency strategy against the PKK's guerrilla warfare, some tribes acquiesced, voluntarily or otherwise, to becoming local auxiliaries of the army.

The Jirkis of Tahir Adiyaman, for instance, were offered an amnesty for their past crimes, including the killing of security agents, in exchange for their collaboration with the State.[27] This force, which numbered some 100,000 men at its peak, was in fact a renewed form of the old Hamidiye cavalries. Since the 1970s – long before the beginning of the PKK's armed struggle – Colonel Nazmi Sevgin, an admirer of Sultan Abdulhamid, had been recommending the establishment of such a force.[28] The salaries of these 'protectors' were three times higher than the minimum wage; however, they were paid not individually but rather to the tribal chiefs, who occasionally could be received by the president of the republic himself.[29] Some of these 'village protectors' – who were, in fact, residing in urban quarters – belonged to tribes that had collaborated with the State in the 1910s, 1920s and 1930s. As their involvement in drug trafficking and inter-tribal violence showed, these auxiliary forces enjoyed a high degree of local autonomy.

However, many other tribes – including those who rebelled in the 1920s and 1930s, such as the Oramar and Pinyanish, or the Geylanis – adopted 'patriotic' positions and became allies of the PKK, and locally constituted the electoral basis of the enfranchised Kurdish parties. As under Abdulhamid II, the tribes' potential military power was used by Ankara in order to divide Kurdish society along the lines of 'anti-' and 'pro-'State forces.

As is well known, in Iraq, too, during the same period, tribal fragmentation or the ability of the State to pressurize some tribes to cooperate with it has considerably weakened the Kurdish nationalist resistance. Some tribes, who were profoundly opposed to Mustafa Barzani, leader of the Kurdish revolt known by his name (1961–75), allied themselves with Bagdad. In the 1980s, some of these tribes, which were organized under the label of Fursan Salahudin (The Knights of Salahudin – ranging from 150,000 to 250,000 men at times), had even participated to the infamous Anfal operations (1988) led by their so-called *mustashars*. Finally, tribes also played an important role in the intra-Kurdish conflicts that would appear later on, during the Kurdish civil war of 1994–6.

Commenting on the role that tribes played in the Kurdish movement during these decades, Michael Hudson coined the term 'tribal nationalism'.[30] While definitively explaining some features of the Kurdish contest, this concept seems to be problematic. It is certain that conflicts between pro-rebellion tribes have at least partly determined the fate of the Kurdish contest. Naturally, Kurdish political organizations had to take into account 'tribal temporalities' – that is, the vicissitudes of tribal circumstances and interests – which were quite distinct from their national agenda.

Whichever strategies the tribes adopted, and whatever their short or long-lasting alliances with the states of the Kurdish movements might have been, it is obvious that they were subordinate actors throughout these decades. They had very limited room for manoeuvre and a 'lower ceiling' for autonomous action than the Kurdish intelligentsia. The latter grew more robust than ever before in numbers and social influence, and asserted its undisputable leading role before giving way to more plebeian urban and rural strata, such as the PKK in Turkey.

The Tribal Factor in the Years 1990–2010

In spite of an abundance of data sets on Kurdistan since 1990, our knowledge of the evolution of its tribal conditions, structures and culture since the Gulf War of 1991 remains rather poor. One reason for this is the evolution of Kurdish society itself, mutating into a much more heterogeneous state than ever before. In Iraq and Turkey, for instance, the proportions of the urban and rural populations have changed dramatically, with urbans constituting 75 per cent of the total population as against 25 per cent just a few decades earlier. Kurdish cities have also become internally differentiated; the former urban notables have disappeared, replaced by modern middle classes with new values, lifestyles, political leanings, modes of organization and action, and expectations. The rural exodus of the 1980s, triggered as it was by economic factors and the State's coercive policies, created new generations of activists who are quite different both from the former intelligentsia and from the plebeian strata that dominated the Kurdish contest in the 1960s–1980s.

More importantly, Kurdish political syntax and values have also changed. As the PJAK's (Free Life Party of Kurdistan) guerrilla warfare in Iran, the second stage of the PKK's armed struggle in Turkey (2005–13) and the PYD's rather self-defensive current military resistance in Syria show, violence has not disappeared from the Kurdish political idiom or agenda; it has, however, ceased to be the main axiological standard of the Kurdish movement. In Iraq and Syria, there is a quasi-state-building process, with institutional durability coupled with the Kurds' well-known shortcomings and deformation – half-patriarchal/half-democratic or half-hegemonic/half-representative. It is true that during the inter-Kurdish civil war in Iraq (1994–6) the tribal world played an important role, as some anti-Barzani tribes, such as the Surchis, supported the Jalal Talabani-led PUK (Patriotic Union of Kurdistan), known to be more 'modern' and 'urban' than the Barzani-led PDK. But the war itself was not a tribal one, and the militarized tribes could neither determine its outcome nor build autonomous power bases, such as militia forces.

Turkish Kurdistan also became a theatre of local-power restructuring, with the majority of its Kurdish cities being dominated by new Kurdish actors who descend from a new, mainly young and largely feminized urban elite.

Only in Iran do the Kurds lack any form of self-rule, however limited. Nonetheless, even there civil resistance has been spreading. While Kurdish society, broadly speaking, has experienced a real empowerment throughout the last quarter-of-a-century, the trans-border Kurdish political space has been reconfigured by two political–military actors: the hegemonic bloc built around the PKK, which also includes PYD and PJAK; and the KRG, centred around the KDP (Kurdistan Democratic Party) of Masoud Barzani, which includes other Kurdish political forces in Iraq and exerts some influence in Iran, Syria and Turkey.

These developments have inevitably affected the tribal world and relations between the Kurdish political movements and tribes. Firstly, in Kurdistan as elsewhere in the Middle East, tribes have become widely urbanized. Although they had never been exclusively rural in the past, this gave them access to new political and economic resources – at the cost, however, of losing their capacity to master time and space, and to regenerate their internal solidarity and control over their fellow tribespeople.

Secondly, compared with the past few decades, the Kurds have lost much of their already-limited autonomy. In the past, they could negotiate some margins of action through a long-term or a limited and elusive cooperation with the states, or with the Kurdish nationalist movements. Such a political game is less likely today: in Iraq, the tribes that had traditionally been allies of Saddam Hussein's regime had to accept Kurdish nationalist authority and try to negotiate their survival at the local level through a complex set of manoeuvres. The Zebaris, Bradost, Doski, Mizuri, Surdchi, Barzanji, Herki and others have certainly not vanished, and could again become active elements in the political arena if the situation deteriorated, but they are obliged for the time being to accept holding a subordinate position.

In Syria, where the PYD has marginalized the KNC (Kurdish National Congress, which mainly represents urban notables) through its access to resources of violence, the tribes have no possible way of undertaking autonomous action. The PYD's influence is strong enough to allow it to build patron–client networks with the country's Arab tribes.

In Turkey, too, while previously the Kurdish struggle was mainly rural-embedded, it was nevertheless led by urban elites; indeed, for more than four decades urban elements constituted both the main fighting force and the leading elite of the Kurdish nationalist movement in the country. It is obvious that many of them are able to maintain *asabiyya* (i.e., solidarity), even in an urban context.[31] But in spite of the fact that some 50,000 'village protectors' are still active in Kurdistan of Turkey, the tribes have had to accept the hegemony of the PKK. While being officially incorporated into the State's security forces, the 'Protectors' also locally develop a 'Kurdish' discourse and many of them try to maintain open channels of communication with the PKK. Thus, tribes not only lose their capacity for accessing resources of violence but, most importantly, also lose their capacity for producing political meaning.[32]

Conclusion

As Martin van Bruinessen argued years ago, the existence of a conflictual environment is a sine qua non for the survival of the Kurdish tribes.[33] But this is not necessarily the case with all conflict environments; tribes can manage low-level conflicts, in which they may establish asymmetric relations of power both with State and among themselves.

As Lale Yalçin-Heckmann suggests, many tribes can also be affiliated with different political parties and forces, and establish clientelist relations with a complex political system.[34] But they unable to manage high-level violent conflicts, such as those in Iraq and Syria, or hegemonic military and political constructions, as one may observe in the Kurdish regions of these two countries or in Turkey.

No wonder, then, that the tribal actor, who has been so widely discussed in the past – not only by scholars but also by political actors – today occupies a rather marginal place in Kurdish debates. As elsewhere in the history of the wider Middle East, when power structures that acquire some degree of supra-social autonomy are strong, tribes are rendered weak. Similarly, when strong political meanings emerge, 'tribal ideologies' lose their impact.

It is obvious that in contrast with the Libyan or Yemeni cases, in which tribes (at least, for the time being) subordinate themselves to the major political actors in order to ensure their survival, the 'patriotic' or nationalist discourse that they adopt allows them to bargain for some 'prestige', to legitimize themselves not only vis-à-vis Kurdish society at large but also vis-à-vis their own young members. In contrast with the Libyan and Yemeni case, Kurdish tribes find themselves in dire need of investing in 'urbanity', not through the formation of militias but by embracing new manners and affiliations, as well as the solidarities that urban life offers.

Notes

1. Taraf, 'AKP'li Alpahan Aşireti'nden 300 kişi HDP', *yegeçti*, 9 May 2015. Available at www.taraf.co (accessed February 2018).
2. T24, 'AKP'liaşiretler HDP', *yegeçmey devam ediyor*, 10 May 2015. Available at http://www.t24.com.tr (accessed February 2018).
3. Fehim Taştekin, 'Kurds abandon AKP'. Available at www.al-monitor.com/pulse/originals/2015/05/turkey-pious-kurds-abandon-akp-in-droves-hdp.html (accessed February 2018).

4. Adnan Gerger, *Daglar in Ardi Kimin Yurdu*, Ankara, 1991&*Anonyme Aşiretler Raporu* (Istanbul: Kaynak, 1998).
5. Cf. mainly, Martin van Bruinessen, *Agha, Shaikh and State: the Social and Political Structures of Kurdistan* (London: Zed Press, 1992) and Lale Yalçin-Heckmann, *Tribe and Kingship Among the Kurds* (Frankfurt/Main: Peter Lang, 1991).
6. Cf. for this concept, Hamit Bozarslan, 'Arab world and Middle East 2010–2015: from revolutionary configurations to the state of violence', in J. Karakoç (ed.), *Authoritarianism in the Middle East. Before and After the Arab Uprisings* (New York, Palgrave, 2015), pp. 67–91.
7. Mohammed Hachemaoui, *Clientélisme et patronage dans l'Algérie contemporaine* (Paris: Karthala, 2013).
8. See, for instance, Najat Abdulla, *Empire, frontière et tribu. Le Kurdistan et le conflit de frontière turco-persan (1843–1932)* (Erbil: Direction culturelle de la Presse, 2013).
9. Boris James, 'Les Kurdes dans l'Orient mamelouk et mongol de 1250 à 1340: Entre marginalisation et autonomie', PhD thesis, University of Paris X, 2014.
10. See Thomas Ripper, *Die Marwaniden von DiarBakr. Eine Kurdische Dynastie imislamischen Mittelalter* (Würzburg; Egon Verlag, 2000).
11. Nejat Göyünç and Wolf-Dieter Hütteroth, *Land an der Grenze. Osmanische Verwaltung im heutigen türkisch-syrisch-irakischen Grenzgebiet im 16. Jahrhundert* (Istanbul: ErenYayincilik, 1997).
12. Jabar, Faleh A., 'Shaykhs and Ideologues: Detribalisation and Retribalisation in Iraq: 1968–1998', MERIP Report no. 215 (1999), pp. 28–31.
13. Mehmed Hurşid Paşa, *Seyahatname-iHudud*, transcribed with the copy of its original manuscript by Alaaddin Eser (Istanbul: Simurg, 1997).
14. Janet Klein, *The Margins of Empire: Kurdish Militias in the Ottoman Tribal Zone* (Palo Alto, CA: Stanford University Press, 2011).
15. In North Africa, notably Morocco, the domains of the kingdom were divided into two segments: the *seeba*, i.e., 'unruly', and the *makhzan*, the controlled. The *makhzan*, literally 'store', signifies the power of the ruling dynasty. Ernest Gellner, *The Saints of Atlas* (London: Weidenfeld and Nicolson, 1969).
16. Joost Jongerden, 'Elite Encounters of a Violent Kind: Milli Ibrahim Paşa, Ziya Gökalp and Political Struggle in Diyarbékir at the Turn of the 20th Century', pp. 55–84; and Jelle Verheij, 'Diyarbékir and the Armenian Crisis of 1895', pp. 85–145 – both in Joost Jongerden and Jelle Verheij (ed.), *Social Relations in Ottoman Diyarbekir, 1870–1925* (Leiden and Boston, MA: Brill, 2012).
17. See Hamit Bozarslan, 'Les relationskurdo-arméniennes: 1894–1996', in Hans-Lukas Kieser (ed.), *Die Armenische Frage und Die Schweiz* (Zurich: Chronos Verlag, 1999), pp. 329–40.
18. Hakan Özoğlu, *From Calipahte to Secular State. Power Struggle in the Early Turkish Republic* (Santa Barbara, CA: Praeger, 2011).
19. Louis Dillemann, 'Les français en Haute Djezireh', unpublished manuscript, Centre des Hautes Études sur l'Afrique et l'Asie Modernes, n.d., n. 50.538, p. 51.

20. İsmail Beşikçi, *Cumhuriyet Halk Fırkası'nın Tüzüğü (1927) ve Kürt Sorunu* (Ankara: Yurt, 1991), p. 228.
21. Martin van Bruinessen, 'Kurdish Tribes and State in Iran: The Case of Simko's Revolt', in his *Kurdish Ethno-Nationalism versus Nation-Building States* (Istanbul: ISIS Press, 2000), p. 139.
22. MetinYüksel, Dengbêj, 'Mullah, Intelligentsia: The Survival of Kurdish-Kurmanji Language in the Middle-East, 1925–1960', PhD thesis, University of Chicago, 2011.
23. Eli Amarilgo, 'The Dual Relationship Between Tribalism and Nationalism', in Ofra Bengio (ed.), *Kurdish Awakening. Nation-Building in a Fragmented Homeland* (Austin, TX: University of Texas Press, 2014), pp. 63–79.
24. H.H. Serdi, *Görüş ve Anılarım 1907–1985* (Istanbul: Med Yayınları, 1994), pp. 43, 149.
25. Jordi Tejel Gorgas, *Le mouvement kurde de Turquie en exil. Continuités et discontinuités du nationalisme kurde sous le mandat français en Syrie et au Liban (1925–1946)* (Berne and Berlin: Peter Lang, 2007).
26. *Hürriyet*, 25 January 1988.
27. Interview with Tahir Adiyaman in Nokta, 6 December 1987.
28. Nazmi Sevgin, *Doğu ve Güneydoğu Anadolu'da Türk Beylikleri – Osmanlı Belgeleri ile Kürt Türkleri Tarihi* (Ankara: TKAE, 1982).
29. See 'PKK ya Karsi Agalar Meclisi', *Gerçek*, no. 36 (1993), p. 15.
30. M. Hudson, *Arab Politics, The Search for Legitimacy* (New Haven, CT and London: Yale University Press, 1977).
31. Michel Seurat, *L'Etat de barbarie* (Paris: Seuil, 1989).
32. See Mehmet Seyman Önder, *Devletve PKK Ikiliminde Korucular* (Istanbul: Iletisim, 2015).
33. M. van Bruinessen, 'Les kurdes, Etats et tribus', *Etudes kurdes*, no. 1 (2000), pp. 9–31.
34. Yalçin-Heckmann, *Tribe and Kingship*.

CHAPTER 8

GENDER, FAMILY, PATRIARCHY AND WOMEN

Sami Zubaida

The subordination of women in family and society – enshrined in religion, law and custom – is an almost universal phenomenon. Campaigns for women's liberation and gender equality were part of the political struggles of modernity in the West, then in other regions, with continuous contentions – some successes and some reverses. However, at the present time, the Middle East continues to be the region most readily identified with the oppression of women and violence against them. While many parts of the region shared, over the course of the twentieth century, measures of liberation, however limited, the end of the last century and the new millennium feature both reverses to these measures and the spawning of many movements, regimes and militias that actively restrict female rights. Although Saudi Arabia never participated in liberation measures, countries such as Iran, Iraq, Syria and Egypt in the middle decades of the last century were home to considerable legal, social and cultural reforms that saw women emerge, however hesitantly, into public life and the labour market. They even enjoyed a presence, often unveiled, in public space. In many countries and regions, these trends have been reversed, beginning with the Iranian Revolution of 1979 and continuing with the mounting public presence of, and control by, religious movements and regimes.

Clerics, salafis and jihadis seem to revel in the control that they exert, often violently, over women's conduct, dress and public presence, and the drastic laws that they impose on family and sexuality.

It is in this context that Kurdish authorities and forces, in their recent wars with the so-called Islamic State of Iraq and Syria (ISIS), have sought to distinguish their efforts as fighters for women's equality and public presence – to the extent of relying on female fighters and commanders in Syrian Kurdistan (Rojava), as we saw in the savage battle for Kobani in 2014–15.

So, does this indicate an exceptional virtue of the Kurds in the struggle for women's rights and equality? Does this virtue pervade Kurdish society in its different regions? Clearly not; Kurdish society is diverse by region, class and culture, and shares many of the characteristics of its neighbours. This is the subject of this essay; but before focusing on the Kurds, let us sketch the background to these issues in the region.

Issues of women, gender and sexuality have come to characterize social conflicts and political struggles in the modern Middle East, and in the Islamic world generally, and have become emblematic in the discourses of difference from the West. At the extremes, we have the spectacle of the Islamic State (IS) demonstrating its 'Islamicity' by savage measures against women, including enslavement. But their rules on women in family and public space are not that different from those of Saudi Arabia. These cases are eccentric to the 'mainstream' countries such as Turkey, Iran, Egypt, Syria, Iraq and even certain North African states – all of which have undergone long processes of socio-economic transformation, secularization and legal reforms over the course of modernity from the nineteenth century onwards.

Legal reforms and social transformations, often modest, have included measures of empowering women in family and society. Education and occupational opportunities, often a necessity for family survival, have played a crucial part.[1]

These measures of women's liberation were part of the transformations of modernity. At the ideological and cultural levels, nationalist and modernizing elites saw women's oppression as part of the 'backwardness' and weakness of their countries vis-à-vis the dominant European world, and saw their liberation as part of progress and national revival. These projects were buttressed by the far-reaching socio-economic transformations brought by modernity: the incorporation of the Ottoman and Iranian worlds into capitalist world markets; the loosening or dissolution of old rural and communal formations; the urbanization of society; the advancement in transport, communications and educational systems; the centralization of political and military institutions vis-à-vis the emerging modern state; and the emergence of the new classes of intelligentsia and urban workers (the proletariat). Equally, the losers in these processes – conservative elites, religious classes, the rural poor and the urban guilds – remained ever responsive to leaders and rulers who sought to curb liberal or revolutionary challenges. They preferred, for example, Ottoman Sultan Abdulhamid II, whose appeal to religion in resisting constitutional demands survived until his removal by the Young Turks' revolution in 1908/9. Subsequently, liberation campaigns and measures were always limited in most countries in the region by the opposition of conservative and religious forces and the tendency of politicians to avoid confrontation on these issues.

As discussed above, in the course of the twentieth century, many countries in the region saw the inclusion of women into public citizenship, which included rights to suffrage and public office. This aspect of liberation, however, was seriously hindered by the limited measures of women's liberation within the family. The subordination of women, by law and practice, to their husbands or male guardians seriously limited or negated their formal rights.

For instance, in many countries the legal provision that women's freedom of movement (including foreign travel) is subject to their husbands' approval negates their citizenship and professional rights. Other provisions of personal-status laws include polygyny, the husband's right to unilateral divorce and custody of children, and rights over the marital home. In addition to these legal hindrances, there are also powerful communal and customary constraints on women such as widespread domestic and communal violence and other forms of exploitation and oppression.

There is also the thorny question of sexuality, which was not part of what modernists and reformers meant by 'liberation'. The ideal modern, liberated woman was, above all, virtuous and modest – maybe unveiled, but well-covered. Sexuality was a taboo subject within the discourse of liberation. While traditional scholars and jurists discoursed on sexuality in detail – regarding the licit and the forbidden, purity and danger – modernists avoided the subject.

The advocacy was merely for women to be unveiled, to come out in public space and to be educated. Advocates differed on, or did not specify, the categories of work or public participation in which women were to engage, or whether they could compete with men on an equal footing. The question of whether they should have the vote or political or judicial office was also not an issue of consensus, and many demurred.[2]

On family relations and personal-status law, the point of general agreement was disapproval of polygyny. The liberated, educated woman was to have a domestic role that was, at the same time, a national duty: to run an efficient and hygienic home as a wife and mother, and to breed a healthy and strong generation to lead the national renaissance.[3]

The Diversity of Kurds

Kurds share in the social and cultural diversity of the region, such as rural–urban–tribal divides, class and religiosity – all issues affecting women and gender. They also live under the different legal and political regimes of the countries of their residence. The KRG (Kurdistan Regional Government) and now Rojava (the Democratic Federation of Northern Syria) have instituted their own, tentative, regimes – and the latter remains particularly favourable to women. Let us consider aspects of some of the countries that incorporate Kurdish regions: Turkey and Iraq.[4]

Turkey

The Turkish Republic enshrined secularism as a fundamental principle of state. It is the only Muslim-majority country to have abolished the Shari'a explicitly. Its secularism, however, was not so much the separation of religion from the State but the State's control of religion. Personal-status law, including family matters, was thus secularized, with provisions adapted from European legal systems. As such, women were 'liberated' from religious impositions of subordination in the family and exclusions from public life to the extent of prohibiting traditional dress and head cover in public institutions and offices, including schools and universities. This ban was only relaxed in recent years under the rule of the pro-Islamic AKP (Justice and Development) Party. As such, this was the first and clearest example of 'state feminism' in the region: the liberation of women by legal enactments and social policy – albeit not always supported by actual belief and practice. Atatürk's secularism, while supported by some educated urban elites in the major cities, was imposed for the most part on a reluctant society – especially the rural areas and the eastern Anatolian regions, including the Kurdish areas.

An early rebellion against the Republic was that of Shaykh Said, a Kurdish religious leader, in 1925. This is usually presented as a Kurdish separatist uprising, but it was also a religious reaction against the imposed secularism. In most regions and sectors, religious and patriarchal family regimes and impositions on women continued under informal social controls. Even polygyny, made a criminal offence, continued to be practised.

Over the course of the twentieth century and up to the present-day, the Kurdish population was spread out. Alongside the rest of the Turkish population, it was largely urbanized – in both provincial cities, such as Diyarbakir, and major cities in the north and west, such as Ankara, Istanbul and Izmir, each of which have Kurdish quarters and institutions. Many have travelled and settled further, in Germany and other European countries. This population is diversified into class, education and culture. Many of its members have maintained or renewed conservative religiosity with attendant gender regimes. In modern, urban contexts, these regimes are reinforced by the perceived threats and temptations of consumer culture and uncontrolled spaces. Educated, middle-class Kurds share the outlooks and lifestyles of their Turkish equivalents.

Of these, Kurdish nationalist activists have tended towards leftist and liberationist ideologies and affiliations – the most notable being the PKK (Kurdish Workers' Party), which holds a Marxist, insurrectionary programme and armed forces. As such, it is secular in ideology and lifestyle and emphasizes gender equality, including within the military ranks. The Syrian/Rojava PYD (Democratic Union Party) and its affiliated YPG (People's Protection Unit) and YPJ (Women's Protection Unit) militias are offshoots of the PKK and have been distinguished by their female fighters, with high-profile women commanders seen in the recent fights against IS in Kobani and elsewhere.

A considerable portion of Kurdish populations, however, support Islamic parties – primarily, the AKP. There is also a Kurdish Hezbollah: a clandestine, Sunni armed group engaged in assassinations and terrorist attacks, and with reported links to IS. The Sunni sectarian identification of conservative Turks – and Kurds – is heightened by antagonism towards the Alevi sect, many of whose adherents are Kurds. Alevi politics has tended towards secular and leftist affiliations, including the ranks of the PKK.

Kemalist secularism has never penetrated deep into the bulk of Anatolian society, including its Kurdish component. Turks remained pious and conservative for the most part. Their support for Kemalism and the Republic was mostly fuelled by Turkish nationalism, of which Sunni Islam remained a vital if implicit component. Conservative piety in politics came to the fore from the 1980s onwards and intensified in the following decades with the rise of pro-Islamic parties and the success of the AKP, which has held a parliamentary majority and the government since 2001.[5]

Recep Tayyip Erdoğan – prime minister, then president, of Turkey – has been confrontational in advocating and enacting socially conservative policies on culture; education; social space; and, crucially, on gender and family issues. He has declared that men and women are not equal, enjoined women to stay in the home and breed children (at least three each), attacked abortion availability even though it remained officially legal, and advocated and enacted gender segregation in university residences.

Since his emergence, religious studies and ethics are being progressively instituted in the education system. Creationism is becoming accepted doctrine, and being taught in schools.[6] These measures are consonant with the world views and lifestyles of many Turkish and Kurdish Sunnis, and are reinforced by a 'resentment' against the previously dominant secular elites. This culture war, between secularists and Islamists, divides Kurds as well as Turks; the AKP, as we have seen, enjoys electoral support from many Kurds who share its conservative outlook, especially on questions of gender and morality.

The novel *Honour*, written in English by the distinguished Turkish novelist Elif Shafak, is a tale of the oppression of women and the patriarchal gender regime in a Kurdish family.[7] It is set in two locations: a Kurdish village by the Euphrates and a London suburb; one as the original home and the other as the new home of one of two twin sisters and her family, while the rest of the family remains in the village. The consideration of gender relations and family honour are carried to London. The mother – abandoned by a drunk and gambling husband, who is courting a dancer – has to fend for the family. Eventually, her cautious and guilty flirtation with a kind man attracts the attention of an uncle, who then sets up the adolescent son to kill his mother for the honour of the family. This sketch does not, of course, do justice to a masterly and subtle tale, but it alludes to the kind of familial conservatism and violence encountered in its setting. This is confirmed by accounts of and statistics on violence and honour killings in many parts of Turkey, and their spread to Kurdish diasporas in Europe.[8] I shall deal further with the question of violence in following section on Iraq.

Iraq and the KRI (Kurdistan Region of Iraq)

Family and gender regimes in Iraq at present are diverse and uncertain, and largely subject to the rule of religious and communal authorities. It was not always thus; Iraq once boasted one of the most liberal regimes in the region, with family and gender considerations and personal-status laws taken seriously. Abdulkarim Qassim, who came to power following a military coup in 1958, enacted family-law reforms in 1959. These reforms, which abolished Shari'a courts, gave women enhanced rights in marriage, divorce and inheritance. They delighted the strong leftist-secularist current of the time, and angered religious conservatives. A mocking rhyme chanted in the streets was: *tali al-shaharmakumahar, wul-qadinthebbabil-nahar* ('come the end of the month there will no longer be dowries, and we shall chuck the *qadi* [Shari'a magistrate] in the river'). Sections of the communists and the left, feeling strong, lost their populist inhibitions regarding religious sentiment and gave full voice to their secularist positions.

The CIA assisted the bloody Ba'athist coup in 1963 and put an end to the relatively benevolent Qassim dictatorship, ushering in the rule of a pan-Arabist and sectarian Sunni regime under the backward Arif brothers. Sure enough, a delegation of venerable clerics – Sunni and Shi'a – prevailed, and Abdalsalam Arif reversed some of the Qassim reforms.

The second Ba'ath coup, in 1968, ultimately brought Saddam Hussein to dominance in the 1970s. This decade was known as the 'golden age' of prosperity and cultural revival, funded by a multiplication of oil revenues and reinforced by the security state and bloody repression. This regime pursued secularism quite seriously and aimed, in part, to weaken religious and patriarchal loyalties in favour of the regime and party.[9] The 1970s and 1980s saw great strides in the empowerment of women in family and society, and the curbing of religious authority over family law – albeit within the limits of a totalitarian security regime that integrated all women's organizations into the Ba'ath Party and the State apparatus.

All this came to an end in the following decades of destructive wars – against Iran in the 1980s, then the 1990 invasion of Kuwait and the subsequent pulverization of Iraq's economy and infrastructure by US and allied bombardment, followed by disastrous UN sanctions. An increasingly weakened regime resorted to tribalism and religion to shore up social controls. As such, it easily bypassed its own reforms to return to patriarchy, 'honour' violence and all kinds of impositions on women. By this time, the class of people who would 'chuck the *qadi* in the river' had been all but eliminated. The violent repression of all politics and civil autonomies had been highly successful in killing, imprisoning and exiling the 'citizen' middle classes; the Ba'ath Party itself had been transformed from an ideological campaign to a passive vehicle of allegiance to the ruling dynasty.

Most importantly, individuals had been driven by the violence and collapse of the economy to seek safety and livelihood in family, clan, patron bosses and religious networks. The only political opposition facing the regime became the Shi'a parties, which were tied to those patrimonial networks and to Iran.

The fragmented electoral 'democracy' imposed by the Americans after the invasion inaugurated chaotic sets of legal and religious practices on family law, and largely restored religious and patriarchal powers over family and women. The dictators thus liberated women in the good days, but retreated under pressure. Critically, it was the populists ushered in by 'democracy' who most assiduously oppressed women.[10]

The breakdown of law and security from the 1990s, the impoverishment of much of the population, and the use of violence by security forces and criminal gangs (not always distinguishable from one another), were intensified after the 2003 invasion. Multiple militias, mostly religious and mixed with security and police forces, added to the violence and destruction of the invasion forces. Women and girls, within patriarchal families and communities, were particular victims. More generally, poverty and violence made them subject to exploitation and trafficking.

In the Kurdish areas, the suffering of the population in the 1980s and until 1991 at the hands of the Ba'ath regime is well known, and includes the genocidal episodes of Halabja and Anfal. Women, after losing many of their menfolk, became particular victims and were forced to relocate to camps.[11]

KRG Policies and Reforms

In 2007, the KRG, the KDP (Kurdistan Democratic Party) and the PUK (Patriotic Union of Kurdistan) became concerned with high-profile incidents of 'honour' killing and, more generally, reports of widespread violence against women in their region.

This concern was heightened by a much-publicized incident in April 2007, when 17-year-old Doa Khalil Aswad was stoned to death in public for falling in love with the wrong man. In the crowd, observers included uniformed police, who merely stood watching.[12] In 2008, the KRG, at the initiative of its then-prime minister, Nechirvan Barzani, commissioned an international research project and report on the subject of honour-based violence in the Kurdistan Region of Iraq (KRI) and the Kurdish diaspora in Europe. The results were published in a report in 2010, and then subsequently in a book.[13] This report drew on interviews with surviving victims; women's-rights activists; police officers; and other officials, lawyers and imams.

KRG Amendments to Iraqi Personal-Status Law

The KRG parties proclaimed their liberal credentials, including a measure of secularity, to put some distance between themselves and the dominant Islamic parties, both Sunni and Shi'a, in Iraq's Arab provinces. These liberal credentials were also symbolic of their pro-Western stance and their proclaimed respect for human rights and the rule of law. Exploiting this stance, women's- and human-rights campaigns were mounted to amend the 1959 Iraqi Personal Status Code, which was still officially federal law in Iraq, to move in a direction more favourable to women. These demands were resisted and opposed by clerics and religious parties, including their female components, who stuck to arguments of the inviolability and fairness of Shari'a provisions.

A committee, including religious and secular advocates and women's-rights activists, was convened to discuss the matter and propose amendments. The amendments eventually passed represented a compromise. Other than Turkey, no Muslim-majority country had found it possible to entirely escape Shari'a provisions, as we have seen, and the KRG attempt was no exception. The amendments, however, included further liberalization of the Iraqi code of 1959. A crucial issue was polygyny.[14]

The Iraqi code placed restrictions on a man's entitlement to a second marriage, making it subject to a court permission and financial capability. The KRG amendment imposed further restrictions, which permitted a second marriage only in the case of the wife's illness precluding sexual contact or her inability to conceive, as attested by medical certification. It also required the permission of the first wife. Crucially, it recognized the provisions of a pre-nuptial contract in which a woman can preclude the husband's further marriage as well as gain the ability to initiate divorce. 'Disobedience', a matrimonial offence confined to the wife, was extended to either spouse. These amendments aroused much controversy in the KRG. Some liberal and women's organizations demanded total separation of the law from the Shari'a, whilst religious advocates declared departure from the Shari'a – especially on polygyny – to be illegitimate and socially destructive.

A question remains: how effective is legislation at the level of social practice and popular sentiment in the conservative and religious sectors of society? For instance, these restrictions on polygyny can be easily evaded by contracting second or further marriages in Iraqi locations outside the KRI; and those marriages are automatically recognized within the region.

On the question of honour killing, the Iraqi Legal Code of 1969 allowed for a reduction of penalties for perpetrators by labelling the offence as *ghasl al-'ar*, or the 'washing away of dishonour'. This loophole was reinforced by a 1990 proclamation from Saddam Hussein recognizing the legitimacy of family honour and morality – in line with the policy of tribalization and religious enforcements adopted at that time. In 2000, the PUK leadership issued an order abolishing these allowances for leniency; in 2002, this was endorsed by the KRG.

In 2011, the Kurdistan National Assembly passed further legislation, entitled the 'Combating Domestic Violence Law', which broadly defined violence to include forced and early marriage, deprivation of education and even non-consensual divorce.[15] These enactments, which were the results of campaigning by women's organizations and activists, were nonetheless resisted from conservative and religious quarters.

Some women activists have expressed scepticism about the effectiveness of this legislation in actual practice, and consider it a public-relations effort aimed at Western audiences to demonstrate the moderation and liberalism of the KRG as distinct from the religious conservatism of Arab Iraq. Given widespread conservative and religious sentiment, it would seem that the Region's police and judiciary are often lax in their interpretation and action. Further, there is a provision in the KRI for tribal tribunals, *solhiashayeri*, allowing tribal and religious dignitaries to settle disputes according to custom – thus bypassing state law. Family affairs, including 'honour', can fall within this jurisdiction.

Violence Against Women

A recent study by Mariwan Kanie[16] critically claims that violence against women falls into different categories, of which killing for honour or any other reason is only one kind. Suicide and death by burning, accidental or suicidal, are the other two. Both suicide and accidental burning are ambiguous and may hide deliberate killing. In supposed accidental burning, for instance, it is suspicious when the fire is confined to one particular victim and causes no other injury or damage.

The numbers of victims, collected from official sources in the three KRG provinces of Erbil, Sulaimaniya and Dohuk (2010–13) are as follows: Total – 1,675 women; 155 suicide; 464 self-burned; 159 murdered; 897 burned by accident. The majority of victims were in the age range of 13–35 years and were urban residents, married and with educational qualifications. Kanie's work follows a comprehensive study by Minoo Alinia, who quotes figures for earlier years: 1991–2002 saw 446 women killed and 155 suicides. In 2011 alone, there were 76 murder or suicide cases and some 330 cases of self-immolation.[17] As we saw, 2000/2002 was when the change in the penal law abolished the leniency of the Iraqi code for honour crime – yet the change has not made much difference to the number of incidents.

Explanations and Analyses

The first line of explanation is the characterization of large sectors of Kurdish society as conservative, patriarchal, religious and tribal, whereby women's sexuality is tightly controlled and policed and where infringements of these controls are considered injurious to family and tribal honour as well as to the masculinity of its men.

These factors are enhanced by events in the region's recent history, including wars, massacres and displacements in Iraqi Kurdistan, which was subject to Ba'athi depredations – notably the Anfal campaign and the Halbja chemical bombing – drawing an armed resistance from the Kurdish peshmerga forces. Alinia dwells on the lasting consequences of these catastrophes and resistances for social relations, attitudes and sentiments.

Militarization and heightened nationalism foster a cult of masculinity and honour, tied up with defence of the homeland and the family. The displacement and oppression of women, including rape, after the massacre of the men during the Ba'athist campaigns heightens sentiments regarding women and their sexuality as tied up with national defence. Alinia identifies the formation of 'Peshmerga masculinity' with members being seen as guardians of honour and the patriarchal order.

However, these forms of social control and attitudes are now operating within an evolved society and polity, in which women have emerged into public space, the labour market, the professions, politics and social activism in women's organizations and non-governmental organizations (NGOs). The legislation reviewed in the foregoing is part of this process; the KRG Constitution grants women 30 per cent of parliamentary seats.

The tension that occurs between the prevalent patriarchal sentiment and control and the modern avenues of liberation generate problems and anxieties contributing to the violence and suicides. Kanie's analysis adds further dimensions; he argues, for instance, that the violence and disruption is not solely due to traditional patriarchy, religion, tribalism or militarized masculinities but that all these factors should be considered in the context of the transformations of society, the polity and the economy since the foundation of the KRG – especially after 2003. Honour killings, as well as suicide and self-immolation, are strongly related to the conflictual atmosphere of family life in the KRI and the crisis of power relations inside the family.

Family life in the Kurdistan Region is transforming rapidly. In many cases, especially those related to the excessive use of violence, the family has lost its integrative functions. New forms of subjectivity are developing that need new forms of family life. Therefore, family life in the KRI should be studied in relation to its internal crisis and gradual loss of power, rather than viewing it in its stable and dominant, patriarchal form.[18]

Rapid economic development and the rise of business elites, which overlap with the political class and leading families; widespread corruption in politics and business; gross inequalities in wealth and power; and limited opportunities of employment for youth have all contributed to the emergence of new tensions, frustrations, and subjectivities. While *Peshmerga* heroism and masculinity is celebrated, the realities of privilege and dominance promote a business masculinity of money, corruption and control. Violence is part of this system of dominance and the suppression of dissent.

Two related developments in recent decades are the emergence of a consumer economy and culture and the sexualisation of public space. These changes affect forms of subjectivity and aspiration, especially those of youth and women, and subvert patriarchal order and control. This fear of loss of control on the part of the patriarchal order, and the family tensions and crises thus produced, is fundamental to the explanation of heightened violence, killings and the more numerically important suicides and burnings.

Kanie points to the rapid economic development of the KRI since 2003 – its emergence as 'the other Iraq', boasting a modern, liberal, dynamic economy with investments and imports from Turkey, China and Europe, and the spaces and culture of shopping malls and diverse public venues for the consumption of food, drink and entertainment. The resulting gross inequalities of wealth and status are made visible in the patterns of consumption, generating tensions and the frustrations of disappointed aspirations – especially for the youth. The consumer culture generates a preoccupation with the self, an individualization that clashes with the communalist ethos and controls of familial and patriarchal culture; this generates further conflicts and personal dilemmas. Women, especially young women, can now range in wider vistas of public space, in work and leisure, and especially the shopping malls – open to both men and women – thus facilitating possibilities of liaisons. These, in turn, are at odds with the patriarchal disciplines.

Consumerism is closely associated with a culture of sexualization, in consumer images themselves and also in the media and public discourses; this includes images, stories, advice columns and programmes on bodies, love and the erotic as well as religious preaching on the licit and the illicit. A sex industry has emerged of prostitution and exploitation, related to money, power and criminal conduct. This sexualization of public space and culture further feeds into the social and psychological disorientation and 'anomie' of aspirations and realities. Kanie concludes,

> A new social and gendered imaginary is emerging in the Kurdistan region, which has [a] difficult relationship with long-standing traditions, familial and communal ties. The codes of conduct that are internalized and routinely followed are now questioned. The social ties that bind different individuals and groups in the region, such as kinship, shared location, religion and nationalism, are undergoing significant changes. Familial ties and identities, religious teaching and institutions, political parties and organization[s] are no longer [a] safe haven for these individuals. Instead, they have become conflictual and contesting social spaces in which preserving the dominant power relations invokes violence.[19]

Violence against women, honour killings, suicides and burning are not just the products of patriarchal culture, tribalism and religion; there are also challenges to these traditions from socio-economic and cultural changes, leading to the increased presence of women in public space and the offering of opportunities.

These developments represent challenges to patriarchy and the violence associated with a fear of loss of control. In addition, they create dilemmas and tensions for individuals, which partly explains incidences of self-harm and suicide. Clearly, these issues are not peculiar to Kurdistan but common to many current situations in the Middle East and elsewhere. But the recent history of wars, persecution and militarization in the KRI heightens the readiness to resort to, and the availability of the means of, violence. Fuelling this trend is the persistence or renewal of tribal formations and authorities with a strong sense of 'honour', and intertwining political and Peshmerga powers.

The KRG and the political class try to present an image to the world of a liberal and secular government, in contrast to the religious authoritarianism of the rest of Iraq and the region. Women's- and human-rights organizations and campaigns are prominent and effective in public life; they press for reforms and publicize infractions. At the same time, the political classes, as well as the related military and police, are involved in complex power relations, patronage and tribal kinships, and communal and religious networks – all of which grant immunity from the law for powerful persons and groups.

To conclude, the Kurdish regions share in the diversity of other Middle Eastern societies with respect to issues of gender, women, patriarchy and reform. They are diverse by elements of region, class, politics and religiosity. Educated middle-class urbanites clash with communal authoritarianism, patriarchy and religious conservatism. The disciplines and controls exerted by these latter groups restrict and oppress women and jealously guard their sexuality and choice – to the extent of violence and murder. The tension between these cultures and modern socio-economic and cultural pressures towards individualization, consumerism and sexual opportunity creates psychological disorientation and social tensions for individuals. In the case of KRI, this leads to honour killings and female suicide.

In the case of Turkey, we saw how the secularism of the Republic and the liberation of women in law and politics represented the classic case of 'state feminism', which was effectively rejected and resisted by reluctant social sectors imbued with patriarchal religious conservatism. The Kurds share in those social contrasts, which fall between modern, liberal and leftist activists and the bulk of the conservative population. Today, under pro-Islamic AKP dominance, Kemalist secularism, including its gender regimes, are under attack – especially from the strident authoritarianism of President Erdoğan. Many sectors of Kurdish society share in this religious reaction.

The vanguards of the national struggle in all Kurdish regions trumpet their support for gender equality and rights. In the cases of the Turkish PPK and the Syrian PYD, they put this advocacy into practice in their ranks. The KRG, in Iraq, is keen to emphasize its support for equality and rights in contrast to the religious rule in other parts of the country.

These proclamations and actions, however, are often at odds with underlying social pressures and sentiments defending patriarchal controls against the transformations of modernity. Let us hope that these pressures, and the women's- and human-rights campaigns, will bring about the necessary changes in cultures, attitudes and practices.

References

Afary, Janet, *Sexual Politics in Modern Iran* (Cambridge: Cambridge University Press, 2009).
Al-Ali, Nadje, *Iraqi Women: Untold stories from 1948 to the present* (London: Zed Books, 2007).
——— *Sexual Violence in Iraq: Challenges for Transnational Feminist Politics* (forthcoming).
Alinia, Minoo, *Honour and Violence Against Women in Iraqi Kurdistan* (Basingstoke, Hampshire: Palgrave Macmillan, 2013).
Altinay, Aysha Gul and Yesim Arat, *Violence Against Women in Turkey* (Istanbul: Punto Press).
Baron, Beth, *The Women's Awakening in Egypt: Culture, Society and the Press* (New Haven, CT: Yale University Press, 1994).
Begikhani, Nazand, Aisha Gill and Gill Hague, *Honour-based Violence: experiences and counter-strategies in Iraqi Kurdistan and the UK Kurdish diaspora* (Farnham, Surrey: Ashgate, 2015).
Begikhani, Nazand, Aisha Gill, Gill Hague and Kawthat Ibraheem, 'Honour-based Violence and Honour-based Killings in Iraqi Kurdistan and in the Kurdish Diaspora in the UK', report for the Universities of Bristol and Roehampton, and Kurdish Women's Rights Watch, 2010. See www.bristol.ac.uk/media-library/sites/sps/documents/honbasedviolenceenglish.pdf.
Daloglu, Tulin, 'Turkish Children Steered Toward Religious Education', *al-Monitor*, 19 August 2013. Available at www.al-monitor.com/pulse/originals/2013/08/turkey-children-steered-religious-education.html.
Finkel, Andrew, 'What's 4+4 + 4?' *New York Times*, 23 March 2012. Available at latitude.blogs.nytimes.com/2012/03/23/turkeys-education-reform-bill-is-about-playing-politics-with-pedagogy.
Ghanim, David, *Iraq's Dysfunctional Democracy* (Santa Barbara, CA: Praeger, 2011).
Kali, Haje, 'Limiting Polygyny in Iraqi Kurdistan', MA dissertation, University of Oslo, 2011. Available at www.duo.uio.no/bitstream/handle/10852/23917/Keli_Master.pdf?sequence=1.

Kandiyoti, Deniz, 'Islam, Nationalism and Women in Turkey', in Deniz Kandiyoti (ed.), *Women, Islam and the State* (Philadelphia, PA: Temple University Press, 1991), pp. 22–47.

——— 'The travails of the secular: puzzle and paradox in Turkey', *Economy and Society* vol. 41, no. 4 (2012), pp. 513–31.

Kandiyoti, Deniz (ed.), *Women, Islam and the State* (Philadelphia, PA: Temple University Press, 1991).

Kanie, Mariwan, *Rethinking Roots of Rising Violence against Women in KRI* (The Hague: HIVOS, 2015).

Kaptan, Ö., 'A Decade of Violence against Women in Turkey', Research Turkey (Centre for Policy and Research on Turkey), vol. IV, issue 9 (2015), pp. 31–45. Available at http://researchturkey.org/9742.

Keddie, Nikki R., *Women in the Middle East: Past and Present* (Princeton, NJ: Princeton University Press, 2007).

Shafak, Elif, *Honour* (London: Penguin Books, 2012).

Tripp, Charles, *A History of Iraq* (Cambridge: Cambridge University Press, (2007).

Zubaida, Sami, *Law and Power in the Islamic World* (London: I.B.Tauris, 2003).

——— 'Women, Dictatorship and Democracy in the Context of the Arab Uprisings', in Fawaz Gerges (ed.), *The New Middle East: Protest and Revolution in the Arab World* (Cambridge: Cambridge University Press, 2014), pp. 209–22.

Notes

1. Sami Zubaida, *Law and Power in the Islamic World* (London: I.B.Tauris, 2003), pp. 144–57, 171–3, 205–7; Sami Zubaida, 'Women, Dictatorship and Democracy in the Context of the Arab Uprisings', in Fawaz Gerges (ed.), *The New Middle East: Protest and Revolution in the Arab World* (Cambridge: Cambridge University Press, 2014), pp. 209–25.
2. A survey of reformist advocacy in the various countries can be found in Nikki R. Keddie, *Women in the Middle East: Past and Present* (Princeton, NJ: Princeton University Press, 2007), pp. 75–101.
3. For discussions and examples of these issues, see ibid.; Beth Baron, *The Women's Awakening in Egypt: Culture, Society and the Press* (New Haven, CT: Yale University Press, 1994); Janet Afary, *Sexual Politics in Modern Iran* (Cambridge: Cambridge University Press, 2009); and Deniz Kandiyoti (ed.), *Women, Islam and the State* (Philadelphia, PA: Temple University Press, 1991).
4. I am not including Iran in this discussion; many of the issues raised here also apply to Iranian Kurdistan, but there are the added dimensions of the Islamic Republic and a distinct history.
5. Deniz Kandiyoti, 'The travails of the secular: puzzle and paradox in Turkey', *Economy and Society* vol. 41, no. 4 (2012), pp. 513–31; Deniz Kandiyoti, 'Islam, Nationalism and Women in Turkey', in Kandiyoti *Women, Islam and the State*, pp. 22–47.
6. Andrew Finkel, 'What's 4+4 + 4?' *New York Times*, 23 March 2012, available at latitude.blogs.nytimes.com/2012/03/23/turkeys-education-reform-bill-is-about-playing-politics-with-pedagogy; Tulin Daloglu, 'Turkish Children

Steered Toward Religious Education', *al-Monitor*, 19 August 2013, available at www.al-monitor.com/pulse/originals/2013/08/turkey-children-steered-religious-education.html (both accessed February 2018).
7. Elif Shafak, *Honour* (London: Penguin Books, 2012).
8. Ayse Gul Altinay and Yesim Arat, *Violence Against Women in Turkey* (Istanbul: Punto Press, 2009); Ö. Kaptan, 'A Decade of Violence against Women in Turkey', *Research Turkey* (Centre for Policy and Research on Turkey), vol. IV, issue 9 (2015), pp. 31–45. Available at http://researchturkey.org/9742.
9. For a historical account of the Qassim regime then the Ba'ath, see Charles Tripp, *A History of Iraq* (Cambridge: Cambridge University Press, 2007), pp. 143–85; 197–202. Nadje Al-Ali, *Iraqi Women: Untold stories from 1948 to the present* (London and New York: Zed Books, 2007) gives vivid accounts of these events as experienced by informants: pp. 56–108 (on the Qassim regime), pp. 109–46 (on the Ba'ath).
10. David Ghanim, *Iraq's Dysfunctional Democracy* (Santa Barbara, CA: Praeger, 2011), pp. 40–9.
11. Nadje Al-Ali (forthcoming), *Sexual Violence in Iraq: Challenges for Transnational Feminist Politics*.
12. Minoo Alinia, *Honour and Violence Against Women in Iraqi Kurdstan* (Basingstoke, Hampshire: Palgrave Macmillan, 2013), p. 1.
13. Nazand Begikahani, Aisha Gill, Gill Hague and Kawthat Ibraheem, 'Honour-based Violence and Honour-based Killings in Iraqi Kurdistan and in the Kurdish Diaspora in the UK', report for the Universities of Bristol and Roehampton, and Kurdish Women's Rights Watch, 2010. See www.bristol.ac.uk/media-library/sites/sps/documents/honbasedviolenceenglish.pdf (accessed February 2018).

    Nazand Begikhani, Aisha Gill and Gill Hague, *Honour-based Violence: experiences and counter-strategies in Iraqi Kurdistan and the UK Kurdish diaspora* (Farnham, Surrey: Ashgate, 2015).
14. Haje Kali, 'Limiting Polygyny in Iraqi Kurdistan', MA dissertation, University of Oslo, 2011. Available at www.duo.uio.no/bitstream/handle/10852/23917/Keli_Master.pdf?sequence=1 (accessed February 2018).
15. Begikhani *et al.*, *Honour-based Violence*, pp. 110–14.
16. Mariwan Kanie, *Rethinking Roots of Rising Violence against Women in KRI* (The Hague: HIVOS, 2015).
17. Alinia, *Honour Violence Against Women*, p. 80.
18. Kanie, *Rethinking Roots of Rising Violence*, pp. 11–12.
19. Ibid., p. 24.

PART III

REFLECTIONS ON THE HISTORIOGRAPHY OF THE KURDS

CHAPTER 9

A CRITICAL OVERVIEW OF EARLY BRITISH KURDISH STUDIES

Michael Gunter

Introduction

The purpose of this chapter is to present a critical overview of how, when and who initiated Kurdish studies in the Anglo-Saxon tradition during the twentieth century. However, it should be noted that earlier work in this genre had also appeared in the nineteenth century. For example, in this magisterial study of the Kurds,[1] C.J. (Cecil John) Edmonds identified 'seventeen British travelers' (among others) who had published accounts of their journeys through Kurdistan. Claudius James Rich[2] and Major-General H.C. (Henry Creswicke) Rawlinson[3] were two in particular whose work stood out. Rich was the East India Company's Resident in Baghdad. He left that city in April 1820 to travel through Kurdistan, not returning until the following March. According to Edmonds, 'Rich was well read in classics, an indefatigable explorer and a keen observer. His *Narrative* is a mine of information on the geography, history and antiquities of all the country through which he passed.'[4] Rawlinson — a British East India Company army officer, later a politician and sometimes called 'the Father of Assyriology' — wrote about his experiences traveling through Kurdistan in 1844. According to Edmonds, Rawlinson's famous article 'gives a detailed and learned description of the geography and people of the whole Zuhab region'.[5]

The Wigrams

During my trip through Iraqi Kurdistan in August 1993, I was told, in reply to one of my numerous questions about the country and its inhabitants, to read the Wigrams' *Cradle of Mankind*.[6] Like most students of Kurdish studies, I had heard of this classic but never read it. Thus, my curiosity was aroused and I acquired a copy upon my return; despite its occasional references to obscure events in Scottish history, I was amply rewarded. More than a century after it was first written, extensive citations from *Cradle of Mankind* constitute a fascinating and innovative introduction to this chapter.

Written by a British Christian missionary and his brother who lived in and travelled through Kurdistan for ten years during the first decade of the twentieth century, *Cradle of Mankind* is a treasure trove of insights and stories despite the inherent Orientalist biases that its authors inevitably possessed. And its subtitle, *Life in Eastern Kurdistan*, notwithstanding, it was written as a paean to the Christian Assyrians who were ultimately decimated by the Muslims during World War I. Nonetheless, the Wigrams' study has every bit as much to say about the Kurds.

In the preface to the first edition, published in 1914, the Wigrams explained the title of their book: 'the country [. . .] is the very *fons et origo* of our Indo-European ancestors. Its traditions connect it with the Garden of Eden, with Noah, and with Abraham' (p. vii). The second edition was published in 1922, and simply added two new chapters 'to bring the story of the Assyrian nation up to date' (p. vi). One of them was pathetically entitled 'Our Smallest Ally'.

Early in their narrative, the Wigrams noted, 'one of the first impressions which besets a traveler in these parts is the reality of the curse of Babel' (p. 10). They counted 'at least six' important languages:

> Arabic is dominant on the plains; Syriac and Kurdish in the mountains; Armenian on the plateaus to the northward; and Greek in western Asia Minor. Turkish, except in Anatolia, is only the official language [. . .] Naturally each of these main stems branches off into dialects by the score. (p. 10)

They also noted that

> [t]he nationalities are as diverse as the languages, and are interwoven together in the most bewildering entanglement [...] None of the component races can be trusted to govern the rest, and [...] all are so inextricably intermingled that it is impossible to parcel them out into distinct homogeneous States. (p. 11)

Thus, although the Kurds 'are a very ancient people' (p. 39n), they 'have no national cohesion' (p. 35) and 'a "United Kurdistan" is a [...] Utopian conception' (p. 37).

The Wigrams journeyed through Kurdistan during the final years of the Ottoman Empire, observing that 'the Turk has the misfortune to be an anachronism in power. His present methods were those of every European Government some five hundred years ago; but European consciences have developed in the interval, and his has not' (p. 260). Everywhere they saw 'that cancer of Ottoman rule – the chronic corruption of the Administration' (p. 38).

Yet even here there was a rationale: 'What is an official to do, whose salary, is in the first place, wholly inadequate; and in the second, not paid?' (p. 77). 'Reform is anathema to the Turk, for he knows (even if he cannot put the matter into words) that reform means subjection of the Turk to the *rayat* [Christian subjects]' (p. 244). And even the reforms that were attempted fell short because 'the Turk is quite satisfied as soon as he gets veneered' (p. 2).

The Kurds themselves were 'uneducated [...] a term of much greater opprobrium than seems quite reasonable in a country where not one man in a hundred is able to read or write' (p. 40). The Wigrams then compared the Kurds to various nefarious Scottish outlaws of the past and concluded that 'the kindly gallows' would make the State 'more gracious' (p. 40), 'for if there is one chance in twenty of trouble ensuing, the Kurd does not raid' (p. 316). When the Jewish serf of one Kurdish *agha* (tribal chieftain or feudal landlord) was robbed by a rival *agha*, for example, the wronged *agha* 'had a brilliant inspiration [...] "I'll go and rob his Jew myself!" That being the way the Kurdish mind works' (p. 318). It was 'less risky [...] to raid your opponents' unarmed Christian villages, than his armed Kurdish ones' (p. 318) (Judaism and

Christianity were linked in the Kurdish mind.) Elsewhere, however, the Kurds were referred to as 'good respectable brigands' (p. 321) who had 'a sport-loving soul' (p. 229). Further unfavourable Kurdish attributes included 'their usual insolent confidence' (p. 223) and 'a certain ruffian swagger [that] is the truest hall-mark of a Kurd' (p. 113). Salahudin was 'the only Kurd whom history is able to mention with esteem' (p. 233).

One of the Wigrams' attempts at humour recorded

> the saying that every Moslem, to be happy, requires at least four wives. A Persian because of her wit, and a Circassian because of her beauty; an Armenian to do the cookery and housework, and a Kurdish woman to thrash, as a wholesome example to the other three. (p. 211n)

The Kurds also had a reputation for toughness and hardiness: 'The writer has known an instance of a Kurd, who was shot through the body in a tribal skirmish; after which he walked home, and observed to his wife, "Beastly nuisance this: here is a brand-new shirt, and two holes in it; and it will want washing too!"' (p. 169). A Syrian told the authors, 'it is very difficult to poison a Kurd at all' (p. 174). This observation was made in elaboration upon the claim that for a medicine to have any effect it was necessary to 'give three times the "book dose" to an Assyrian, and five times the amount to a Kurd; for then you may produce some sort of effect' (p. 173).

Some individual Kurds, however, came out better in the Wigrams' estimation, such as Shaykh Abdul Salam II of Barzan ($c.$1882–$c.$1915), who was the older brother of the legendary Mullah Mustafa Barzani (1903–79) and an uncle of Masoud Barzani, the president of the Kurdistan Region of Iraq (KRI) (born 1946). Another example was Abdul Salam II, who was only in his twenties when the Wigrams met him around 1910:

> Like most mountaineers he is of medium height, with a slight and active figure and a grave but pleasant face [...] By his own immediate followers his commands are obeyed instantly and without question; and we have not the least doubt that had he ordered us to be shot, instead of entertaining us graciously, the

sentence would have been executed unhesitatingly, Europeans though we were. (p. 143)

Unfortunately, the Turks executed Abdul Salam II during World War I for reputedly dealing with the Russian enemy. 'He had been enticed down to Mosul by the Vali Haidar Beg and there secretly put to death' (p. 369), in the spring of 1915.

The Wigrams used such descriptions for the shaykh as 'merciful overlord' (p. 138) and 'tolerant' (p. 369), noting that he was also called '"the Shaykh of the Christians," because he treats his Christian vassals so well' (p. 153). They also pointed out that the shaykh 'reaped the fruit of his good treatment of his villagers, for not a man, Christian or Moslem, ever dreamt of betraying him to his foes' (p. 139). He was 'not only one of the most powerful but one of the most respectable of the mountain chieftains' (p. 136).

Unfortunately for subsequent Barzani–Christian relations, some of the earliest fighting between the Barzanis and the new Iraqi Government established from the ruins of the Ottoman Empire after World War I occurred in the early 1930s when the government tried to settle some Assyrians on hereditary Barzani land. The main theme of the Wigrams concerned the often desperate struggles of the Christian Assyrian minority against their then-inveterate Kurdish foes.

In one place, for example, the authors compared the Assyrian Patriarch to the legendary Prester John: 'while a very good imitation of the harpies that tormented Prester John are found in the Kurds that ravage the land' (p. 262). Indeed, most, but not all, of the Christian villagers were 'little better than serfs to the Kurds near whom they live' (p. 265).

The famous Bedir Khan Beg (c.1800–68), often mentioned as a precursor of modern Kurdish nationalists by other scholars,[7] 'attacked these Christian tribes in 1845 – and perpetrated a massacre so appalling that the years are dated from it to this day' (p. 279). Ismail Simko Agha, another noted Kurdish nationalist of the early twentieth century, treacherously murdered his guest, the Assyrian leader Mar Shimun, at the end of World War I.

Foreign residents referred to the process of Kurds quartering themselves in Christian villages and gradually expropriating them as 'the hermit crab Act' (p. 177). 'If ever one sees a Kurdish village which has good fields, and signs of good cultivation, one can be sure that it was originally Christian, and that it has gone through this process' (p. 178). In this regard, the Wigrams related 'a weird belief but [one . . .] fully accepted on all hands' that a Kurd 'does not himself expect to sleep quiet in his grave unless some Christian places a rag on it in token of forgiveness' (p. 319).

Although seasoned travellers, the Wigrams owned to having 'some misgiving' when entering 'those formidable mountains where [one] has been promised enlightenment as to what "real rough travelling" means' (p. 134). 'Nothing that runs upon wheels can enter the Kurdistan highlands. And the "heir of all the ages," travelling there in A.D. 1900, finds himself no better off than his forerunners of B.C. 1100, whose amazed Great King recorded on slabs of imperishable granite the fact that "I, Tiglath-Pileser, was obliged to go on foot!"' (p. 111).

The Wigrams' conversation with Shaykh Abdul Salam II was through an interpreter. He 'bewailed the universal lawlessness, which, he said [. . .] was as bad for Kurds as for Christians. "You have gone to India," he protested, "and you stay there, though you are not wanted. Why cannot you come to us who do want you? You would be welcomed everywhere here"' (p. 145). Today, similarly, the Kurds would welcome the protection a strong Western (i.e., US) presence. Before departing, the Shaykh of Barzan also consulted the Wigrams about his suffering eyes, a general malady common in those parts due to 'dust and want of cleanliness, and aggravated by persistent neglect' (p. 146n). In this particular case, however, the patient turned out to be suffering from trachoma.

In sharp contrast to the Shaykh of Barzan, the wandering Heriki Kurds resembled a 'horde of human locusts' (p. 127) who 'were regarded much in the light of an annual migration of wolves by all the villages on the road' (p. 159): 'It is not a good thing for a village to lie in the track of the Heriki, for everything that is not too hot or too heavy they annex and carry away' (p. 127). Ironically, 'those *hastes* [sic] *humani generis* the Heriki Kurds' (p. 149), 'if legend tells true [. . .] were Christians once' (p. 162). According to the 'old Nestorian priests', the Herikis still carried the head of 'one of the several saints George of Eastern legend. This is the palladium of their tribe, and is borne about in a chest' (p. 163).

A Critical Overview of Early British Kurdish Studies 211

Illustrating the lack of an adequate work ethic, the Wigrams told a story about their inability to get a pair of boots repaired in Akra over a period of three days:

> Friday (it was explained) had been the Mohammedan Sabbath, and Saturday the Jewish, and Sunday the Christian; and no doubt a Bank Holiday on Monday was only averted by the fact of the boots being prematurely reclaimed. Tuesday, it may be added, is esteemed inauspicious by Christians, because on that day Judas Iscariot made his covenant with the chief priests. Wednesday is the Yezidi Sabbath. (p. 133)

The Wigrams incorrectly considered the Yezidis[8] not to be Kurds and claimed that '"Devil worshippers" they are indeed' (p. 88). They referred to the Yezidi temple at Shaykh Adi as the 'unhallowed Hoodoo House' (p. 106) and 'this Domdaniel of Sorcery' (p. 97). Today, of course, most scholars consider the Yezidis to be Kurds who still follow an ancient and indigenous, pre-Islamic Kurdish religion. To their credit, the Wigrams did note that the Yezidis had 'a religion of Faith, and not of Works. They are under no obligation to make evil their good' (p. 88). Additional observations regarding ancient Kurdish religions[9] concerned 'that oldest faith of the land, the aboriginal tree-worship, [which] still lingers in the villages; and indeed is only despised by the townsfolk when the foreigner is within hearing [...] A rag from the garments of any sufferer from any disease has only to be tied on to one of its branches to secure relief infallibly' (p. 205).

Mark Sykes

The famous Mark Sykes, of the Sykes–Picot Agreement of 1916 that created many of the artificial state borders of today's Middle East while denying the Kurds a state, was one of the early British political officers (intelligence agents) who, to a large extent, constituted the first set of writers on the Kurdish issue in the twentieth century.[10] For the most part, these officers were tasked with surveying Kurdish tribes and land at the end of the Ottoman Empire. They were brave and adventurous men who, for the most part, gave us a variety of strikingly detailed accounts of the Kurds. Sykes authored the lengthy – despite the misleading word 'short' in its subtitle – *Caliphs' Last Heritage*.[11] The first half of this tome is an overview of the political geography of the Middle East, while the second half is an account of Sykes' travels in Asia Minor and the Middle East between 1906 and 1913. According to Edmonds,

> Sykes was interested in Ottoman administration and collected much tribal information which, elementary and incomplete as it may now seem, was for many parts of Kurdistan an important source of our knowledge when Turkey entered the war in 1915. His highly developed sense of the ridiculous adds spice to the narrative of what was then a useful piece of exploration.[12]

Sykes wrote rather simplistically, 'with regard to the Kurds I think they may be divided into three classes. Class I [...] who are the semi-nomads of the plains and southern hills; Class II [...] who are the sedentary mountain tribes; [and] Class III, the semi-nomadic mountaineers comprising the remainder of the tribes' (p. 555). He found that the Kurdish tribes in Class I were 'mentally [...] far superior to the majority of Kurds, being apt to education, astute men of business and very industrious' (ibid.). Those in Class II 'are industrious agriculturists [...] They live under the rule of tribal chiefs and [...] are constantly at war with one another' (p. 556). The Kurds in Class III 'are of thievish disposition, bloodthirsty, cowardly, and often cruel. Their women are ugly and hard worked' (ibid.). Sykes devoted many subsequent pages to enumerating various Kurdish tribes, noting, 'years and years ago the Kurds were divided into two branches, the Milan and Zilan' (p. 574). He added, 'the legend to me is extremely interesting, but the way in which Milan Kurds would suddenly grow vague or change the subject while relating fragments of it was more than maddening. The reader would be surprised if he knew the months of toil I endured in collecting the above small paragraph' (p. 575).

Sykes and his associates on the de Bunsen Committee, advising the cabinet on Middle Eastern affairs during World War I, revived ancient Greek and Roman names for the region, including Syria, Palestine, Iraq and Mesopotamia. He also designed the Arab-revolt flag, which was a combination of green, red, black and white. The contemporary flags of Jordan, Iraq, Syria, Egypt, Sudan, Kuwait, Yemen, the United Arab Emirates and the Palestine Liberation Organization all use variations of this theme. Sykes died suddenly of the Spanish flu during the peace negotiations in 1919. Eighty-eight years later, his body was exhumed for samples of the virus to be used in research.

C.J. Edmonds

In the preface to his rightfully famous and lengthy study *Kurds, Turks and Arabs*,[13] Edmonds told his readers that 'the framework of this book is the diplomatic history of the Mosul dispute between Great Britain and Turkey, enriched (in the architectural sense of the word) with an account of my own experiences as a Political Officer in the contested territory' (p. xi). His 457-page analysis then proceeded to provide detailed and sophisticated insights into the geographical, political, social, demographic and linguistic conditions then prevalent in Kurdistan. It also presented fascinating photographs and valuable maps.

For example, Edmonds pointed out that 'in Kurdistan a distinction is drawn between villagers who claim tribal origin and those who do not. In Mosul and Arbil non-tribal villagers are called Kirmanj' (p. 12), but they are called Misken and sometimes even Gorran in other parts of Kurdistan. Misken is a more appropriate term because the other two words also confusingly refer to different Kurdish dialects. 'Such Misken are sometimes almost serfs of the owner of the village and are supposed to submit meekly to the oppression of their tribal neighbours' (ibid). Although 'in the villages Kurdish women probably have as bad a time as any of their neighbours in the Middle East, being saddled with much of the drudgery', Edmonds also perceptively noted, 'it is quite common for strong-minded women to come forward and play an important part in tribal politics' (p. 14).

With his 'learned Kurdish friend' (p. xii), Taufiq Wahby, Edmonds also worked out a special Roman alphabet in Kurdish and compiled an early Kurdish–English dictionary, the first in a Western language since 1879.[14] Edmonds finally left Iraq in 1945 after serving as an adviser to the Ministry of the Interior for the preceding ten years. In 1951, he became a lecturer in Kurdish at the University of London. However, as late as 1957, Edmonds mentioned Mullah Mustafa Barzani only in passing as a 'fugitive rebel from Iraq'[15] and incorrectly concluded that 'with every year that passes any concerted armed revolt becomes more improbable'. Two years later, although now realizing that 'the event which perhaps more than any other has caught the popular imagination is the return of Mullah Mustafa',[16] he could only argue that 'it is difficult to explain this rapid build-up into a national all-Iraqi figure [...] otherwise than as the work of a well-organized chain of communist propagandists long established throughout Iraq'. Nevertheless, one could assert that Edmonds would be more than pleased with the Iraq Kurds' progress in the twenty-first century.

Other British Political Officers

A number of other British political officers served with distinction in Kurdistan during the 1920s and left useful accounts of their experiences. Major W.R. (William Rupert) Hay (1893–1962) served for two years in Erbil. Like those of his colleagues, Hay's book *Two Years in Kurdistan* (1921)[17] was as much political and anthropological as it was military. Thus, the first six chapters of his study discussed everything from flora and fauna to the structure of village life to the roles of women in society, tribes, agriculture and commerce. The next eight chapters segued into a biographical travelogue, as the author journeyed through Kurdistan. The last two chapters detailed an unsuccessful revolt among some Kurdish tribes against the British administration that Hay had helped to construct.

Major Edward W.C. Noel was the British political officer in Sulaimaniya in 1919. He supported the Kurds so strongly that he was disparagingly called the 'Second Lawrence' by some officials in the Colonial Office. As such, Noel worked for either an independent Kurdish state or some type of viable Kurdish autonomy – either one of which would have been under British control. He made extensive trips throughout Kurdistan during 1919, and played an important role in bringing Shaykh Mahmood Barzinji (1878–1956) to power in the area around Sulaimaniya. However, his efforts in what is now southeastern Turkey failed to win the support of his own government because of Shaykh Mahmood's refusal to cooperate with Britain and the Kemalist revival in Turkey. Indeed, the Turks suspected Noel of trying to incite the Kurds to attack the aborning Kemalist government. Noel wrote a 77-page report on his experiences among the Kurds,[18] and also participated in the famous Cairo conference on the future role of Great Britain in the Middle East held in March 1921.

Major Ely Bannister Soane (1881–1923) was a politically controversial writer and traveller who replaced Noel in 1919 and served as political officer until March 1921. Although he considered Shaykh Mahmood Barzinji a rogue, Soane was deeply committed to Kurdish autonomy and eventually lost his post as a result. After the Shaykh's first defeat in June 1919, Soane strictly administered the area but also initiated public-works projects and encouraged what was then considered the novel use of written Kurdish in newspapers and the schools. When the Cairo conference in March 1921 finally decided to abandon the idea of Kurdish autonomy, as part of an overall policy of maintaining British control as cheaply as possible, Soane was summarily dismissed.

By 1912, Soane had authored a 400-page book on southern Kurdistan based on his travels, which recorded what he had heard and seen – from ancient tribal enmities to modern customs, such as drinking in coffee houses.[19] The astute Edmonds wrote that 'Soane collected a mass of historical material regarding the country [...] His previous experience of the neighbouring districts of Persian Kurdistan, his knowledge of the languages, and the fact of his passing as a Muslim, combined to give the contemporary information he recorded a special authority.'[20]

Following the death of Soane's widow, Lynette Lindfield-Soane, in 1994, the Soane Trust for Kurdistan was established to promote projects dealing with Kurdistan. Sheri Laizer, who was a British/New Zealand author and friend of the Kurds, administered the trust. Lazier found Soane's book 'wonderful', and wrote that its pages 'abound in lively camaraderie, jokes at the expense of Ottoman officials and idle soldiers and intimate accounts of the author's days passed among Kurds and Persians dressed in their own guise, his fluency in their languages rarely creating suspicions as to his true English identity'.[21]

Lt Colonel Arnold Wilson (1884–1940) was yet another important political officer stationed in Iraq after World War I, who helped to determine the policies that eventually led to the incorporations of the Kurds of the Mosul *vilayet* (province) into Iraq. He based his policies on the belief that, given Britain's financial difficulties, Mesopotamia could be most economically defended from the Kurdish foothills. Following the failure to implement indirect British control through a pliant Shaykh Mahmood Barzinji, Sir Percy Cox, the British high commissioner, replaced Wilson in October 1920. Wilson wrote a detailed and valuable study of his experiences.[22]

Wallace Lyon (1892–1977) served in various capacities as a British administrator in Iraqi Kurdistan from 1918 until the end of 1944 – an exceptional length of time, which gave his memoirs a special value. He wrote them after retiring, but they remained for his son-in-law to edit and publish early in the twentieth-first century under a title that was 'a deliberate echo of the title of C.J. Edmonds's *Kurds, Turks and Arabs*'.[23] Although there already was a 'large literature [...] on the Kurds as an ethnic group and political problem' in the first quarter of the twentieth century, 'very little existed on how the British actually ran or manipulated the Kurdish region of northern Iraq during the period of the Mandate to 1932, or thereafter while Britain had extensive treaty rights there' (p. viii). It is here that the importance of Lyon's memoirs lie: they dealt with the problems of a mixed Arab, Turkish and Kurdish population, and especially with the feuds of the Kurdish shaykhs, which were complicated by Turkish irredentism and an open Persian frontier. The result filled a large gap in the history of Iraq's evolution, and threw considerable light on the origins of contemporary and subsequent Kurdish problems. The Lyon memoirs also contain a number of interesting photographs, including ones I had never seen before of a very young Mullah Mustafa Barzani on horseback in 1923 as well as another of the famous Lady Adila Khan in her later years. Lyon recorded that Barzani 'was one of those very few men who delight in battle for its own sake and, as he afterwards confessed to me, he would much rather shoot Arab soldiers than either ibex or chikoor [hill partridge]' (p. 190).

Although not a political officer, A.M. (Archibald Milne) Hamilton was a New Zealand engineer who built the strategic military highway that bears his name and still runs today from Erbil to the Iranian frontier. In October 2014, I travelled along much of the Hamilton Road when I journeyed from the modern new airport in the KRG capital, Erbil, to the newly created Soran University near the Iranian border to give the commencement address. No less an authority than the great Russian Kurdologist Vladimir Minorsky (1877–1966) wrote of Hamilton's book[24] about his construction and the travails involved that

> in this colourful and engaging account, Hamilton describes the four years he spent overcoming immense obstacles – disease,

ferocious brigands, warring tribes and bureaucratic officials – to carve a path through some of the most beautiful but inhospitable landscape in the world. Road through Kurdistan is an enthralling story, packed with adventure, of one man's determination in the face of adversity: a classic of travel writing. It is also an invaluable portrayal of the Iraqi Kurds themselves, and of the Kurdish regions of Northern Iraq [...] a book which conquers the reader by its freshness, warm sympathy to men and a keen gift for observation.[25]

The renowned Gertrude Bell (1868–1926) – an English writer, traveller, political officer, administrator, spy and archaeologist who explored, mapped and became highly influential in British imperial policy-making due to her knowledge and contacts developed through extensive travels in Syria, Mesopotamia, Asia Minor and Arabia – helped to establish the Hashemite dynasties in what is today Iraq as well as Jordan. However, less well-known were her penetrating insights into such Kurdish issues as anti-British unrest in the Amadiya and Zibari-Barzan areas, Kurdish attitudes towards the Russians, and insights regarding Shaykh Sayyid Taha II and Shaykh Mahmood Barzinji published in a British government document.[26]

Unfortunately, space does not permit mention of any other worthy authors in the Anglo-Saxon tradition who wrote in the early decades of the twentieth century.

Concluding Remarks

This chapter has sought to give an account of the 'how, when and who' of the initiation of Kurdish studies in the Anglo-Saxon tradition. As was made clear, the first set of writers on the Kurdish issue were largely British political officers tasked with surveying the Kurdish tribes and land at the end of the Ottoman Empire. Looking back on their work almost a century later, one is very impressed with its quality and quantity. This is due perhaps to their deep first-hand knowledge of the subject, often interpreted through the kind of prior, thorough academic study sometimes lacking in today's scholarship. In many ways, these earlier studies have not been equalled let alone surpassed by subsequent generations of researchers. Indeed, a review of the work of these British political officers would pay rich dividends to new scholars seeking to study and write about the Kurds.

However, it should be recalled that almost all of the first generation of authors were government employees and intelligence agents. Surely these connections influenced their research and insights, not only in favour of whom they were working for but also in ways that can only be partially imagined. This is not necessarily a negative fact. Indeed, it may well have grounded them better to reality than the succeeding generations of scholars, who came more often from the world of academia and thus might not have been as well versed in the real world as garnered from years of actual field experience. Of course, when exactly these second and succeeding generations of scholars emerged is a matter of interpretation.

Probably it would be best to view the first generation of political officers blending into the next generation rather than constructing a strict separation between them. In addition, these second and succeeding generations also had government and intelligence ties. It is doubtful that experts in Kurdish studies ever cut their ties completely with the interests of their government and its funding.

On the other hand, one must also quickly admit that so much has occurred in the past century – and, especially, in the past decade – that new work has become a prerequisite. Indeed, there has been an explosion of recent studies, some of them based on innovative political and sociological theories and frameworks, that have enabled us to open up new scholarly horizons.[27] *Kurdish Studies*, a new scholarly journal that has been published in English biannually since 2012, does not limit itself to political and historical work but covers all different fields of Kurdish studies and brings together a truly international board of editors. The Kurdish Network connects scholars of Kurdish studies almost instantaneously via the internet. Thus, modern scholarly communications suggest that the idea of an Anglo-Saxon tradition in Kurdish studies is no longer valid given the interconnections among Kurdish scholars today. Indeed, in trying to trace the Anglo-Saxon tradition in Kurdish studies into modern times, I was often faced with the quandary of how to consider writers who were not born in Britain or the United States but who had been educated there and were doing their work there.[28] Such scholars might be considered 'converts/accessions' to the Anglo-Saxon tradition. To a large extent, they have been subsumed by the Anglo-Saxon tradition while at the same time broadening it to include new ethnicities and scholarly traditions thriving in our modern, global, epistemic networks of scholarship.

Notes

1. C.J. Edmonds, *Kurds, Turks and Arabs. Politics, Travel and Research in North-Eastern Iraq 1919–1925* (London: Oxford University Press, 1957), pp. 22–8.
2. Claudius James Rich, *Narrative of a Residence in Koordistan*, 2 vols (London: James Duncan, 1836).
3. H.C. Rawlinson, 'Notes on a Journey from Tabriz, Through Persian Kurdistan, to the Ruins of Takhti-Soleiman', *Journal of the Royal Geographical Society* 10 (1841), pp. 1–158.
4. Edmonds, *Kurds, Turks and Arabs*, p. 23.
5. Ibid., p. 24.
6. Edgar T.A. and W.A. Wigram, *The Cradle of Mankind: Life in Eastern Kurdistan*, 2nd edition (London: A. & C. Black, 1922). The following citations from this source are indicated in the text in parentheses.
7. See, for example, David McDowall, *A Modern History of the Kurds* (London: I.B.Tauris, 1996), pp. 89–91. McDowall's book is arguably the single best history of the Kurds that exists in English. Bedir Khan's three grandsons – Sureya (1883–1938), Jaladet (1893–1951) and Kamuran (1895–1978) – were each noted figures in Kurdish literature and devoted to the Kurdish nationalist cause. Bedir Khan himself famously had anywhere from 40 to 90 sons!
8. On the Yezidis, see Nelida Fuccaro, *The Other Kurds: Yazidis in Colonial Iraq* (London: I.B.Tauris, 1999); and Khanna Omarkhali, 'Yezidism, the National Religion of the Kurds', PhD dissertation, St Petersburg State University, Russia, 2006, p. 1.
9. For an analysis of the pre-Islamic religions and their continuing residual influence in the land, see Mehrdad R. Izady, The Kurds: A Concise Handbook (Washington, DC: Crane Russak, 1992), pp. 131–66. Most scholars argue that Izady greatly exaggerates the historical role of the Kurds in general and in particular the number of those who still follow pre-Islamic religions.
10. Cahal Milmo, 'A Cure for Flu (from Beyond the Grave)', *Independent*, 16 September 2008. Available at www.independent.co.uk/a-cure-for-flu-from-beyond-the-grave-933046.html (accessed February 2018).
11. Mark Sykes, *The Caliphs' Last Heritage: A Short History of the Turkish Empire* (London: Macmillan and Co., 1915). The following citations from this source are indicated in the text in parentheses.
12. Edmonds, *Kurds, Turks and Arabs*, p. 25.
13. For the full citation to this work, see endnote 1. The following citations from this source are indicated in the text in parentheses. The Mosul *vilayet* of the

14. Taufiq Wahby and C.J. Edmonds, *A Kurdish-English Dictionary* (Oxford: Clarendon Press, 1966). For more recent dictionaries, see Shafiq Qazzaz, *The Sharezoor: Kurdish-English Dictionary* (Erbil, Kurdistan: Aras Press and Publishers, 2000); and, arguably the best yet, Michael L. Chyet, *Kurdish-English Dictionary/Ferhenga Kurmanci-Inglizi* (New Haven, CT: Yale University Press, 2003).
15. This and the following citation were taken from C.J. Edmonds, 'The Kurds of Iraq', *Middle East Journal* 11 (Winter 1957), p. 61.
16. This and the following citation were taken from C.J. Edmonds, 'The Kurds and the Revolution in Iraq', *Middle East Journal* 13 (Winter 1959), pp. 4 and 8.
17. W.R. Hay, *Two Years in Kurdistan: Experiences of a Political Officer, 1918–1920* (London: Sidgwick and Jackson, 1921). Ninety years later, Hay's book was edited and re-released by Paul Rich, (Lanham, MD: Lexington Books, 2008) – see the review by Michael Rubin in *Middle East Quarterly* (Winter 2011), available at www.meforum.org/2863/to-years-in-kurdistan (accessed February 2018).
18. 'Diary of Major Noel on Special Duty in Kurdistan, from June 14th to September 21st, 1919', and available in the archives of the Public Record Office, Kew, as FO 371/5068.
19. E.B. Soane, *To Mesopotamia and Kurdistan in Disguise. With Historical Notices of the Kurdish Tribes and the Chaldeans of Kurdistan*, 2nd edition (London: John Murray, 1926), reprinted as Ely Bannister, *To Mesopotamia and Kurdistan in Disguise* (New York: Cosimo, Inc., 2007) almost a century after it was first published in 1912.
20. Edmonds, *Kurds, Turks and Arabs*, p. 26.
21. Sheri Laizer, *Into Kurdistan: Frontiers under Fire* (London and NJ: Zed Books Ltd, 1991), p. 79.
22. Arnold T. Wilson, *Mesopotamia, 1917–1920; A Clash of Loyalties: A Personal and Historical Record* (London: Oxford University Press, 1931).
23. D.K. Fieldhouse, *Kurds, Arabs and Britons: The Memoir of Wallace Lyon in Iraq 1918–44* (London and New York: I.B.Tauris Publishers, 2002), p. vii. 'Political Adviser to the Forces in Northern Iraq (at this time "Paiforce")' was one of Lyon's titles. Ibid., p. 227. The following citations from this source are indicated in the text in parentheses.
24. A.M. Hamilton, *Road through Kurdistan: The Narrative of an Engineer in Iraq* (London: Faber & Faber, 1937).
25. Valdimir Minorsky, blurb cited in one of the editions of the Hamilton book on books.google.com/books?id=dRsBAwAAQBAJ&dq=A+M+Hamilton+Road+through+Kurdistan&source=gbs_navlinks_s (accessed February 2018). In any study of the Kurds, of course, the work of Martin van Bruinessen, *Agha, Shaikh and State: The Social and Political Structures of Kurdistan* (London: Zed Books Ltd, 1992); and Wadie Jwaideh, *The Kurdish National Movement: Its*

Origins and Development (Syracuse, NY: Syracuse University Press, 2006) – originally completed in 1959, and submitted as a PhD dissertation to Syracuse University in early 1960 – are still considered pre-eminent, although they are not literally in the Anglo-Saxon tradition.

26. Gertrude Lowthian Bell (Great Britain, Office of the Civil Commissioner, Iraq), *Review of the Civil Administration of Mesopotamia, 1914–1920* (London: H.M. Stationery Office, 1920).

27. For examples, in alphabetical order, of surnames, see Denise Natali, *The Kurds and the State: Evolving National Identity in Iraq, Turkey, and Iran* (Syracuse, NY: Syracuse University Press, 2005); Robert Olson, *The Goat and the Butcher: Nationalism and State Formation in Kurdistan-Iraq since the Iraqi War* (Costa Mesa, CA: Mazda Publishers, 2005); and David Romano, *The Kurdish Nationalist Movement: Opportunity, Mobilization and Identity* (Cambridge: Cambridge University Press, 2006) among many others.

28. See, for example, Amir Hassanpour, *Nationalism and Language in Kurdistan, 1918–1985* (San Francisco, CA: Mellen Research University Press, 1992); Hakan Ozoglu, *Kurdish Notables and the Ottoman State: Evolving Identities, Competing Loyalties, and Shifting Boundaries* (Albany, NY: University of New York Press, 2004); Cengiz Gunes, *The Kurdish National Movement in Turkey: From Protest to Resistance* (London and New York: Routledge, 2012); and Joost R. Hiltermann, *A Poisonous Affair: America, Iraq, and the Gassing of Halabja* (Cambridge: Cambridge University Press, 2007) among many others.

CHAPTER 10

KURDISH HISTORY – NOT A NEUTRAL PURSUIT

Janet Klein

At the very turn of the twentieth century, one interested Kurdish-Ottoman notable wrote in his Kurdish-Ottoman gazette,

> Despite the fact that Kurds possess special human qualities such as wit and mental acuity, courage and industriousness, are altruistic and sacrificing, and have a love for liberty as if they worshipped it, in world history their name is not frequently mentioned. And in a century in which civilization has reached its peak, other nations do not really know much about the general history of this noble people.[1]

While Abdurrahman Bedir Khan was lamenting the lack of attention paid to the Kurds, hindsight shows us that 'national' histories were certainly not the norm then, if they existed at all, although Kurds at this moment found themselves on the brink of a historical/national turn. But over a century later, Kurds still find themselves marginalized in mainstream works devoted to Middle Eastern history, during a moment when every 'noble people' has its own history. Exemplifying this denialist position, one twentieth-century Turkish scholar wrote, 'If I have to be frank, there is no such thing as Kurdish history.' It only consists of, he claimed, 'various stories that recount tribal events and actions'.[2]

Kurdish history does exist, of course — every bit as much as the histories of their neighbours (Turks, Armenians, Arabs etc.) do. However, I propose the question: to what extent are 'ethnic' histories helpful? They certainly are, for unacknowledged groups, but does 'a history of the Kurds' on its own do the Kurds justice in term of presenting Kurdish history in a nuanced light? This chapter will situation this question against historical developments and will explore how Kurds in the late-Ottoman period viewed Kurdish history in their ongoing exploration of Kurdish identity and Kurdish sociopolitical and geopolitical aspirations. I argue that Kurdish history must be seen as relational. It must also be seen as something that has developed for Kurdish writers and for others in dialogue with the histories of the Kurds' neighbours as each group has travelled down the path of identifying and expounding on distinct 'national' histories, and has worked to make cultural and political claims accordingly in the nineteenth century and beyond.

Kurds have truly emerged onto the global map in recent years due to the Kurdistan Regional Government's (KRG's) support of US-led efforts to topple Saddam Hussein and his regime, which earned them greater coverage in the mainstream press. Even more recently, the Kurdish forces in the Kurdistan Region of Iraq (KRI) and northeastern Syria (Rojava) have proved to be the most effective forces fighting Da'esh (Islamic State of Iraq and Syria, or 'ISIS'), with significant assistance from the PKK (Partîya Karkerên Kurdistan/Kurdistan Workers' Party — originally of Turkey, but now 'transnational'). But due to the fact that the Kurds do not have a nation state of 'their own',[3] their history — if, and when, it is presented in the mainstream media — tends to place them not in the leading role in their own history but as pawns or other agents juxtaposed against their 'Others' — neighbouring communities, dominant groups within the states in which they live or the states themselves.

Off the mainstream map, however, the pursuit of Kurdish history is thriving. This is a very recent development, but it speaks volumes about wider trends in Middle Eastern history and beyond; scholars are now ignoring their nation-state imperatives to study their *own* history, and are branching out to focus on neglected, suppressed, framed and denied histories. As a friend of mine recently put it, in the past decade or two, '[s]cholars [began to ask] different questions, studied the languages and the cultures their nation states suppressed, ignored, or had purposely forgotten, and changed how we think [about] modernity, nationalism, sectarianism and empire in the 19th and 20th century'.[4] What scholars in the past two decades have established is not only that Kurdish history is a valid, compelling and relevant topic but, more importantly, that it *exists*, even though Kurds do not have a state of 'their own'.

One key reason Kurdish history has been marginalized arises from this very point – because Kurds don't have a state of 'their own'. Most 'official' histories these days are about nation-state peoples. As Andreas Wimmer and Nina Glick Schiller point out, scholars have tended to naturalize, or take 'for granted that the boundaries of the nation-state delimit and define the unit of analysis', and they also engage in 'territorial limitation which confines the study of social processes to the political and geographic boundaries of a particular nation-state', thus 'forming a coherent epistemic structure, a self-reinforcing way of looking at and describing the social world'.[5] To the extent that Kurds are included in these histories, it is in relation to the dominant groups in their respective nation states (mainly Turkey, Iraq, Iran and Syria, with some attention also being paid to Kurdish groups in the diaspora in Europe and North America). But this situation is also part of Kurdish history. Indeed, it is part of the history not only of the Kurds, but of their neighbours.[6]

One guiding feature of many expressions of Kurdish history today is the fact that the Kurds represent a 'nation without a state'. This expression is *guiding* because it conditions the reader to think in a nation-state framework – to imagine that the Kurds somehow failed at the nation-state goal, and to see them only as minorities within the states in which they live. Calling the Kurds a 'nation without a state' may reflect their reality on one level but it also ignores their history. It assumes that the nation state is natural and dominant, and that those who have no nation state of their own are somehow less 'natural' communities. Yes, Kurds have been non-dominant groups in the states in which they live (with nuance), but no less 'natural' than the dominant identity (if there ever was one, in the case of the Ottoman Empire). There is a history behind this phenomenon.

Before the modern era, Kurds lived in regions that were divided between the Ottoman Empire and Iran. Until the middle of the nineteenth century, this was a frontier zone. Modern state-making processes began to transform it from a frontier zone to a borderland, and indeed, a *bordered* land.[7] While Kurds in the borderlands had certainly felt the need to choose one side or another centuries earlier when the Ottomans and Safavids were vying for the loyalty of the population of eastern Anatolia, things continued to change, and by the nineteenth century both the Kurds and the Ottoman state found themselves looking for new arrangements. Previously, on the Ottoman side, where most of the Kurdish population lived, in the region inhabited by Kurds (and also Armenians and other groups), Kurds were bound by an agreement with their notables by which local Kurdish chiefs and dynasts were granted significant autonomy by the Ottoman state. They were supposed to acknowledge the Ottoman sultan's sovereignty, to provide troops when needed, and sometimes to submit tribute – although the extent to which any of these happened varied from one tribe/dynasty to another, and from one period to another.[8]

While tribal identification was strong during this period, Kurdish producers (nomadic producers of livestock and their products – things like butter, wool, meat and rugs) and Kurdish agriculturalists continued to identify with their more immediate overlords, who tended to be Kurdish *beys* and *aghas*. As such, the Ottoman 'conquest' of Kurdistan was not terribly meaningful for most peasants and tribespeople in the region as they remained under the authority of the tribal chiefs and local dynasts under whom they had lived previously. Indeed, the notion of 'conquest' in the case of the Kurds needs to be nuanced just as it has been for other groups. Kurdish agency has often been neglected in the story of the battle between the Ottomans and Safavids as well as that of the Kurds' own role in their incorporation into the two empires, and in subsequent arrangements of governance.

Another major transformation in this relationship occurred in the nineteenth century. The regions that the Kurds inhabited began to experience a new relationship with the Ottoman state as the empire faced territorial losses and threats (real and perceived) from both inside and beyond its borders. State officials began to rethink their 'Kurdish' policies. Part of this new vision was not just regional but for the empire at large; the central Ottoman Government hoped to reclaim (or, in some cases, actually gain) authority over imperial regions that had either drifted beyond the grasp of the central government or that had never really submitted – beyond a nominal measure – to state authority. This was part of modern Ottoman state-building. But in this larger picture, the Ottoman East[9] – the main population of which consisted of Kurds and Armenians – came under special scrutiny. This region, after all, bordered the Ottomans' greatest rival – Russia – which had been expanding its territory westwards for some time. It also bordered Iran, with whom the Ottomans had been in the process of demarcating a boundary.[10] As frontiers morphed into borderlands and as borderlands were transformed into bordered lands, states began to view their populations and the issue of loyalty in a different light. As nation states emerged, and as empires themselves began 'thinking' like nation states, borders became contested and the identity of the people within them did too. Concomitant with these changes was the new notion of Ottoman citizenship. Who would be loyal citizens, and who would be suspect?[11] 'Borders' had meant very little to nomadic Kurdish tribes, who crossed them freely and had family and tribe on both sides. A nomadic lifestyle was indeed anathema to the need to count, monitor, discipline and require loyalty of the people within one's borders.

The Ottoman Army moved against the Kurdish dynasts in the early to mid-nineteenth century, but the result was a power vacuum in the region. Shaykhs replaced the dynasts and gathered their own followings, and the region experienced a significant measure of re-tribalization. The Kurdish population of the empire might have seemed 'out of control' in the eyes of the State, but after the war with Russia (1877–8) and the Treaty of Berlin that followed, it was the Armenian population of the empire that the central Ottoman Government brought into focus. The Treaty of Berlin designated the six eastern provinces (*vilayet*s) as regions where reform was necessary. The Armenians were now seen increasingly as a minority (a new concept), and Europeans and Russians vied to 'protect' them. Although most Armenians lived their daily lives much as they had before, and saw their loyalties and allegiances in similar terms to what they had experienced previously, now Ottoman authorities began to regard Armenians as a whole group whose loyalties needed to be questioned. Many believed that Armenian revolutionaries were conspiring with neighbouring Russia to sever the Ottoman East from the empire, and that the average Armenian supported this project.

The Ottoman authorities' novel Kurdish policy cannot be separated from their new view of Armenians within the empire, and their loyalty.

Ottoman authorities modified their arrangement of accommodation with the Kurds. They continued their goal of courting and controlling them at the same time, but now with a new institution that was built around fears of this 'Armenian threat'. In an updated version of its long-standing 'special' relationship with the Kurds, the central Ottoman Government created a Kurdish tribal militia (the Hamidiye Light Cavalry) through which the State hoped to boost the Kurds' loyalty to it (through privileges and to squash the emerging 'Armenian threat'. The leaders of this militia, however, began to use their state backing and weapons for their own agenda. Soon, they were able to acquire the property of poorer Kurdish tribespeople and non-affiliated, settled Kurds, but were especially adept in looting and usurping the properties of Armenians because they could now allege that the latter were traitors, and, in so doing, could rationalize and justify the appropriation of their property and violent acts against Armenians.[12] This anti-Armenian violence added fuel to the fire, and increased Armenians' need for protection, particularly by Armenian revolutionaries. It also prompted foreign powers to expand their reach into internal Ottoman affairs, which, in turn, brought more Ottomans (and also local Kurds) to see Armenians as traitors who were responsible for increased foreign intervention. Indeed, many Kurds believed rumours that the Sultan — in cahoots with the Europeans, who were seen as the puppetmasters — were going to grant the Armenians their own independent principality (*beylik*).[13] The idea of the 'foreigner' began to take root among people who had previously not had such a concept of their neighbours. Kurdish identity, as such, was itself sharpened in the process.[14]

Kurds responded to these changes in a variety of ways, but, significantly, many Kurdish thinkers began to formulate their own new ways to envision their identities as Kurds and Ottomans, and to disseminate their views to others — especially with the goal of 'awakening' other Kurds to their own history. In the Kurdish-Ottoman press, in which these Kurdish-Ottoman writers published their thoughts on Kurdish history, the subject itself became part of a larger effort to explore Kurdish identity, to advocate for the Kurds and to influence the wider changes under way in the empire.

Eric Hobsbawm, a well-known historian of nationalism, offered a colourful comment on the link between his profession, in the field of history writing, and nationalism:

> Historians are to nationalism what poppy-growers in Pakistan are to heroin-addicts: we supply the essential raw material for the market. Nations without a past are contradictions in terms. What makes a nation is the past, what justifies one nation against others is the past, and historians are the people who produce it. So my profession, which has always been mixed up in politics, becomes an essential component of nationalism.[15]

This was something that Kurds began to recognize nearly a century before Hobsbawm wrote these words. As Abdullah Cevdet, a Kurdish-Ottoman intellectual, put it, 'we are in an era in which the nationalities are being decided and recognized'.[16] He knew that the purpose of history writing and historical research had changed, and that 'national' histories were coming to dominate the pursuit of history. As Prasenjit Duara later suggested, 'Nations emerge as the subject of History, just as History emerges as the ground, the mode of being, of the nation.'[17] Tessa Morris-Suzuki, who studies Japan, submits that her studies of Japanese frontiers go further than the bounds of Japanese studies. They touch upon the whole way in which we deal with space in history. The modern practice of history writing began side by side with the rise of the nation state, and the study of history in schools and universities has largely meant the study of national histories (above all the history of one's own nation).[18] Morris-Suzuki notes that '[t]he nation therefore casts a long shadow backwards on our vision of the past, and channels our perceptions into a particular spatial framework'.[19] As such, she draws attention to her own bookshelves, and in particular to the 'volume on the history of Thailand since the tenth century, which, considering the repeated political and culture realignments within the space we now label "Thailand", seems only a little more bizarre than its neighbour on the shelf, a history of the Soviet Union from palaeolithic times to World War II'.[20] Those of us who study West Asian history have no doubt encountered similarly peculiar volumes on places like Iraq and Turkey – themselves only nation states for less than a century, but whose various histories date back centuries, even millennia (to a time when, indeed, Turkic peoples were not even in Anatolia)!

Although Abdullah Cevdet was writing in the 1910s, before the Ottoman Empire was dismembered into independent nation states or mandates, he was acutely aware that he and other Ottoman compatriots were writing in the midst of this historical/national turn in which every people (if it were to be considered a 'nation' – with all of the rights that this came to imply) needed to assert its 'nation-ness' through history writing. Beginning just a decade later, histories of newly formed countries like Iraq and Turkey were used to not just to claim 'nation-ness' but also in competing visions of *what kind* of nation they would be (and who would be considered full citizens, as will be discussed below). But in this moment, Kurdish-Ottoman writers started by asserting the Kurds' worthiness as historical subjects and the necessity of participating in the writing of history in their national(ist) project. In a very colourful piece, Cevdet put it this way:

> [Just] as an individual who does not possess a certain clearly-defined personality, a nation [which] does not possess a personality cannot be considered anything other than a group of speaking animals who are not called by a name [...] History plays the role for nations that memory plays for individuals. The human life and even the life of animals can be continued by adding memory. A person who has *amnésie complète* is nothing more than a plant in our gardens and mountains, [which] blows its leaves from one direction to another [...] If a nation does not have an excellent history, it is as if that nation has never lived [...] Do the Kurds have a history? [...] The century we live in, no joke, is the twentieth century. A nation that does not possess its history of the past and its future history does not have an identity. Nations and individuals who do not have their own identity will become slaves – the property of others [...] I said the future history [...] Many readers might be surprised by this strange phrase; yes, nations must possess their future history in addition to their past histories, and the former is more important.[21]

From the beginning of the first Kurdish-Ottoman gazette in 1898, Kurdish writers worked to highlight Kurdish history as such, and to draw attention to the historical importance of Kurds in the past as well. They were aware that histories were becoming 'national', and that, while many of them still hoped for a more cosmopolitan and inclusive Ottoman history, they needed to emphasize the more particular (here, the 'Kurdish' element) even within that broader Ottoman framework.

And in drawing attention to nations and individuals possessing 'their future history in addition to their past histories', it was clear that Abdullah Cevdet saw the writing on the wall.

For the moment, however, Kurds remained in an imperial setting (even in Iran, across the border), and they joined other Ottoman groups in constructing 'national' histories for themselves and finding new ways in which to situate themselves in the larger histories of the empires in which they lived, past and present, but *as Kurds*.[22] Articles in the Kurdish-Ottoman press underlined the Kurdish element and Kurdish contributions to the greatness of these empires. As one Kurdish writer described it,

> It is certain through the testimony of today and the past that the Kurdish nation is one of the most important pillars of the large family of Islam. The position of a noble nation, producer of very well-known rulers, administrators, ulema, and poets to Islam, throughout 1300 years is by no means inferior to other Islamic nations [...] The historic position of the Kurds, who make their brains and biceps, their swords and pens, servants of Islam within the Ottoman family is by no means less glittering that their position in the history of Islam.[23]

The Kurds' most important contribution to Islam, according to writers in these gazettes, was Salahaddin Eyubî. But this well-known figure in Islamic history, and even in the history of the Crusades, was transformed in the Kurdish press into a distinctly Kurdish figure who represented an individual aware of his Kurdishness and motivated to serve not just Islam, 'and even all of merciful humanity',[24] but particularly the Kurds and Kurdistan.[25] Elsewhere, writers emphasized the historical contributions of Kurds to science, art and religion.[26] In this vein, another author described the Kurds as 'one of the strongest pillars of Ottomanism and humanity'.[27] An important element of 'national' history writing was the effort to highlight 'national' groups' awareness of themselves as such, not only in the present but also in the past. In this endeavour, contributors to the Kurdish-Ottoman press drew attention to the *Sharafname* – a Kurdish epic in the oral tradition, which recounts the histories of various Kurdish tribes and dynasties and which was written down by Ehmed-ê Khanî in the late sixteenth century.

The *Sharafname* was important because it not only highlighted Kurds' self-awareness *as Kurds* in the past, but it also was used as a *source* for new research on Kurdish history. Kurdish intellectuals were part of the larger, global, intellectual trends that engaged in this new approach to history writing, and sought to document their findings with as many 'reputable' sources as they could muster. Now, historical research required a 'scientific' methodology that no longer relied solely on, or repeated uncritically, the narratives in older chronicles. The *Sharafname* was extremely important in this regard, but eventually seemed insufficient on its own. Like other intellectuals around the world, Kurdish-Ottoman writers tended to be strong positivists, and embraced the Young Turk *Weltanschauung* of 'science and progress'.[28] While the strength of their commitment to positivism may have varied from one writer to the next, many adopted and practised the wider 'science and progress' motto. History was supposed to be an 'objective science', but a number of thinkers also believed that it was the duty of the historian to underscore issues of morality and progress as humans advanced.[29] For Ottoman intellectuals and their colleagues elsewhere, the social sciences saw history in terms of 'laws' and evolutionary stages,[30] which would eventually classify and place people onto some rung of an evolutionary ladder of civilization, and, concomitantly, bestow upon them rights to recognition as a nation. Social engineering (addressed below) was also wrapped up in these new views on history and peoplehood. Kurdish intellectuals saw it as their mission to intervene and assert their own agency in the historical/national(ist) turn.

As such, while the *Sharafname* was officially regarded as the most important source of all for those researching Kurdish history,[31] Kurdish thinkers also (and, perhaps, more committedly) explored the writings of Russian and other European Orientalists whose works included studies of the Kurds and their neighbours. Indeed, Halil Hayali (writing under the pen name, Kurdîyê Bitlîsî), believed that Russian sources were especially valuable because Russians had, for their own reasons, taken a particular interest in the Kurds.[32] Halil Hayali also argued that the latest research methods (of which Kurdish writers were aware) could stand up to those who were already beginning to deny that the Kurds had a distinct (let alone distinctive) history, or even a separate identity from Turks. In a series of articles that he composed, he attacked those parties and suggested that their spurious claims were the product of outdated research methods and hearsay.[33] Upon the conclusion of Halil Hayali's round of rebuttals, *Jîn* published a long letter addressed to this author, in support of his research. The letter's author, Süleymaniyeli Tevfik, wrote, 'I do not know who it is who is denying Kurds or what they are saying; in your journal there are replies to those who attack Kurdishness. Therefore, I am leaving the meat of the problem for you to explain. But just in order to clarify your ideas, I offer these few lines', and proceeded to draw precisely on the range of sources that Halil Hayali had been praising (including citations from Persian, Arabic, French, German and American sources) to illustrate what a historic nation the Kurds were, how autonomous they had been throughout history and even how modern ethnology proved that Kurds were not Turks but related to Armenians, Persians and Nestorians – all members of the same 'race' (*ırk*).[34] Interestingly, the works that seemed to interest Kurdish writers the most tended to be more anthropological (dealing with culture) rather than historical. Perhaps they were unaware that on some level, in using these anthropologically focused works, they were unintentionally placing themselves into the more particular, 'small, static, "primitive" societies whose destiny was to be swallowed up by modernity's relentless advance' rather than among the 'large, complex "historical" societies which participated in the process of evolution culminating in "modernity."'[35] Or possibly, by highlighting the Kurds' essential role in the larger, more complex Ottoman society, they were attempting to subvert this paradigm and claim a historical role rather than a mere cultural (primitive) role in history, thus assuring their place at the future 'table' of recognized nations.

Kurdish writers' focus on a unique Kurdish identity and the Kurds' ethnic 'family' (or 'race', as they put it) came not simply in response to those who were denying the Kurds a peoplehood separate from that of the Turks but was part of the larger historical context that served as the backdrop against which they were writing. Foreign intervention plus changing ideas on notions of peoplehood combined to produce an environment in which many Kurds began to fear that the eastern regions of the Ottoman Empire (which were mainly inhabited by Kurds and Armenians) would be severed from the empire and given to the Armenians. In other words, new historical thinking and international (and domestic) politics were at play together, and informed one another. This concern about foreign intervention and its impact on the Kurds grew steadily after the provisions of the Treaty of Berlin (1878), which designated eastern Anatolia as 'six Armenian provinces', and the Armenians as a minority group who needed protection. As mentioned above, this sharpened the Kurds' awareness of themselves *as Kurds* – particularly now in relation to those ruling the Ottoman state ('Turks') and to their Christian neighbours, who were increasingly seen as a threat by Ottoman officials. While this perception continued to take shape over the following decades, it was really World War I and its aftermath that propelled Kurdish thinkers to use Kurdish history (and other kinds of research on Kurds) to jostle for an advantageous position for Kurds in the postwar settlements. The Armenian Genocide, in particular, loomed large in their minds as they engaged in this endeavour.

The Armenian Genocide resulted in the murder and displacement of most of the Kurds' Armenian neighbours during World War I. Those questions of loyalty and citizenship were tested with the Armenians, and although most of the latter remained loyal to the empire (or were, at least, not traitors by any stretch of the imagination), decades of ideas surrounding citizenship, loyalty and social engineering brought the new regime in power to eliminate the Ottoman-Armenian community.[36] Many Kurds were horrified at what they saw happening to their neighbours, and tried to protect them. Others – who drew on their state connections, an interest in profiting from Armenian losses (indeed, creating those losses for their own profit) and/or a genuine belief that the Armenians were indeed traitors and a threat to their existence – participated in the rounding up, deportation and murder of their neighbours near and far. This series of tragic events served to further sharpen a Kurdish identity. After the war, many Kurds feared retribution for their participation in the wartime violence against Armenians. But even for those Kurds who did not engage in anti-Armenian violence, the war and its aftermath brought them to consider 'their' position in the growing uncertainty about what would remain of the empire.

In the period following World War I, the European victors of the war – mainly Britain and France – carved out a new map for the former Ottoman regions, and took several of these new states as their own 'mandates'. Although ethnic nationalism was far from the minds of most inhabitants of the empire, some among their leaders adopted 'nationalist'[37] idioms as they recognized that it was increasingly the most powerful political discourse of their day, and they joined the global dialogue on the nationality question. The various ways in which Kurdish writers portrayed Kurdish identity in their journals were not only *not* uniform but were also sometimes fraught with contradiction in terms of how those writers sought to align Kurds' identities with others (or distance themselves from others) and how they articulated the Kurds' geopolitical aspirations for a future settlement. After the war, like others, some Kurdish leaders agitated for an independent Kurdistan, but found that their claims for territory and sovereignty competed and overlapped with lands sought by their neighbours. They had been inspired by the twelfth US President Woodrow Wilson's Fourteen Points (see below), and some were also mindful of what might happen to them if they found themselves under Armenian rule, given their role in the Armenian Genocide. Other Kurds fought for the Ottoman Empire.

This time of confusion and uncertainty made Kurds hedge their bets and explore various outcomes, and the seemingly contradictory positions expressed by Kurdish writers about the Kurds' identity and future must be seen in this light; the Kurds were engaged in a survival strategy, not a bout of indecision, and they were exploring their options.[38] The efforts of Süleymaniyeli Tevfik to position the Kurds 'racially' in the same family as Armenians and other Iranic peoples was probably his way of highlighting the Kurds' *non-Turkishness*, perhaps with the goal of seeking a separate existence for Kurds in the postwar settlements. It appears that other writers had a similar agenda. A number of Kurds reacted to a publication by the General Office of Tribes and Emigrants about the Kurds, which some writers alleged was designed to deprive Kurds of their unique Kurdish identity and their 'Iranian' ancestry by claiming that the Baban family (a Kurdish dynastic family) was Turkish.[39] An article in *Kurdistan* similarly critiqued the Ottoman official Suleyman Nazif for 'the evil policy which evidently aims at Turkifying Kurds, and [...] makes the life of an innocent nation a plaything'. Its author wrote that he wished 'that each and every Kurd knew the enemies surrounding them, who play with their destiny and belittle their future'.[40] Elsewhere, Kurdish writers began to separate themselves from Armenians and to highlight the uniqueness of the Kurds and their right to Kurdistan. One writer penned 'An Open Letter to the Present Government', denouncing the policy by which Kurdistan was 'constantly referred to by such strange names as "the Eastern provinces", "the Eastern regions", "Eastern Anatolia", "the frontier", and even "Armenia"' without calling it by its real name.[41]

A heightened urgency to explore options for the Kurds in the postwar settlements came after Woodrow Wilson issued his Fourteen Points, the twelfth of which read, 'The Turkish portions of the present Ottoman Empire should be assured a secure sovereignty, but other nationalities which are now under Turkish rule should be assured an undoubted security of life and an absolutely unmolested opportunity of autonomous development.'[42] A number of Kurds began to explore the possibility of an independent Kurdistan, and worked to distance themselves from Armenians with specific reference to what they interpreted as being promised to the Kurds. One writer admitted, 'Yes, until now we Kurds have not felt the need to leave the government of the Turkish state, in other words, the Ottoman commonwealth.' Citing the Fourteen Points, he continued,

> [But] now we see that Wilson is saying, We will not give non-Turks to the Ottomans [...] [t]hey call our place Kurdistan; there, there are no Turks other than two or three who have come and settled as *memur*s [government officials] [...] As for the Armenians, they do not amount to one fifth of us. Others only amount to two per cent. Therefore, there is no nation other than the Kurds. Therefore, Kurdistan is the right of the Kurds, and is the right of no one else but the Kurds.[43]

Elsewhere, Kamuran Ali Bedir Khan actually called on the 'Turkish government' to assist the Kurds in gaining their national rights!

> In Wilson's fourteen principles, it is declared how the principle of each nation's self-determination in the world will now be accepted and it is made clear that humanity will no longer be a toy for political purposes [...] In this most important period in our world history, in the beginning of the establishment of a new order, now we want to assert our ideas as openly as possible [...] morally and materially with this living nation's individual appearance. Finally, the previous government that ruled our country and did not depend in any way upon the principles that knowledge has accepted, has fallen along with its program [...] Now, I am calling

out to the Turkish government which is behind the regions of the Crimea, Georgia, and Armenia, whose people are adamant about independence, who are far away from them, and who promises warm and friendly support for those nations whose rights have been seized: In these most crucial moments, remember the cities of the east, some other regions, and Iran as well, in their entirety, and the traditions and national qualities of the Kurds and Kurdistan, who for the sake of religion and virtue, protecting all of their moral and material values, listen to the echoes of the voice of freedom from rough, rocky mountains, and who do not hesitate to do anything to uphold their national dignity [...] Kurdistan, who [once] desired, with a religious ideology and in a national admiration, peaceful unification and obedience to Yavuz Sultan Selim, today also hopes to receive support from the Turkish nation [...] The Kurdish nation, in order not to meet this [negative] end, from falling into this dark situation, sees in itself the power and ability to hold itself together [...] Kurdistan is going to attend, in a way to advance the elevation and progress of all its national strengths, the Peace Conference, whose decisions and negotiations are still unclear.[44]

The Kurds had representation at the Peace Conference, and although the Treaty of Sèvres (1920) made provisions for an independent Kurdistan it was superseded by the Treaty of Lausanne (1923), which recognized Turkish independence based on the new Republic of Turkey that incorporated much of geographic Kurdistan into its borders – an achievement for the Turkish nationalist leaders who had led the Turkish War of Independence. The British mandate of Iraq, which comprised three Ottoman provinces – Mosul, Baghdad and Basra – was created in 1920 after the British decided that a viable Iraq needed to include the Mosul province for economic, ethnic and strategic reasons. A smaller number of Kurds was incorporated into Syria – and, of course, Iran, which was not part of the Ottoman Empire, retained the Kurds already within its boundaries. From that point forward, Kurdish identities shifted further in response to the new nation/state-building practices of the new states in which they lived.[45]

Returning to one of my original questions: how helpful is it to see the Kurds in terms of an 'ethnic' history? 'Ethnic' histories have largely lost their analytical significance, but we nonetheless *can* still speak of a 'Kurdish history' (and indeed, several Kurdish histories) even beyond the paradigm of methodological nationalism as critiqued by Wimmer and Glick Schiller.[46] Kurdish history exists on its own, and is also relational. In other words, the history of the Kurds *as such* today finds its significance in relation to the history of the neighbours of the Kurds *as such*. Indeed, Turkish identity – perhaps more than that of any others among the Kurds' neighbours, I would argue – developed closely in relation to the process through which Turks' relationship with their 'Others' emerged (and continues to develop along this path). These 'Others' have, most prominently, been Armenians and Kurds.[47] As noted above, this process was intimately connected with the larger transition to a modern state, to new notions of citizenship and to the practices through which majorities and minorities were constructed in the late-Ottoman Empire – and, particularly, in the nation states that emerged from the fallen empire after World War I.[48] And this whole course of action has been comfortably united with changing trends in historical research and the political (particularly nationalist) uses of history.

Today, there is a growing and increasingly rich and nuanced body of works on Kurdish history (and in related disciplines as well) that demonstrates that scholars of 'non-dominant' groups frequently find themselves at the cutting edge of fresh theoretical approaches to their subjects of study. Part of this may be attributable to the fact that scholars in the early years of this new trend (namely, the 1990s and early 2000s) encountered difficulties accessing archival sources from Kurdish-inhabited countries (mainly for political reasons) and were forced to evaluate accessible sources from fresh angles. This situation led them to explore new methodologies by scholars working on other groups, and even in other disciplines, to investigate these new approaches in the Kurdish context and to produce studies that have not only brought students of Kurdish history into conversation with a wider body of scholarship (frequently outside of the 'Middle Eastern Studies' orbit) but that also have, in the process, produced fresh theoretical proposals with which other scholars now engage. Some recent works, for example, demonstrate that studying the histories of non-dominant groups and groups on the 'margins' of societies, states and empires (whether geographically or for their subalternity) is indeed essential for a better understanding of the larger dynamics of the states and societies in which they live as well as the histories of the dominant groups themselves. In other words, scholars thereby understand the *relational* dimension of these histories.[49] The interconnectedness of the histories of various groups in the same society has also brought historians of Kurdish societies to continue to question the utility of 'ethnic histories' and to propose new frameworks of analysis.

History writing is never a neutral pursuit, but in the case of the Kurds it has been particularly fraught with tension. From the late Ottoman period, when Kurdish researchers joined other groups in the pursuit of documenting their 'national' history, to the present, those who research Kurdish history have been faced with roadblocks laid down by states, individuals and institutions who believe that the study of the Kurds somehow constitutes a threat. These obstacles have included restricted access to research fields and archives, the persecution of scholars and the banning of books and articles. In recent years, many scholars have been able to overcome these obstacles – sometimes through their own creativity, and sometimes through the lifting of restrictions on access to relevant materials. But now that 'Kurdish history' as such has become a more 'acceptable' subject of study, the trend in history is turning away from ethnic histories as meaningful categories of analysis and towards thematic topics. The newest generation of scholars is showing wonderful promise in navigating both ongoing obstacles and new opportunities for innovative research.[50]

Notes

1. Abdurrahman Bedirkhan, 'Kurdistan ve Kürdler', *Kurdistan* 24 (19 Ağustos 1316/1 September 1900), in M. Emîn Bozarslan's collection, *Kurdistan: Rojnama Kurdî ya pêşîn/İlk Kürd Gazetesi*, vol. 2 (Uppsala: Weşanxana Deng, 1991), transliteration from Ottoman, p. 431. I use the original reproductions when they are included in the reprints produced by Bozarslan, but when they are not included I must rely on his transliterations.
2. Abdülhaluk Çay, *Türk Milli Bütünlüğü İçerisinde Doğu Anadolu Aşiretlerinin Sosyo-Ekonomik ve Kültürel Yapıları ve Bölücülük Meselesi* (Ankara: Türk Tarih Kurumu Yayınları, 1995), p. 23, cited in Cevdet Ergül, *II. Abdülhamid'in Doğu Politikası ve Hamidiye Alayları* (İzmir: Çağlayan Yayınları, 1997), p. 5.
3. The concept of statelessness emerged as a meaningful legal category after World War I. Although there was such a concept before the war, it had not really been a principle of international law (see 'International Law—Nationality—Stateless-

ness', *Yale Law Journal*, vol. 27, no. 6 (April 1918), (pp. 840–1). Between the two world wars, however, and particularly after World War II, the 'condition' of statelessness grew to affect not just individuals but large communities, who began to consider themselves as stateless – see Jane Perry Clark Carey, 'Some Aspects of Statelessness Since World War I', *American Political Science Review*, vol. 40, no. 1 (February 1946), (pp. 113–23). Today, the UN definition of statelessness sees a *de jure* stateless person as 'a person who is not considered as a national by any State under its domestic law', available at www.unhcr.org/en-us/protection/statelessness/46d4387f2/protection-stateless-people-prevention-statelessness-legal-information.html (accessed February 2018). The case of the Kurds is complicated. Although there are some 200,000–300,000 Kurds in Syria who have been stripped of their citizenship, other Kurds are citizens of the states that they live in. The policies and practices of minoritizing Kurds and making them feel like they are less-than-equal citizens has caused many Kurds to see themselves as stateless; while this is certainly important for understanding Kurdish oppression and identity, in the case of the Kurds, statelessness is more of a political statement than a legal reality.
4. Orit Bashkin, personal communication/social media, 27 August 2015. This was a remark made in honour of Vangelis Kechriotis, scholar of Ottoman History, who passed away on 27 August 2015 but who was a true pioneer in this effort.
5. Andreas Wimmer and Nina Glick Schiller, 'Methodological Nationalism, the Social Sciences, and the Study of Migration: An Essay in Historical Epistemology', *International Migration Review* 37:3 (Fall 2003), p. 578. These authors also point out that the 'naturalization' of the nation state also 'owes its force to the compartmentalization of the social science project into different "national" academic fields, a process strongly influenced not only by nationalist thinking itself, but also by the institution of the nation-state organizing and channeling social science thinking in universities, research institutions and government think tanks [...] In most states universities are linked to national ministries of education that favor research and teaching on issues of "national relevance"' (p. 579).
6. This may be true not only of Kurds' other 'non-dominant' neighbours but also of the segments among the 'dominant' groups (in this case, Turks), whose complicated and multi-identificational histories have also not been written.
7. See Sabri Ateş, *Ottoman-Iranian Borderlands: Making a Boundary, 1843–1914* (New York: Cambridge University Press, 2015). See also Jeremy Adelman and Stephen Aron, 'From Borderlands to Borders: Nation-States, and the Peoples in Between in North American History', *American Historical Review* vol. 104, no. 3 (June 1999), pp. 814–41.
8. See my *Margins of Empire: Kurdish Militias in the Ottoman Tribal Zone* (Stanford, CA: Stanford University Press, 2011), esp. pp. 53–63.
9. For a new, historiographical, perspective on the 'Ottoman East', see the innovative volume edited by Yaşar Tolga Cora, Dzovinar Derderian and Ali Sipahi: *The Ottoman East: Societies, Identities and Politics* (London and New York:

I.B.Tauris, 2016). Its authors engage in writing a regional history 'as an Ottoman history rather than a chapter of it' (p. 1), and take the Ottoman East as a geographical unit of analysis that appreciates 'the coeval presence of Armenia, Kurdistan and Turkey in the lives of every people in the region' (p. 2).
10. See Ateş, *Ottoman-Iranian Borderlands*.
11. Gyanendra Pandey's concept of 'marked citizens' is relevant here. See his *Routine Violence: Nations, Fragments, Histories* (Stanford, CA: Stanford University Press, 2006), esp. chapter 6.
12. See my *Margins of Empire*, esp. chapter 4.
13. Sami Önal (ed.), *Sadettin Paşa'nın Anıları: Ermeni-Kürt Olayları (Van, 1896)* (Istanbul: Remzi Kitabevi, 2003), p. 21.
14. See my 'De la tribu à la nation, genèse d'une identité', special issue on the Kurds, *Qantara* 88 (July 2013).
15. E.J. Hobsbawm, 'Ethnicity and Nationalism in Europe Today', *Anthropology Today*, 8:1 (February 1992), p. 3.
16. Dr Abdullah Cevdet, 'Bir Hitab' [An Address], *Rojî Kurd* 1 (2 Haziran, 1329/15 June 1913), p. 3.
17. Prasenjit Duara, *Rescuing History from the Nation: Questioning Narratives of Modern China* (Chicago and London: University of Chicago Press, 1995), p. 27, cited in Daniel Woolf, 'Of Nations, Nationalism, and National Identity: Reflections on the Historiographic Organization of the Past', in Q. Edward Wang and Franz L. Fillafer (eds), *The Many Faces of Clio: Cross-cultural Approaches to Historiography* (New York: Berghahn Books, 2007), p. 73.
18. Tessa Morris-Suzuki, 'The Frontiers of Japanese History', in Heinz Tonnesson and Hans Atlöv (eds), *Asian Forms of the Nation* (Richmond, Surrey: Curzon, 1996), p. 42.
19. Ibid.
20. Ibid.
21. Dr Abdullah Cevdet, 'Bir Hitab', p. 3.
22. As John Hutchinson notes, 'Cultural nationalism can result in conflict over heritages and territories, where ethnic populations are mixed [...] or where populations share important cultural elements' – 'Re-Interpreting Cultural Nationalism', *Australian Journal of Politics and History* 45:3 (1999), p. 395.
23. Babanzâde İsmail Hakkı, 'Müslümanlık ve Kürdlük', *Rojî Kurd* 2 (7 Temmuz, 1329/19 July 1913), p. 5.
24. [Unsigned], 'Salahhadin Eyubî', *Rojî Kurd* 3 (1 Ağustos 1320/14 August 1913), pp. 13–14.
25. Abdurrahman Bedir Khan, 'Selahedînê Eyûbî', *Kurdistan* 15 (22 Nisan, 1315/4 May 1899), pp. 3–4 (original reprinted in Bozarslan, *Kurdistan*, vol. 1). See also Kerkuklu Necmeddin, 'Kürd Talebe Cemiyeti ve Kürdlerin Makam-ı Hilafete Hizmetleri', *Rojî Kurd* 1 (2 Haziran, 1329/15 June 1913).
26. Abdurrahman Bedir Khan, 'Kürdistan ve Kürdler', *Kurdistan* 24 (19 Ağustos, 1316/1 September 1900); Bozarslan's reprints of *Kurdistan*, vol. 2, pp. 431–3. As I will discuss below, some of these glorifications of Kurds in history were

penned with the purpose of contrasting Kurdish greatness in the past with their decline under the oppressive regime of Abdulhamid II. *Kurdistan* was, after all, an Ottoman opposition journal, and its founders were involved in the Ottoman Committee of Union and Progress.
27. Article signed 'Rojî Kurd', *Rojî Kurd* 1 (2 Haziran, 1329/15 June 1913), p. 2.
28. See M. Şükrü Hanioğlu, *The Young Turks in Opposition* (New York: Oxford University Press, 1995), esp. chapter 9.
29. Q. Edward Wang, 'Introduction', in Wang and Fillafer, *The Many Faces of Clio*, pp. 1–2. See also Hutchinson, 'Re-Interpreting Cultural Nationalism', for his view of cultural nationalists as 'moral innovators'.
30. Donald R. Kelley, 'Ideas of Periodization in the West', in Wang and Fillafer, *The Many Faces of Clio*, p. 22.
31. Kurdîyê Bitlîsî (Halil Hayali), 'Kürdler Münasebetiyle', *Jîn* 3 (20 Teşrin-I Sanî 1334/20 November 1918), pp. 1–4, reprinted in M. Emîn Bozarslan, *Jîn: Kovara Kurdî-Tirkî/Kürdçe-Türkçe Dergi, 1918–1919*, vol. 1 (Uppsala: Weşanxana Deng, 1985).
32. Ibid. He did not seem to judge the Russian sources on many other scholarly merits.
33. Kurdîyê Bitlîsî (Halil Hayali), 'Kürdler Münasebetiyle', *Jîn* 3 (20 Teşrin-i Sanî 1334/20 November 1918), pp. 1–6, and ibid.
34. Süleymaniyeli Tevfik, '"Jîn" Dergisi Aracılığıyla Kurdîyê Bitlîsî Kardeşime', *Jîn* 4 (28 Teşrin-i Sanî 1334/28 November 1918), pp. 1–4, reprinted in Bozarslan, *Jîn*, vol. 1. Süleymaniyeli Tevfik continued on these lines in subsequent issues in order to highlight the fact that Kurds were not Turks but were from the Iranic branch of people, and that the cities in Kurdistan were, and had been historically, inhabited by Kurds. Of course, this – as I will highlight, below – was significant during the postwar negotiations over what would happen to the empire and the peoples within it. See Süleymaniyeli Tevfik's articles, 'Kürdistan'daki Şehirler Sekenesi Türk müdür?' *Jîn* 6 (25 Kanun-i Evvel 1334/25 December 1918), pp. 1–9, reprinted in Bozarslan, *Jîn*, vol. 2 (1985); and 'Kürdler (Iran)î değil midir?!' *Jîn* 18 (8 Mayıs 1335/8 May 1919), pp. 1–8; *Jîn* 19 (22 Mayıs 1335/22 May 1919), pp. 5–8; *Jîn* 20 (4 Haziran 1335/4 June 1919), pp. 13–14, reprinted in Bozarslan, *Jîn*, vol. 4 (1987); and *Jîn* 21 (18 Haziran 1335/18 June 1919), pp. 9–11, reprinted in Bozarslan, *Jîn*, vol. 5 (1988). See also 'Dehak Efsanesi', *Jîn* 1 (7 Teşrin-i Sanî 1334/7 November 1918), pp. 7–11, reprinted in Bozarslan, *Jîn*, vol. 1. Some pages of this last-named article are illegible; see Bozarslan's transliteration, pp. 189–92.
35. Morris-Suzuki, 'Frontiers of Japanese History', p. 44.
36. Üngör, *The Making of Modern Turkey*; and Taner Akçam, *The Young Turks' Crime Against Humanity: The Armenian Genocide and Ethnic Cleansing in the Ottoman Empire* (Princeton, NJ: Princeton University Press, 2012).
37. I put this in quotation marks because it is difficult to classify the kind of identity politics that Kurdish-Ottoman intellectuals embraced (and that many Kurds continue to embrace) as merely nationalist, since they have been complex

and have incorporated many shifting goals and symbols. While I have explored this elsewhere, I will rely on the less-nuanced term, nationalism, here.

38. Hutchinson draws attention to the fact that those whom he calls 'cultural nationalists' may 'experiment with several alternative visions of the nation over an extended period' and that 'the never ceasing elaboration of options is not a sign of opportunism but rather of the preparedness of nationalists to face contingency' – 'Re-Interpreting Cultural Nationalism', pp. 397–8.

39. Y[usuf] Ziya, 'Kürd Tarihinden Baban Hanedanı', *Jîn* 9 (16 Kânûn-î Sanî 1335/16 January 1919), reprinted in Bozarslan, *Jîn*, vol. 2, p. 445; and Kurdîyê Bitlîsî (Halil Hayali), 'Mühacirin Müdiriyeti Neşriyatından "Kürdler" Münasebetiyle Dehak Efsanesi', *Jîn* 1 (Teşrin-i Sanî 1334/7 November 1918), reprinted in Bozarslan, *Jîn*, vol. 1, pp. 7–11. Some pages are illegible; see Bozarslan's transliteration on pp. 189–92.

40. Barzinicizade Abdulvahid, 'Gönül İsterki', *Kurdistan* 8 (29 Mayıs, 1335/29 May 1919). Please note that although the title of this journal is the same, it is not the same publication as the *Kurdistan* gazette that was published between 1898 and 1902.

41. Hizanizade Kemal Fevzi, 'Hükümet-i Hazıraya Açık Mektub', *Jîn* 13 (10 Mart, 1335/10 March 1919), p. 3, reprinted in Bozarslan, *Jîn*, vol. 3 (1986).

42. 'President Woodrow Wilson's Fourteen Points', 18 January 1918. Available at avalon.law.yale.edu/20th_century/wilson14.asp (accessed February 2018).

43. Abdurrahim Rahmî, 'Halê me yê Hazir' [in Kurdish], *Jîn* 6 (25 Kânûn-î Evvel, 1334/25 December 1918), pp. 14–15, reprinted in Bozarslan, *Jîn*, vol. 2 (1985).

44. Kamuran Ali Bedir Khan, 'Kürdistan İçin', *Jîn* 3 (20 Teşrin-î Sânî, 1334/20 November 1918), p. 5, reprinted in Bozarslan, *Jîn*, vol. 1. Parts of Kurdistan were incorporated into the Ottoman Empire during the reign of Sultan Selim I (r. 1512–20).

45. See my 'The Minority Question: A View from History and the Kurdish Periphery', in Will Kymlicka and Eva Pföstl (eds), *Multiculturalism and Minority Rights in the Arab World* (Oxford: Oxford University Press, 2014), pp. 27–51.

46. Wimmer and Glick Schiller, 'Methodological Nationalism'.

47. See Üngör, *The Making of Modern Turkey*, on this point.

48. I have explored this topic elsewhere. See my 'Minorities, Statelessness, and Kurdish Studies Today: Prospects and Dilemmas for Scholars', *Journal of Ottoman Studies* [*Osmanlı Araştırmaları Dergisi*], special issue in honour of Rifa'at Abou-el-Haj (December 2010), pp. 225–37. This special issue has also been reprinted as a book: Donald Quataert and Baki Tezcan (eds), *Beyond Dominant Paradigms in Ottoman and Middle Eastern/North African Studies: A Tribute to Rifa'at Abou-El-Haj* (Istanbul: İSAM, 2010).

49. For a few examples in the Ottoman context, see Christine Philliou, *Biography of an Empire: Governing Ottomans in an Age of Revolution* (Berkeley, CA and Los Angeles: University of California Press, 2010); Bedross Der Matossian, *Shattered Dreams of Revolution: From Liberty to Violence in the Late-Ottoman Empire* (Stanford,

CA: Stanford University Press, 2014); and Üngör, *The Making of Modern Turkey*. I have also attempted to contribute to this in my *Margins of Empire*.

50. Some of the themes explored in this chapter were also touched upon in my 'Kurdish identity in the Ottoman Empire', in Wolfgang Taucher, Mathias Vogl and Peter Webinger (eds), *The Kurds: History – Religion – Language – Politics* (Vienna: Austrian Federal Ministry of the Interior, 2015), pp. 7–20, and were first developed in my Master's thesis, 'Claiming the Nation: The Origins and Nature of Kurdish Nationalist Discourse, A Study of the Kurdish Press in the Ottoman Empire', Princeton University, Princeton, NJ, 1996.

CONTRIBUTOR BIOGRAPHIES

Faleh A. Jabar was Director of the Iraq Institute for Strategic Studies in Beirut and Research Fellow at the School of Politics and Sociology, Birkbeck College, University of London. His publications in English include: *The Shi'ite Movement in Iraq* (2003), *Tribes and Power in the Middle East* (2002), and *Ayatollahs, Sufis and Ideologues* (2002). He wrote a number of books in Arabic as well as contributions to peer-reviewed edited collections and journals.

Renad Mansour is Research Fellow at both The Royal Institute of International Affairs, Chatham House, and the Cambridge Security Initiative at the University of Cambridge. He has previously been Lecturer of International Studies in the Faculty of Politics at Cambridge University and Senior Fellow at The Iraq Institute for Strategic Studies, Beirut.

Gareth Stansfield is Professor of Middle East Politics and the Al-Qasimi Chair of Arab Gulf Studies at the University of Exeter. He is also a senior associate fellow with special reference to the Middle East and Islamic world at the Royal United Services Institute (RUSI).

Michiel Leezenberg is Associate Professor in the Department of Philosophy (chair of Philosophy of Science) at the University of Houston-Downtown (UHD).

David Romano is Assistant Professor of International Studies at Rhodes College. He is the author of *The Kurdish Nationalist Movement*, in addition to numerous articles on Middle Eastern politics, the Kurdish issue, forced migration and globalization.

Contributor Biographies

Martin van Bruinessen is Professor of the Comparative Study of Contemporary Muslim Societies at the University of Utrecht. He was trained as a theoretical physicist but later switched to anthropology, and has conducted many years of field research in Kurdistan, Afghanistan and Indonesia.

Hamit Bozarslan is Associate Professor at the École des Hautes Études en Sciences Sociales, Paris. He is the author of the book, *La Question Kurde: États et Minorities au Moyen-Orient*. He is currently working on issues surrounding violence in Turkey and the Middle East.

Sami Zubaida is an emeritus professor of Politics and Sociology at Birkbeck, University of London, with extensive works on the politics and sociology of the Middle East.

Michael M. Gunter is an authority on Kurds in Turkey and Iraq, and has written seven books on the Kurdish struggle. He is frequently consulted by media members for analysis and comment on breaking news in the Middle East.

Janet Klein is Associate Professor of History at the University of Akron, Ohio, and author of *The Margins of Empire: Kurdish Militias in the Ottoman Tribal Zone*.

INDEX

Abadi, Haidar, 110
Abdulhamid, Sultan, 145–149, 174, 178, 187
Activism, 12, 77, 196
Agha, Ismail Simko, 209
Ahmed, Ibrahim, 44, 51, 77, 142
AKP. *See* Islamist Justice and Development Party (AKP)
Alaka, Karim, 54–55
Alevi Kurds, 125
Algiers Agreement (1975), 41, 45
Alinia, Minoo, 195
al-Mardini, Arif Pasha, 43
Al Qaeda Iraq (AQI) group, 79
Amarilogo, Eli, 176
American Federation of Labor and Congress of Industrial Organizations (AFL-CIO), 59
Anatolia
   European-style revolution in, 125
   provinces, 91
   Tigers, 99
Anderson, Benedict, 20, 88
Anglo-Saxon tradition, 13, 205, 217–219
   Kurdish studies in, 205
Ankara's decentralization reforms, 9
Ansar al-Islam, in Iraq, 137n44
Anthropology, 149, 151

Anti-Arab sentiment, 109
Anti-Armenian violence, 227, 233
Anti-KDP coalition, 159
Arab
   nationalism, 96
   tribes, 146
Arab-Iraqi, in Baghdad, 23
Arabs of Iraq, 29
Arab Spring, 1, 9, 86
   Kurds and, 4–7
Arif, Abdul Salam, 50
Armed conflict, 88, 118, 120, 130, 132
Armenian Genocide, 233, 234
Armenian revolutionary activities, 174
Armenian rule, 234
Armenian threat, 227
Artificiality, 20
Asal, Victor, 71
Askari, Ali, 46
Atatürk, Mustafa Kemal, 6, 92, 125, 135n26, 175
Authoritarianism, 8, 27, 86
   communal, 199
   dividing effect of, 32
   religious, 13, 199
Authoritarianpatrimonial system, Syria, 8
Authorities, 92, 103, 128, 148, 152, 155, 171, 176, 216

INDEX

central, 74, 120, 174
clerical, 126
communal, 191
federal, 5
and forces, 186
imperial, 172
Kurdish, 103, 181, 186
Kurdistan Regional Government (KRG), 104
Ottoman, 226–227
political, 172
religious, 42, 54, 191, 192
state, 120, 121, 132, 149, 163, 225
in Tehran, 126
tribal, 77
tribal formations and, 199
Turkish, 98
Autonomous democracy, 2, 5
multi-ethnic, 2
Autonomy Agreement, 61
Azar, Edward, 119

Ba'ath coup, 192
Ba'athist rule, 95, 96
Ba'ath party control, 158
Ba'ath single-party regime (1968–2003), 27
Baghdad
Arab-Iraqi in, 23
armed confrontation with, 156
conflicts with, 157
discontinuation of oil payments (2014), 110
electoral and political cooperation in, 31
failure of Shi'i leaders in, 121
Kurdish tribal leaders loyal to, 96
leadership, 59
new Arab government in, 124
Talabani's legitimacy, 47
Baris ve Demokrasi Partisi (BDP), 107
Barzani–Christian relations, 209
Barzani-led KDP, 30
Barzani, Masoud, 102, 177

Basrite kingdom, 22
Bates, R.H., 89
Bazargan, Mahdi, 126
Bedir Khan, Abdurrahman, 222
Bedir Khan, Emin Ali, 73
Bedir Khan, Kamuran Ali, 235
Bedouin tribes, 149, 150
Bell, Gertrude, 217
Boucek, Francoise, 69
British Colonel French, 43
British colonial administration, 21
British colonial army, 29
British mandate rule, 94–95
British political officers, 214–217
Bucak, Celal, 178
Burton, John, 119

Capitalism, 20
crony, 32, 95
industrial, 7
print, 20, 88
state, 95
Central authorities, 74, 120, 174
Cevdet, Abdullah, 228, 229
Chandra, Kanchan, 89–90
CIA, 60, 97, 168n33, 191
Civil war, 6, 53
inter-Kurdish civil war in Iraq (1994–6), 180
Kurdish civil war of 1994–6, 179
post-civil war, 172
in Syria, 3, 10
Clerical authorities, 126
Coercion, 48
Mullah Mustafa Barzani, 50–51
post-1975, 51–53
post-World War I, 48–50
1991–present, 53–54
Colonial rule, 22, 24, 90
Combating Domestic Violence Law, 195
Communal authorities, 191
Communitarian theories, 119
Consumerism, 198, 199
Cox, Percy, Sir, 22, 23, 215

Cradle of Mankind (Wigrams), 206
Crony capitalism, 32, 95
Cultural cohesive system, 20
Cultural conflict, 23
  linguistic–cultural conflict, 33
Cultural-linguistic ethnicity, 4
Culture, 2, 179, 186, 189, 197, 228
  patriarchal, 198
  political, 72
  of sexualization, 198
  Turkish, 92, 146

Davos, 62
Demirel, Süleyman, 177
Demirtas, Selehattin, 94
Democracy, 88–91
  autonomous, 2, 5
  patronage-democracy, 89, 90, 102–106
Democratic claim, 42–43
Democratic mandate, 43
Democratic Union Party (PYD), 5, 86
Dersim, 148
Detractors of Kurds, 68
Dichotomy, 20, 55, 91
Diversity of Kurds, 188
  Iraq, 191–193
  Turkey, 188–191
Diyarbakir Province, 99
Dobbs, Henry, Sir, 22
Dohuk, KRG provinces of, 195
Dominant national group, 3
Dynasty, 54
  Mullah Mustafa Barzani, 55
  post-1975, 55–56
  post-World War I, 54–55
  1991–present, 56

Edmonds, C.J., 205–206, 212–216
Entessar, Nader, 126, 136n31
Erbakan, Necmettin, 100
Erbil
  economic vulnerability of, 110
  Harir Plain north of, 96

KRG provinces of, 195
Kurds in, 28
  regional government in, 86
Erdogan, Recep Tayyip, 9–10
Ethnic identity, 4, 88, 93
  Kurdish, 158–160
  self-ethnic-identity, 3
  tribes and, 141–164
Ethnicity, 88–91, 119
  cultural-linguistic, 4
  and ethnic pursuits, 18
  Kurdish, 89
  politicization of, 88, 121
Ethnic loyalties, 154–155
Ethnic mobilization, 88, 103, 108
Ethnic pursuits, ethnicity and, 18
Ethnic segmentation, 72–75
Ethnic violence
  causes of, 88
  contrasting patterns of, 107–111
  in Iraqi Kurdistan, 108
  between the Kurdistan Workers' Party (PKK), 87
Ethno-Kurdish-ness, 3
Ethno-linguistic nationalism, 7
Ethno-nationalism, 7
Ethno-political movements,
  segmentation and fragmentation in, 70–71
European-style revolution, in Anatolia, 125
Evans, Peter, 89
Eyubî, Salahaddin, 230

Factionalism, 68, 69, 71
  in established democracies, 69
  internal, 79
  of Kurdish, 78
  legacies of, 80
Fearon, James, 88, 89
Federal authorities, 5
Federalism, 3, 28, 32
Food-distribution system, 104

INDEX

Fragmentation
 in ethno-political movements, 70–71
 impact of, 70
 political, 72–75
Free-market economy, 32
Frustration–aggression theories, 119

Galtung, Johan, 119
Gamal Abdel Nasser of Egypt (1952), 6
Gellner, Ernest, 18, 19, 88
Ghassemlou, Abdul Rahman, 45, 55, 61
Gökalp, Ziya, 145–150
Gorran Movement, 76, 79
Great National Assembly, 175
Greenhouse, F.S., 49
Group identity, 134n12
 Kurdish discourse of, 3
 theories, 119
Gulf War, 3, 9, 26, 28, 120, 177, 179

Hachemaoui, Mohammed, 172
Hafeed, Mahmood, 29, 30
Halkin Emek Partisi (HEP), 94
'Hamidian' empowerment, 148
Hamidiye, 147, 163
Hamidiye Light Cavalries, 174
Hamilton, Archibald Milne, 216
Hashemite dynasties, 217
Hayali, Halil, 231
Hay, William Rupert, 214
HDP, 4, 5, 8, 101, 107
HEP. *See* Halkin Emek Partisi (HEP)
Heriki Kurds, 210
'the hermit crab Act,' 209
Hobsbawm, Eric, 227
Hussein, Saddam, 47, 61, 95, 157, 181, 194, 223

ICP. *See* Iraqi Communist Party (ICP)
Ideational segmentation, 75–78

Identity
 ethnic (*see* Ethnic identity)
 group, 3, 119, 134n12
 tribal, 143
IKF. *See* Iraqi Kurdistan Front (IKF)
IMK. *See* Islamic Movement of Kurdistan (IMK)
Imperial authorities, 172
Industrial capitalism, 7
Industrialism, 19, 20, 29
Integration, overlapping systems of, 20
Internal conflicts, 151
Internal schism, 45–46, 178
International community, 46, 53, 62, 70, 118
International Monetary Fund (IMF) loans, 93
International Support, 56
 Mullah Mustafa Barzani, 58–60
 politicization of, 60–61
 post-1975, 60–62
 post-World War I, 56–58
 1991–present, 62–63
Intra-Kurdish fighting, 53
Investment laws, liberal, 106
Iran
 Kurdish nationalist movements in, 33
 Kurdish Republic of Mahabad in, 142
 Kurdish resistance to Islamic Republic in, 125–127
 Kurds in, 18, 87
 state elites in, 120
Iranian Revolutionary Guards, 18, 126
Iranian Revolution of 1979, 185
Iran–Iraq War, 26, 61, 74, 95, 144, 158
Iraq
 Ansar al-Islam in, 137n44
 Ba'ath regime in 1991 Gulf War, 9
 dilemma of state-formation and nation-building, 21–28

diverging and converging
  trajectories, 91–97
diversity of Kurds, 191–193
economic development, 95
emerging patronage democracy,
  102–106
ethnic violence in, 108
inter-Kurdish civil war in (1994–6),
  180
KDP- PUK conflict in, 74
KRG in, 17
Kurdish aspirations in, 5
Kurdish leaders in, 10, 41
Kurdish policies of, 148
Kurdistan Democratic Party, 52
Kurds in Iraq since 1991, 102–106
Legal Code of 1969, 194
Shaykh Barzinji revolt in (1920–32),
  124
state elites in, 120
Iraqi–British Treaty, 23
Iraqi Communist Party (ICP), 52, 95
Iraqi Kurdistan, 158–160
Iraqi Kurdistan Front (IKF), 102
Iraqi Personal Status Code, 194
Iraqi personal-status law, 193–195
Irredentism, 216
Islamicity, 186
Islamic Movement of Kurdistan
  (IMK), 78
Islamic Republic, 122
  in Iran, 125–127
Islamic Revolution (1979–80), 6, 8
Islamic Shari'a law, 31
Islamic State (IS), 87, 186
  fight against in (2014–17), 17
  global war against, 5
  'IS factor,' 6–7
Islamic State of Iraq and al-Sham
  (ISIS), 79
Islamic State of Iraq and Syria (ISIS), 28,
  186, 223
Islamism, 28, 79
  political, 78

Islamist Justice and Development Party
  (AKP)
  government, 97, 107
  rule, 98
Islamist politics, impact on, 155

Jabar, Faleh Abdul, 113n1
Jalal Talabani-led Patriotic Union of
  Kurdistan (PUK), 30
James, Boris, 172
Jash tribes, 158–159
Jirkis of Tahir Adiyaman, 178

Kanie, Mariwan, 195, 196
KCK. *See* Koma Civakên Kurdistan
  (KCK)
KCP. *See* Kurdistan Conservative Party
  (KCP)
KDP. *See* Kurdistan Democratic Party
  (KDP)
KDPI. *See* Kurdistan Democratic Party
  of Iran (KDPI)
Kemalism, 160, 190
Kemalist government, 214
Kemalist republic, 92
Kemalist secularism, 190, 199
Kermanji-speaking tribes, 33
Khaddaj, Abir, 113n1
Khaldun, Ibn, 149, 150, 173
Khan, Adila, 216
Khan Beg, Bedir, 209
Khan, Hero, 31
Khanî, Ehmed-ê, 230
Khan, Sureya Badr, 43
Khomeini, Ayatollah, 126
Kinaci, Zeynep, 137n45
King Faysal, 23, 24
KIU. *See* Kurdistan Islamic Union (KIU)
KNA. *See* Kurdistan National Assembly
  (KNA)
Koma Civakên Kurdistan (KCK),
  99–100
Komeley Xwendi karani Kurd Le
  Europa (KSSE), 45

INDEX

KRG. *See* Kurdistan Regional Government (KRG)
KRI. *See* Kurdistan Region of Iraq (KRI)
KSSE. *See* Komeley Xwendi karani Kurd Le Eurupa (KSSE)
Kurd-focused insurgency, 122–123
Kurdish armed struggles, 122–123
future prospects for, 130–132
Kurdish authorities, 103, 181, 186
Kurdish autonomy, 26, 43, 103, 124, 126, 127, 158, 177, 214, 215
Kurdish axiom, 29
Kurdish community, 2, 7–9
Kurdish Democratic Party, 43
Kurdish dilemmas, expectations and bewilderment, 28–34
Kurdish discourse of group identity, 3
Kurdish disunity, 127
Kurdish ethnic identity, 158–160
Kurdish euphoria, 32, 126
Kurdish forces, 17, 127, 223
Kurdish identity, 11, 125, 131, 227, 234
politics, 4
Kurdish leaders, 43, 49, 52, 55–58, 61, 64, 118, 124, 234
in Iraq, 10, 41
of the KDP-I, 45
Kurdish leadership, 42, 55
Kurdish movement, 143, 144, 156, 158–161, 175, 179, 180
Kurdish National Congress (KNC), 181
Kurdish nationalism, 4, 23, 33, 131, 132, 143, 176
Kurdish nationalist movement, 33, 54, 74, 118, 148, 158, 161, 181
Kurdish nationalist party, 123, 142
Kurdish particularism, 126
Kurdish political segmentation, origins of, 71–72
Kurdish population, 42–43, 45, 47, 50, 74, 118, 123, 131, 163, 189, 190, 216, 225, 226

Kurdish pro-government militias, 158–160
Kurdish provinces, 129, 161
Kurdish realities, 42
Kurdish Regional Government (KRG), 172
amendments to Iraqi personal-status law, 193–195
policies and reforms, 193
provinces, 195
Kurdish Republic of Mahabad, 142, 177
Kurdish resistance, 121
to Islamic Republic in Iran, 125–127
Kurdish social groups and entities, 8
Kurdish society, 31, 151, 155, 161, 174, 180, 182, 186, 196
Kurdish Spring, 9
Kurdish tribalism, 71
Kurdish tribal leaders, 96
Kurdish tribesmen, 164
Kurdish uprisings, 118, 121, 122, 154, 158, 175
Kurdish Workers' Party (PKK), 5, 6, 75, 87, 94, 118, 137n50, 160
insurgency in Turkey, 128–130
Kurdism, 177
Kurdistan Conservative Party (KCP), 159
Kurdistan Democratic Party (KDP), 28–29, 41, 46, 47, 52, 94, 141, 193
Kurdistan Democratic Party of Iran (KDPI), 122, 126, 127
Kurdistan Democratic Party–Patriotic Union of Kurdistan (KDP–PUK) conflict, 74
Kurdistani community, 41
Kurdistan Islamic Union (KIU), 79
Kurdistan National Assembly (KNA), 42, 195

Kurdistan Regional Government (KRG), 4, 6, 11, 13, 28, 42, 87, 109, 111, 223
  authorities, 104
  in Iraq, 17, 33
Kurdistan Region of Iraq (KRI), 191–193, 223
Kurds–Leftists and Shi'i Islamist groups, 26
Kurds, Turks and Arabs (Edmonds), 216
Kuwait war, 158

Laitin, David, 88
Laizer, Sheri, 215
Land conflicts, 163, 164
Land registration, 163
Law and security, 192
Leninism, 76
Liberal investment laws, 106
Liberalization, 93, 95, 97, 197
Liberation, 42, 185, 187, 196
  campaigns, 187
  of Raqqa, 5
  women, 185–187, 189, 199
Lindfield-Soane, Lynette, 215
Lineages, 151
Loyalties, ethnic and religious, 154–155
Lyon, Wallace, 216

Mahmood Barzinji, Shaykh, 22, 29, 44, 48–50, 54, 73, 155, 214, 215, 217
Maoism, 76
Maoist-style guerrilla movement, 129
Marxism, 76
Marxist-Leninist Komala, 46, 77
Marxist–Leninist principles, 94
Masculinity, Peshmerga, 196
Masoud Barzani, 17, 28
McDowall, David, 54, 127
Military-dominated National Security Council, 93

Militias
  multiple, 193
  tribal, 163
  tribe, 158
Minorsky, Vladimir, 216
Mono-ethnic political pattern, 7
Morris-Suzuki, Tessa, 228
Mosaddegh, Mohammad, 6
Mosul Province, 23, 49, 105, 236
Mosul Vilayet Council, 159
Muhammad, Qazi, 44
Multi-ethnic autonomous democracy, 2
Multiple militias, 193
Mustafa Barzani, Mullah, 44–45, 50–51, 55, 58–60, 141, 142, 156, 178, 208, 216
Mustafa, Falah, 62
Mustafa, Noshirwan, 106, 168n32

Najaf insurrection (1916–18), 22, 77
Naqshbandi Sufi movement, 123
Naqshbandi Sufi order, 141
Nationalism
  Arab, 96
  ethno-linguistic, 7
  Kurdish, 4, 23, 33, 131, 132, 143, 176
  Pan-Kurdish, 33
  tribal, 179
Nationalist revolts, 118
National Security Council, 56
  military-dominated, 93
National unity, 20, 26, 31
Neo-liberal Turkish economy, 91
New Kurdish Society, 9–10
Noel, Edward W.C., 214
Nomadism, 148
  pastoral, 145, 146, 150, 162
Non-tribe-based guerrillas, 128
Nur, Riza, 145

Öcalan, Abdullah, 6, 9, 53, 61, 77–78, 90, 94, 98, 101, 128, 130
Olson, Robert, 123

INDEX

Open market economy, 35
Organizational segmentation, 75–78
Ottoman-Armenian community, 233
Ottoman Army, 226
Ottoman authorities, 226–227
Ottoman civilian administration, 147
Ottoman Empire, 73–75, 88, 92, 153, 173–175, 207, 211, 217, 224, 232, 236, 237
Ottoman–Persian war, 173
Ottoman society, 232
Özal, Turgut, 93, 146
Özoglu, Hakan, 175

Pahlavi monarchy, 126
Pahlavi, Reza, 176
Palestine Liberation Organization, 212–213
Pan-Arabism, 18
Pan-Iraqi phenomenon, 32
Pan-Kurdish endeavours, 18
Pan-Kurdish nationalism, 33
Parliamentary debate, 106
Particularism, 126
  regional-linguistic, 33
Pasha, Ibrahim, 175
Pasha, Sherif, 43, 73
Pastoral nomadism, 145, 146, 150, 162
Patriarchal culture, 198
Patriarchy, 1, 13, 192, 198, 199
Patriotic Union of Kurdistan (PUK), 41, 47, 52–55, 142, 180, 193
Patronage-democracy, 89, 90
  emerging, 102–106
Persian empire, 173
Peshmerga masculinity, 196
Pitkin, Hanna, 42
PJAK (Free Life Party of Kurdistan) attacks, 118, 180
PKK. *See* Kurdish Workers' Party (PKK)
Pluralism, 4, 7–8, 27
  political, 92

PMF. *See* Popular Mobilization Force (PMF)
Political authorities, 172
Political culture, 72
Political economy, 88, 113
  of Kurdish-majority regions of Turkey and Iraq, 87
  twenty-first-century, 90
Political fragmentation, 72–75
Political Islamism, 78
Political parties, sufi orders to, 155–157
Political schism, 31
Political segmentation, 79–80
Popular mandate, 42–43
  Mullah Mustafa Barzani, 44–45
  post-1975, 45–48
  post-World War I, 43–44
  1991–present, 48
Popular Mobilization Force (PMF), 17
Post-World War I, 43–44, 48–50, 56–58
Print capitalism, 20, 88
PYD. *See* Democratic Union Party (PYD)

Qadir, Abdul, 43
Qassim, Abdulkarim, 95, 191

Radicalism, 107
Rahman, Sami Abdul, 46
Rasool, Kusret, 31
Rawlinson, H.C., 205–206
Rebellious leaders, 148
Religious authorities, 42, 54, 191, 192
Religious loyalties, 154–155
Rentierism, 32
Republic of Turkey, 123–124, 145
Re-tribalization, 144
Re-tribalization of society, 162
Rich, Claudius James, 205
Rizgari, Ala, 129
Roe, Paul, 120
Rojava, 86

administration of, 5
multi-ethnic 'autonomous democracy' in, 2
PYD, 189
Russian Empire, 174
Russian–Ottoman War, 147

Sabbath, Mohammedan, 211
Sadr, Bani, 126
Said, Nouri, 44
Scepticism, 86, 195
Schiller, Nina Glick, 224, 237
Schism, 32
  internal, 45–46, 178
  political, 31
  third, 78–79
Secularism, 189, 192
  Kemalist, 190, 199
  Turkish Republic enshrined, 188
Segmentary-lineage theory, 151
Segmentation
  ethnic, 72–75
  in ethno-political movements, 70–71
  ideational and organizational, 75–78
  Kurdish political, origins of, 71–72
  legacies of, 80
  political, 79–80
Seko, Mobutu Sese, 89
Self-determination, 4, 118, 235
  demanding, 159
  Kurds' struggle for, 142
  Wilsonian principles of, 4
Semele Massacre of 1937, 25
Settlement Law, 146
Seufert, Günter, 164
Sevgin, Nazmi, 178
Sèvres Treaty 1920, 30
Sex industry, 198
Sexuality, 186–188, 196, 199
Sexualization, 198
Seymour, Lee J.M., 70
Shah's dictatorship, 126
Sharafname, 231

Shaykh Said Revolt of 1925, 122–126, 137n50
Sheikhmous, Omar, 47, 52–53
Siddiq, Muhammad, 155
Sisyphean efforts, 3
Soane, Ely Bannister, 215
Social glue, 119
Social-movement logic, 121
Spiral-anarchy theories, 120
Sri Lanka, Tamil Tigers (LTTE) in, 130
State authorities, 120, 121, 132, 149, 163, 225
State capitalism, 95
State feminism, 199
Sufi orders *(tariqa)*, 154
  to political parties, 155–157
Sulaimaniya
  KRG provinces of, 195
  Ottoman agents in, 48
  Sulaimaniya–Rawanduz axis, 29
Sultan, Ottoman, 147
Surchi, Umar Khidr, 159
Sykes, Mark, 211–213
Sykes–Picot Agreement of 1916, 74, 211
Syria
  authoritarianpatrimonial system, 8
  civil wars in, 3
  Kurdish aspirations in, 5
  Kurdish population in, 74
  Kurds in, 17–18
  militarization of Kurds in, 6–7
  state elites in, 120

Taha, Saiyid, 55
Talabani, Jalal, 41, 44, 46, 47, 51, 53, 61, 77, 102, 142, 156, 157, 180
Talabani Praetorian Guard, 157
Talabani, Qubad, 62
Tamil Tigers (LTTE), in Sri Lanka, 130
Tanzimat, 174
Tehran
  authorities in, 126
  military, 126

Territorial partition, 72–75
Tevfik, Süleymaniyeli, 234
Tilly, Charles, 132
TOKI. *See* Turkish Housing Development Agency (TOKI)
Transcending tribal boundaries, 154–155
Treaty of Berlin, 233
Treaty of Sèvres (1920), 236
Tribal actors, 173, 182
   in Kurdistan, 172
Tribal authorities, 77
Tribal boundaries, transcending, 154–155
Tribal factor
   imperial past and, 172–175
   in the years 1990–2010, 179–181
Tribal identity, 143
Tribalism, 1, 71, 143
   in Kurdistan, 171–172
Tribal militias, 163
Tribal nationalism, 179
Tribal organization, 163
Tribes, 43, 143, 145–154
   and ethnic identity, 141–164
   and Kurdish contest from 1946 to 1991, 177–179
   segmentary and hierarchical principles, 150–154
   structural features of, 149
Türk, Ahmet, 177
Turkey
   authorities, 98
   culture, 92, 146
   diverging and converging trajectories, 91–97
   diversity of Kurds, 188–191
   economic policies, 93
   irredentism, 216
   Kurdish autonomy within, 124
   Kurdish-majority provinces of, 107
   Kurdish policies of, 148

Kurds in, 97–102
   military and intelligence services, 162
   modes of integration in, 160–162
   neo-liberal Turkish economy, 91
   PKK insurgency in, 128–130
   Republic of Turkey, 123–124, 145
   security forces, 107
   state elites in, 120
   White Kurds in, 107
Turkish Housing Development Agency (TOKI), 98, 99, 102
Turkish–Iraqi border, 101
Two Years in Kurdistan (1921) (Hay), 214

Union of Communities in Kurdistan, 99–100
Urbanization, 2
Urban leaders, 43–44

Vali, Abbas, 33
van Bruinessen, M.M., 164n1, 182
Vested-interest theories, 120
Violence, 88–91
   anti-Armenian, 227, 233
   ethnic (*see* Ethnic violence)
   against women, 195–196

White Kurds, 90, 100, 107, 111
Wigrams, W.A., 206–211
Wilson, Arnold, 50, 215
Wilson, Woodrow, 234, 235
Wimmer, Andreas, 159, 224, 237
Women
   liberation, 185–187, 189, 199
   rights activists, 144
   violence against, 195–196

Yalcin-Heckmann, Lale, 182
Yildirim, A. Kadir, 98
Yilmaz, Nurettin, 177

www.ingramcontent.com/pod-product-compliance
Lightning Source LLC
Chambersburg PA
CBHW062129300426
44115CB00012BA/1858